Marco Bussagli

Understanding Architecture

Architecture

VOLUME I

SHARPE REFERENCE
an imprint of M.E. Sharpe, Inc.

Contents

VOLUME 1

What is Architecture?

VOLUME 2

Civilizations, Architectural Achievements, Outstanding Figures

What is Architecture?

Architecture is the art and technology of realizing, from design through construction, physical spaces that meet the basic necessities of human existence—beginning with, but not limited to, habitation—on the individual and collective levels. The urge to build, following the natural and essential need to find suitable shelter, involves a number of aspects that constitute the subject matter of this book. Such considerations have, from the very beginning, guided and determined the practice of architecture. It is impossible, for example, to design any building without sufficiently considering the geographic location, the climate, and the available materials and how they will affect the interior and exterior construction. Obviously, these must take into account the anatomical structure of humans as well as the specific function of the building. A stadium designed to hold tens of thousands of people, for example, will have different characteristics from those of a private home or a church.

Another important aspect is that of building technology, which has varied over the centuries according to the diversity of materials at hand and the ability to exploit their properties.

The style of a building is, moreover, influenced by its historical context and by the artistic and cultural trends of its time.

All of these elements combine to create an architectural language that bears the same relationship to an individual building as literature does to a single written work.

LE MODULOR

People and Space

The relationship between people and space is conditioned by the anatomical structure of the human body. Humans, unlike the other animals, stand upright and feel constantly at the center of the perceived world. Their upper limbs stretch out from the medial axis of their bodies to conquer the surrounding space, placing them at the center of two complementary halves and allowing them to distinguish between right and left. In the same way, their ability to perceive the space in front of and behind them enables them to discover another two halves. In other words, since the time humans first stood upright, they have perceived space as divided into four parts: right, left, front, and behind (as well as "above" and "below"). Especially eloquent in this regard are Leonardo da Vinci's famous drawing of a man inscribed in a circle and a square and Le Corbusier's *modulor*. The latter is a system of measurement, based on the figure of a man with a raised arm, defined by the French architect as "a range of harmonic dimensions on a human scale which is universally applicable to both architecture and mechanics."

The concept of four-way space, innate in humans, is shared in many different cultures. We find it, for example, in images of Brahma (the four-headed creator god of Hinduism) and in medieval prints depicting the earth and its cities. Also divided into four parts was the layout of the Roman military camp (*castrum*), on which major cities of the Western world were established.

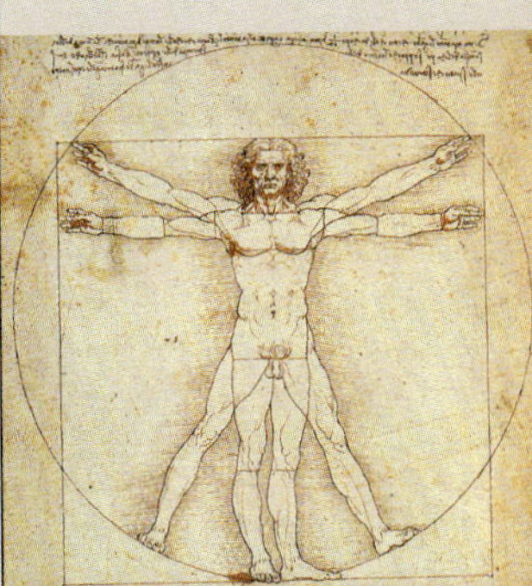

Top:
Leonardo da Vinci, *Homo Vitruvianus*, c. 1492. Venice, Gallerie dell'Accademia.

Above:
Khmer culture, *Head of the god Brahma*, tenth century. Paris, Musée Guimet.

Left:
Diagram of Le Corbusier's modulor, 1948.

Natural Environment and Human Environment

Traditional hut in the South Sahara. Burkina Faso.

Both humans and animals, in order to survive, interact with the physical landscape and make use of its resources. Humans, however, differ from the other animals, which are forced to migrate from hostile environments. Since the agricultural revolution of the Neolithic Age, humans have striven to create the best conditions for their habitats by transforming the natural environment into a human one. The transformation of the environment may lead to serious disruptions, many of them strikingly apparent today. The global climate is now subject to severe changes, and widespread hydrogeological imbalances (destruction of the natural balance between the ground and water system) have become a cause of serious concern. Since the 1970s a new discipline has emerged—ecology, literally the "science of the house"—which pertains not only to specific geographical areas (town, regions, or countries) but also to the entire globe, our common "home," now viewed by scientists as a spaceship of limited resources that must be treated with care and respect.

● PROBLEMS OF THE ENVIRONMENT

Uncontrolled development can wreak havoc on the environment, as exemplified by the "mushroom-city," a form of community based on exploitation of the land. The ecological balance is also disturbed by sites established in the desert to exploit oil fields which, when abandoned due to the depletion of those resources, become lifeless ghost towns.

Many other wounds to the landscape include hills eaten out by quarries and mines, woodlands stripped of trees abandoned strip mines, and rivers choked by pollution.

Realistic solutions to these problems and new approaches to development must be found, without attempting to turn the natural landscape into a kind of museum.

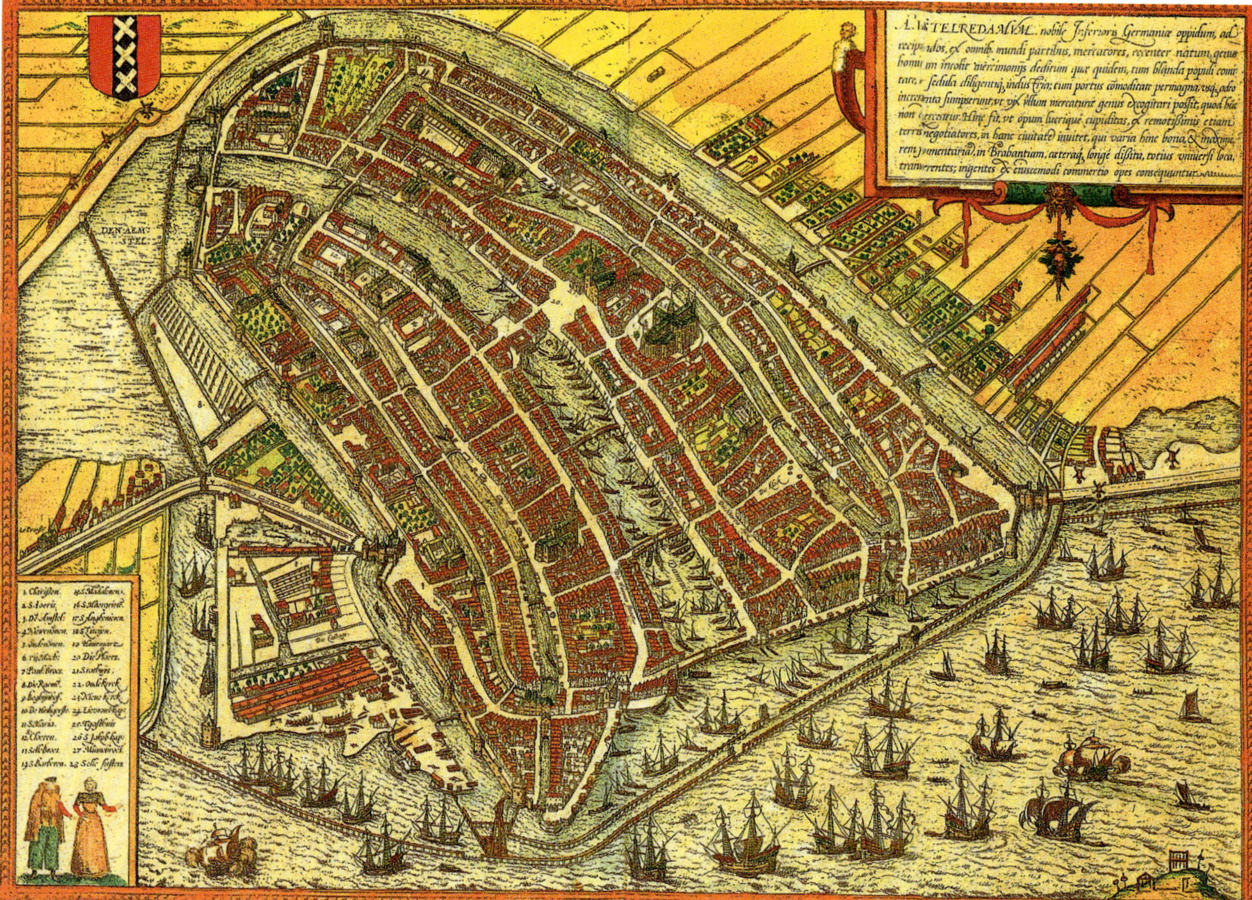

Georg Braun and Frans Hohenberg, *Map of the city of Amsterdam,* from the atlas *Civitates orbis terrarum,* 1572.

Sassi of Matera, Italy.

View of Istanbul. The domes of the Topkapi palace complex overlook the Bosporus strait.

In many places, meanwhile, the natural and human environments are perfectly integrated, with nature itself dictating modes of integration and forms of architecture.

● THE TERRAIN

Architectural initiatives and urban development are determined by a number of geomorphologic factors. Cities facing the sea, for example, tend to develop along the coastline. Such is the case with Istanbul, which extends along the coasts of the Golden Horn and the Bosporus strait, at the entrance to the Black Sea.

The Dutch city of Amsterdam, instead, developed on the swamplands along the Amstel River. Its famous artificial canals are a fine example of the fusion that can be achieved between the natural and human environment.

In the Italian region of Basilicata, the urban centers of Matera and I Sassi (Civita, Sasso Caveoso, Sasso Barisano) lie at different altitudes, adapting perfectly to the uneven slopes of the mountainous terrain.

In far northern Greenland, the largest island in the world, where ninety percent of the land is covered by ice, tens of thousands of inhabitants live exclusively along the rocky coastline.

Below: *Arctic houses suspended on a cliff.* Island of Uummannaq, northwestern Greenland.

From Territory to City

Ideograms representing the concept of city:

a. cuneiform characters, archaic pictogram
b. Hittite hieroglyph
c. Egyptian hieroglyph Njw.t
d. archaic Chinese pictogram yì

a

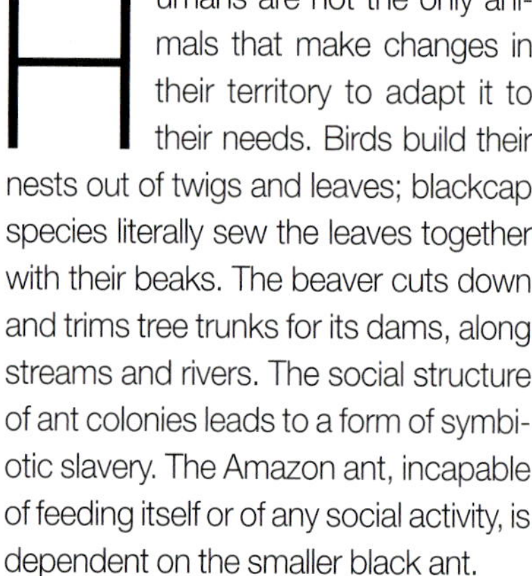

b

c

d

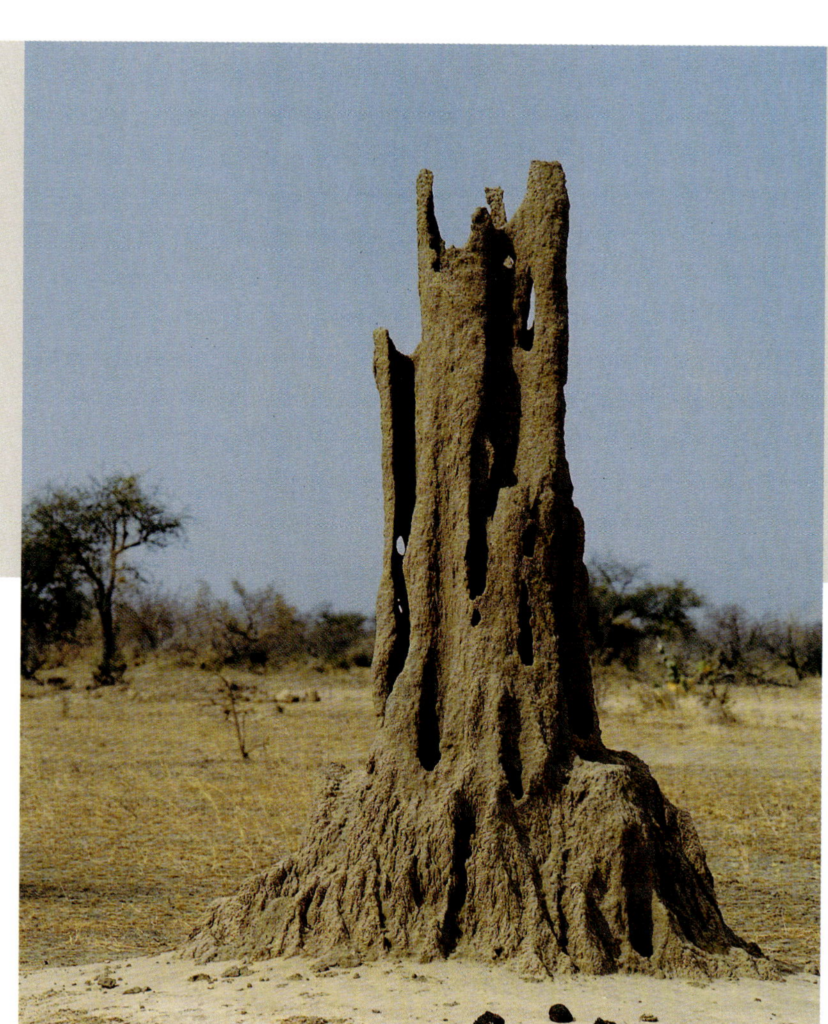

An anthill on the Kenyan savanna.

Humans are not the only animals that make changes in their territory to adapt it to their needs. Birds build their nests out of twigs and leaves; blackcap species literally sew the leaves together with their beaks. The beaver cuts down and trims tree trunks for its dams, along streams and rivers. The social structure of ant colonies leads to a form of symbiotic slavery. The Amazon ant, incapable of feeding itself or of any social activity, is dependent on the smaller black ant.

The complex social life of ant communities takes place in a well-organized anthill, a structure that considerably transforms the surrounding terrain. Like miniature skyscrapers, anthills can rise to a height of 30 feet and can hold as many as ten million individuals. Such similarities, while superficial, suggest that the systematic exploitation of the landscape is implied, for animals and well as humans, by the need for permanent settlements.

● AGGREGATION

No systematic exploitation of territory can be planned while moving continuously from place to place. The human instrument still best suited to this purpose is the city, which in fact can be considered a kind of "specialized territory."

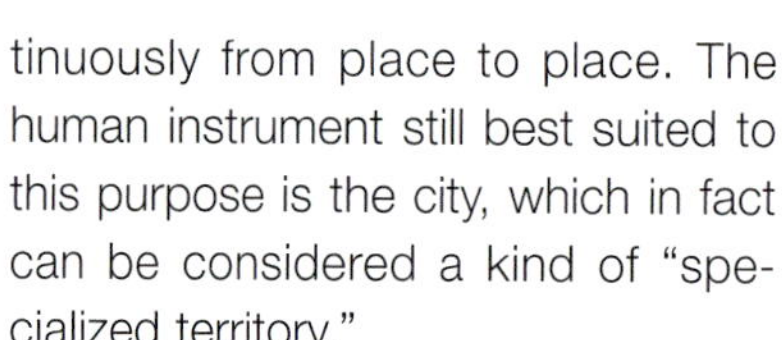

"Before the city," wrote the urban historian Lewis Mumford, "there was the group of houses, the sanctuary, and the village; before the village, the field, the cave, and the stone quarry; and before them all a tendency to social life that humans clearly share with other animal species."

The urge to band together has led humans to seek out the places most suitable to cohabitation for their climatic, economic, and religious conditions. In his *Republic*, Cicero comments on the fortunate geographical position of Rome and the reasons for its foundation: "Romulus knew how to exploit the advantages offered by the sea and to avoid the disadvantages by building his city on the banks of a river whose waters flowed abundantly. Rome could therefore import everything it needed not only from the sea but also from the land.... It is clear to all, in fact, that the location is favored by nature."

Starting from these premises, the Romans worked to put their natural

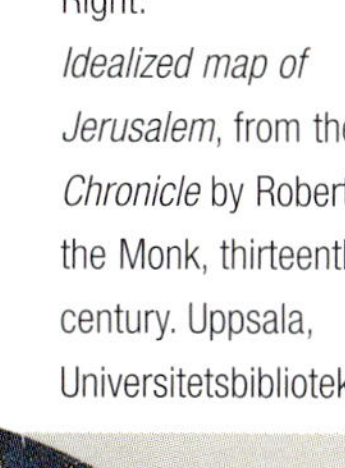

Below:
Taddeo di Bartolo, *Map of Rome,* second decade of the fifteenth century. Siena, Palazzo Pubblico.

Right:
Idealized map of Jerusalem, from the *Chronicle* by Robert the Monk, thirteenth century. Uppsala, Universitetsbibliotek.

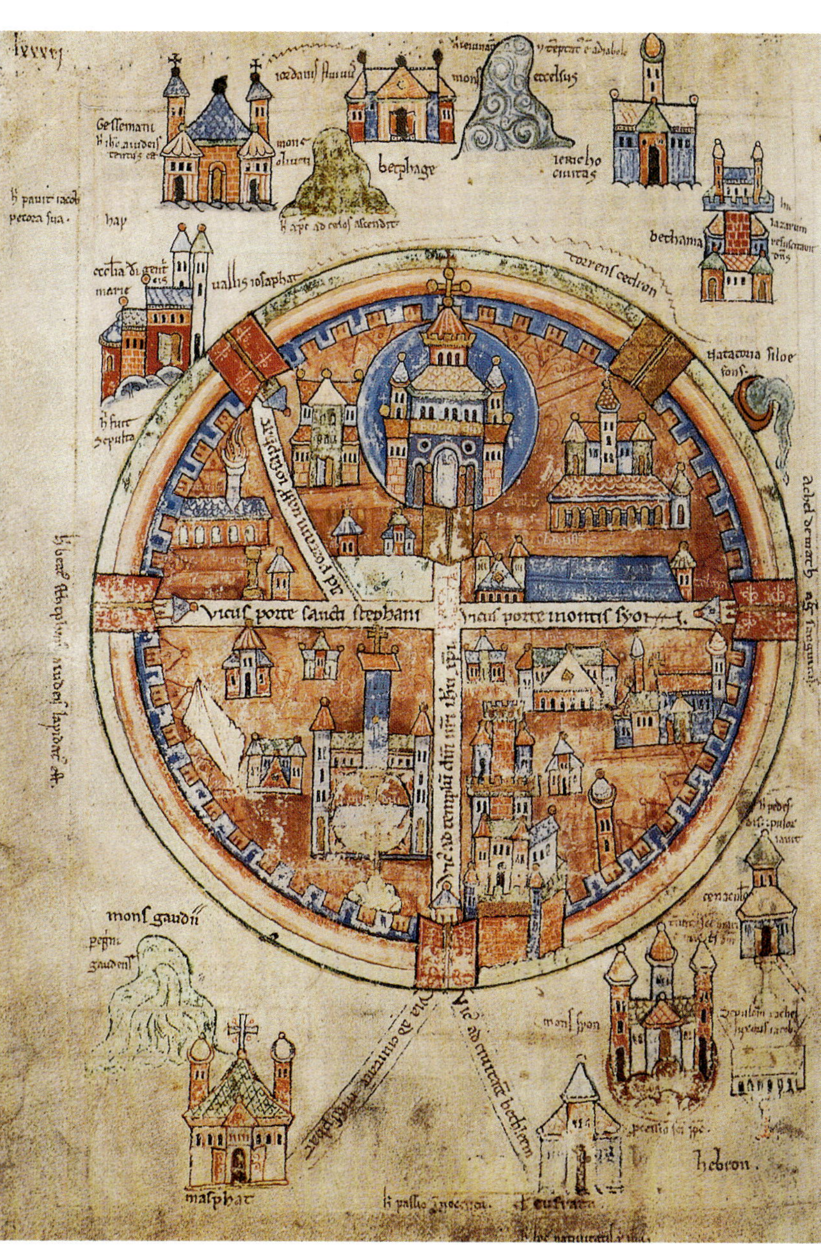

resources to even better use. The plan of Ancient Rome, as still seen in medieval prints, is basically a tract of land suitably enclosed—at first by the furrow traced by Romulus's plow, according to tradition, and later by its defensive walls.

● THE CITY AS AN ISLAND

The study of Hittite and Egyptian hieroglyphics, cuneiform characters, and Chinese pictograms confirms how the concept of "city" came to be expressed by a line that enclosed and isolated a surface area. The Egyptian hieroglyphic for "city," *Njw.t*, shows roads converging at the center of a circular urban space. In ancient Chinese, the character *yì* indicates the access road to the city, perceived as a regular space in contrast to the natural disorder of the world outside.

● THE SACRED AREA

The city was also a sacred area, at times considered the home of the divinity to which it was dedicated. This divinity could even represent an entire people: Assur was not only the god of the Assyrians but also of a city and a nation; the goddess Athena was identified with the city-state of the Athenians. As a sacred place, the city was regarded as a unique and separate territory, set apart from the outside world. It could be dangerous to enter without permission, as in the case of Remus, killed by his brother Romulus, who had forbidden him to cross the furrow traced by his plow. The city was also a concentration of specialized, contiguous precincts. While the public square (the *agorà* of Greek cities) was the place dedicated to meetings and political activity (from *pólis*, and thus *politiké téchne*, "the art of governing," a citizen's most important activity), the *templum* was the area consecrated to a particular god or goddess.

The Greek term for this site was *thémenos* (meaning "a separate, circumscribed area"); the temple was therefore a circumscribed, enclosed place of sanctity. Some religious sites have remained intact for centuries, consecrated under a succession of different faiths, suggesting that such places may always be held sacred.

● THE PUBLIC SQUARE

There are many types of public squares, differing in function, shape, and size. The oblong layout of Piazza Navona in Rome clearly reveals that it was originally a stadium, built under the Emperor Domitian (r. 81–96 C.E.). In a typical example of how a monarchical power could appropriate urban space and use it for a different purpose, Pope Innocent X (1644–1655) decided to turn Piazza Navona into a "family living room." A different intention but the same absolute authority lay behind the rearrangement of the Kremlin and Red Square in Moscow, conceived by Soviet leaders as the nerve center of the country. Clustered together in dramatic confrontation are the vestiges of Russian history, from the Imperial Palace to Lenin's Mausoleum, from the cathedrals inside the Kremlin to Red Square. The latter was designed for military parades and served as the chief venue of Soviet political representation until 1991, when the Soviet empire dissolved.

Left:
St. Basil's Cathedral on Red Square. Moscow.

Above:
The Jema al Fna square. Marrakesh, Morocco.

Left:
Piazza delle Erbe.
Padua, Italy.

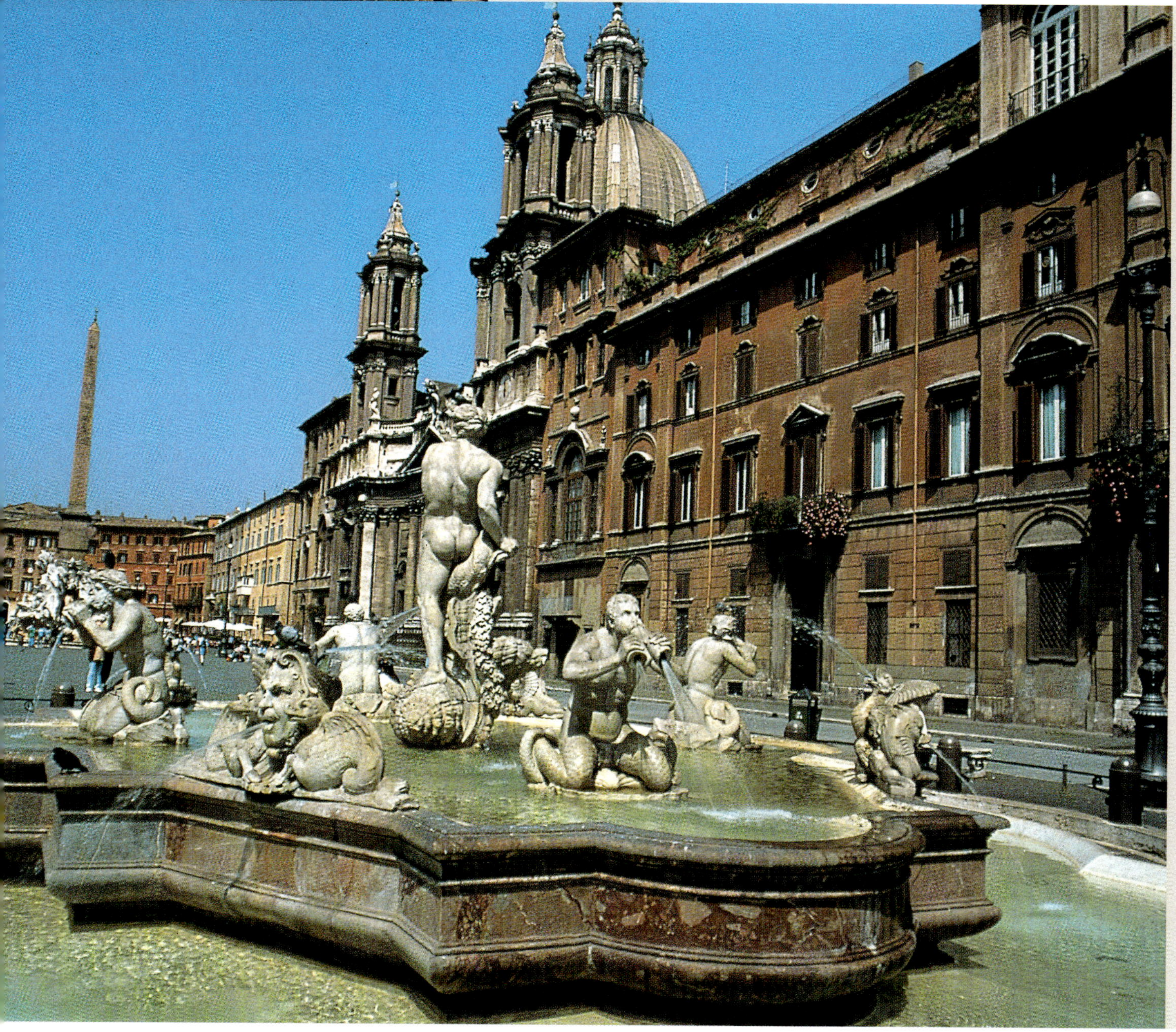

Below:
Piazza Navona. Rome.

In addition to its official role, a public square can serve as a market and meeting place. Such is the case with the vibrant Jema al Fna in Marrakesh, Morocco, and of Piazza delle Erbe in Padua, dominated by the Palazzo della Ragione, site of the city's Republican government from 1256 to 1318. Politics, commerce, and the community converge in the public square, an urban nerve center where architectural styles may confer a variety of forms, interpreting a historic age with the political and social requirements of the times.

A Brief History of Urban Planning

Top:
Remains of a nuraghi site. Barumini, Sardinia, Italy.

Above:
Remains of a Celtic-Iberian village. Debriteiros, Citania, Portugal.

The Latin word *urbs*, from which the English word "urban" derives, means "city." It differs from *civitas*, a concept that is more complementary than synonymous. *Urbs* is the constructed city, *civitas* the inhabited one; thus, every human settlement reflects, within certain limits, the beliefs, social life, and needs of all of its inhabitants.

● FROM THE CIRCLE TO THE SQUARE

The oval or circular plan, typical of Neolithic settlements from Cyprus to England, is common to other civilizations as well. It is found not only in the *nuraghi* (stone tower) sites of Sardinia (1400 B.C.E.) and in prehistoric Celtic-Iberian and Portuguese villages, but also in many settlements from equatorial and southern Africa to Borneo, where archaic structures, practices, and customs survive from the ancient world. Urban plans based on a linear scheme presented more complex problems, in particular the rational organization of demographic growth.

In 2000 B.C.E., the city of Ur in Mesopotamia covered an area of more than 300 acres, with about 20 houses per acre, indicating a population of about sixty thousand. If the Babylonian palace at Mari (1700 B.C.E.) was already imposing in size, the Minoan palace-cities on the island of Crete were truly gigantic.

At Knossos, eight hundred rooms were grouped together in a kind of enormous plaza (180 x 90 feet), surrounded by buildings, that seems to have anticipated the Greek *agorà*. At Mycenae, by contrast, small rural groups living outside the Minoan palace complex formed their own towns, not suffocated by a highly centralized system.

The cities of Ancient Greece were distinguished by monumental areas and complexes designed for social purposes; theaters, gymnasiums, and other buildings were distributed freely throughout the territory, conferring a unique character on each city.

The Romans developed the urban and architectural system still further with amphitheaters, stadiums (p. 56), and public baths (p. 60). The city plan was rationalized in blocks (*insulae*) and sometimes organized, like military camps (*castrum*), along a north-south thoroughfare (*cardo*) and an east-west thor-

Left:
View of the city of Brasília.

produced a wealth of monuments and squares, such as the *places royales* built to glorify the absolute power of the Sun King (Louis XIV) in seventeenth-century France.

And while Georges-Eugène Haussmann's plan for the *boulevards* of Paris (1853–1870) was inspired by the Enlightenment, industrial cities were developing elsewhere in response to the fast-growing demands of production. In the twentieth century, somewhere between the precisely designed city and the one exploding in urban sprawl was Brasília (1960), conceived by the architect Lucio Costa (1902–1963) in an attempt to solve the problems of the megalopolis.

Today as in the past, urban development depends largely on the specific territory, with planning based on a variety of factors. The principle usually applied in modern cities is that of locating production (factories, refineries, farms) as well as port facilities, airports, and railway stations in outlying districts, while businesses, social services (schools, hospitals), and entertainment are kept within the city limits.

oughfare (*decumanus*). The hill towns of the Middle Ages were perfectly adapted to a different landscape and social climate. The village of Monteriggioni near Siena, for example, is a fortified *vicus* (village) well suited to the political unrest of the times. From the ninth to the thirteenth centuries, the phenomenon of *incastellamento*, the transformation of a castle into a village, was widespread.

The Renaissance rediscovered the public square as a meeting place and reorganized the system of streets, as exemplified by the urban plan of Pope Sixtus V for Rome. The Baroque city

Fortified town. Monteriggioni, Siena, Italy.

Building for Beauty

The beauty of a building, obviously, depends not only on the harmony of its shapes and proportions but also on the sense of balance conveyed by the rhythmic arrangement of its elements.

● A QUESTION OF RHYTHM

Humans are attracted by visual impressions, as well as sounds, in which diverse elements alternate in recurring rhythms. Already in prenatal life, the fetus is accustomed to hearing its mother's heartbeat. Our biological existence is marked by precise rhythms: of sleep and of waking, of breathing, and of the beating of the heart.

It is this sense of rhythm, innate in the human species, that provides the physiological basis for a correct architectural formulation, understood as the harmonious coexistence of diverse elements.

● FULLNESS AND VOID

Since a perfectly flat wall arouses little visual stimulation, it is necessary to bring it alive and to exploit the openings that are inevitably required to make the building functional.

In a Greek temple (p. 46), structured around a sacred cella (*náos*), the walls are rhythmically articulated by columns that satisfy both aesthetic and structural requirements.

A sense of harmony is produced by a balanced relationship between the fullness of the columns and the voids of the intercolumns, or spaces between them; the latter are "filled in" at the back by the wall of the naos. Columns standing very close together would make the side or front of

the temple appear too "full," while columns placed too far apart (beyond the limits of structural support) would convey a sense of emptiness.

The same problems, albeit in different terms, pertain to buildings of other types. In the Palazzo Venezia, built in Rome by Pietro Barbo (then Pope Paul II) between 1455 and 1464, the façade overlooking the public square, which includes the Annibaldi Tower, has three rows of hierarchically arranged windows: medium-size and arched in the bottom row, large and cruciform on the piano nobile (main floor), and small and square at the top. As a matter of architectural composition, the vertically rising windows serve the same functions as the empty spaces of the intercolumns, i.e., lightening the mass of the wall and imposing a visual rhythm.

The relationship between fullness and emptiness applies as well to masses, as in the cubic structure of Villa Moller in Vienna, designed by the Czech architect Adolf Loos (1870–1933).

● SPACE AND TIME

An architectural structure also possesses a temporal dimension, consisting of the time required to scan or traverse its space. A structure imposes tempos and rhythms on those who experience it, which should be accompanied and enhanced by an appropriate spacing of elements. This is the only way to bring the building truly alive.

View of the bell tower and the apse of the Duomo, twelfth century. Pisa. A harmonious relationship between fullness and void distinguishes the elegant architectural structures of Piazza dei Miracoli.

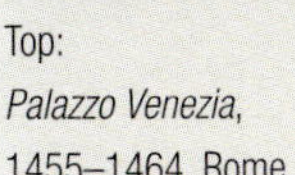

Top:
Palazzo Venezia, 1455–1464. Rome.

Above:
Adolf Loos, *Villa Moller in an old photograph*, 1927–1928. Vienna.

Left:
Idealized rendering of the color scheme of a Greek temple, from the *Expédition Scientifique de Morée*, Paris 1831–1838. Originally the temples were brightly colored, heightening the contrast between filled-in spaces and voids.

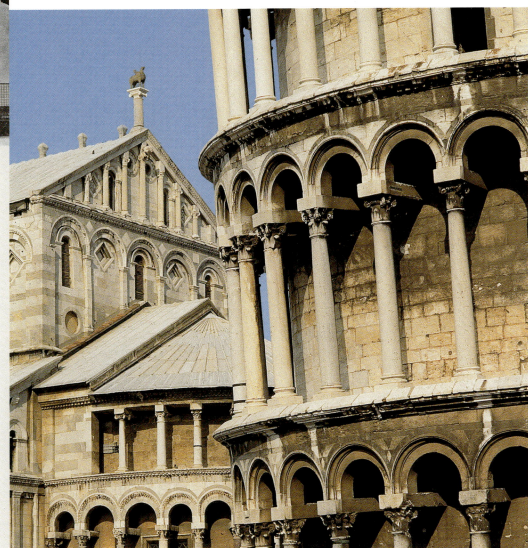

Music and Architecture

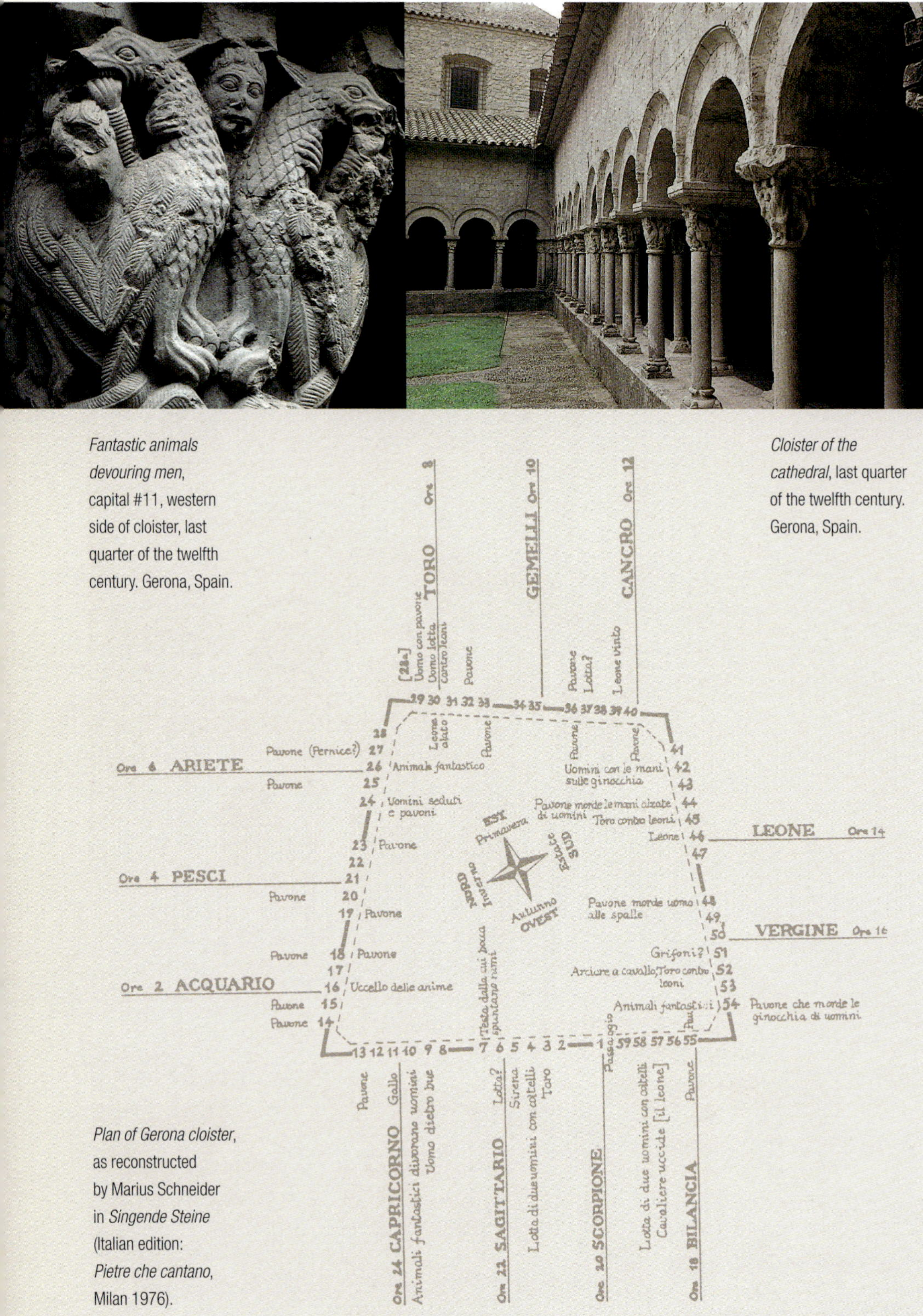

Fantastic animals devouring men, capital #11, western side of cloister, last quarter of the twelfth century. Gerona, Spain.

Cloister of the cathedral, last quarter of the twelfth century. Gerona, Spain.

Plan of Gerona cloister, as reconstructed by Marius Schneider in *Singende Steine* (Italian edition: *Pietre che cantano*, Milan 1976).

The analogy between music and architecture is based on two assumptions; first, that the geometric relationships between architectural spaces and the arithmetical ones of musical notes and tempo can be reduced to simple numerical concepts; and second, that a building, conceived as a sort of small universe, reflects the musical harmony of the cosmos.

● MUSIC AND COSMOLOGY

For centuries, many Western and Eastern civilizations have thought of music as a reflection of the harmony of the cosmos. Plato described the universe as an immense carillon, producing an endless melody from the motion of the planets. According to an ancient Chinese manuscript called the Yo Ki, "Music is the harmony of the sky and the earth... Through harmony all beings are born and are transformed.... Music draws its effective virtue from the heavens."

A medieval Indian text regards music as a sign of immortality. Everything, then, joins in the celestial music, which humans try in vain to replicate.

Various sacred buildings, as we shall see, have been designed according to this symbolism.

● SINGING STONES

In his book *Singende Steine* ("Singing Stones"), the German ethnomusicologist Marius Schneider notes a curious resemblance between symbols in the carved reliefs on capitals in the cloisters of St. Cugat and Gerona in Catalonia, Spain, and a thirteenth-century musical text from India. While any direct relationship between the cloisters and that text is extremely unlikely, it may be that

Jubal, Pythagoras, and Philolaus, from *Theorica Musice* by Franchino Gafurio, Milan 1492.

Dosso Dossi, *Allegory of Music*, c. 1530. Florence, Horne Foundation Museum.

both are based on a common knowledge of music that was later lost. The Indian text establishes precise relationships between certain animals and specific musical notes; for example, D is represented by the peacock, E by the ox, and B by the horse.

The same animals are found on the capitals of two Romanesque cloisters in Catalonia, where they seem to "compose" the sequence of notes of a medieval hymn dedicated to the regional saint, St. Cucufate. Surprisingly, the musical strophe (melodic unit or stanza) of the hymn reiterates the succession of forty notes appearing on seventy-two columns, represented by the animals carved on the capitals.

● ALLEGORICAL FIGURES

During the Middle Ages and the Renaissance, philosophical and theological reflections on musical relationships and symbolism often evoked the figures of Pythagoras and Tubalcain. For his painting *Allegory of Music*, Dosso Dossi (1479–1542) was inspired by the biblical character of Tubalcain (Genesis 4: 19–22), the smith who was held to be the inventor of music throughout the Middle Ages, and his brother Jubal, a harp player.

The identity of the two women in the painting is still uncertain. The nude figure probably represents Music, while the seated woman may be the musician's sister Naamah. The latter is shown holding a tablet bearing a sort of pentagram, a circular shape marked off by six lines, which undoubtedly alludes to the music of the celestial spheres. Pythagoras is also linked to Tubalcain and Jubal, as seen in the frontispiece to Franchino Gafurio's *Theorica Musice*, published in 1492. In this drawing, Jubal supervises the work of the smiths in his brother's shop, while Pythagoras, with his follower Philolaus, experiments with musical relationships by beating a succession of numbered hammers, plucking strings of different lengths, and sounding vases filled with water to different levels. Such proportional and numerical relationships also play a fundamental role in architecture, as will be seen in the succeeding pages.

Architecture and the Theory of Proportions

The basis of harmony, according to the Greek philosopher Philolaus, is "discordant agreement," meaning the accord between unequal consonances represented by dissimilar proportions, such as the ratio between 3 and 4 or between 2 and 3. In playing the monochord, his master Pythagoras had discovered that musical harmonies derive from ratios of small numerical units. Thus, the Platonic triangle or *lambda*, considered the secret of music and therefore universal harmony, offers two progressions starting from 1: in the ratio of doubling (1, 2, 4, 8) and of tripling (1, 3, 9, 27). In Christian thought, Pythagoras's hypotheses seem borne out by passages from the Bible. In Genesis (6:15), Jehovah dictates the dimensions of the ark to Noah: 300 cubits long, 50 cubits wide, and 10 cubits high, according to ratios of 6:1 and 30:1. In Exodus (25:10), Jehovah tells Moses that the Ark of the Covenant should measure 2.5 cubits in width, 1.5 cubits in length, and 1.5 cubits in height. Lastly, the Temple of Solomon

Raphael, *Pythagorean slate*, detail from *The School of Athens*, 1509–1510. Rome. Vatican Palaces. A disciple of Pythagoras holds a slate illustrating the musical relationships between the four-chord zither (at top) and the *lambda*, or Platonic triangle.

Right: *Method for determining* entasis *in columns.* A perpendicular line is drawn down the middle of the column, from the upper base to the lower base (or scape). From the resulting center, a circle concentric to the perimeter of the lower scape is then traced. The semicircles are overturned on the vertical plane to identify a section of arch, which is then divided into three equal parts (points a, b, and c) in the portion of the column extending from the lower scape to the projection of the edge of the upper base. From here depart three half-lines, which will produce a swelling, or *entasis*, along the contour of the column at about one-third its total height.

(1 Kings 6:2) is to extend 60 cubits long, 20 cubits wide, and 30 high, or ratios of 3:2 and of 2:1. These are all symbolic images of the universe based on proportional relationships, in keeping with the biblical affirmation, "But you have arranged all things according to measure, number, and weight (Wisdom 11:20).

● THE SENSE OF HARMONY

The "secret" of musical harmony was translated into spatial, or geometric, relationships that were used in antiquity and throughout the Middle Ages and the Renaissance to construct buildings in accordance with the laws of the universe.

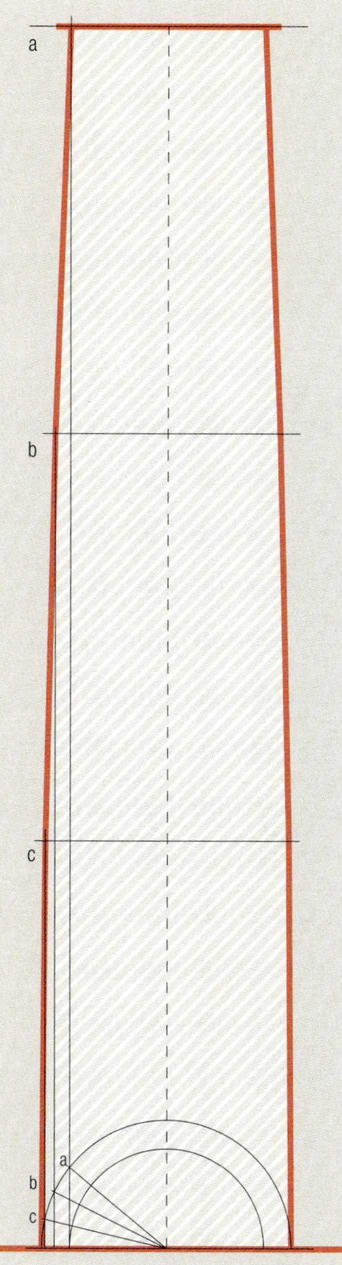

The interest of Greco-Roman architects in the problem of proportions is demonstrated by their geometrical calculations to determine the swelling of a column, or *entasis*, which served to correct the optical effect of a colonnade as viewed from below and to confer on matter a sense of elasticity, as if the columns were actively responding to the weight of the lintel. Another geometrical calculation was employed by Vitruvius in establishing the proportions of a theater design.

Medieval architects were well aware of these teachings. The plan for a Cistercian church sketched in the notebooks of Villard de Honnecourt (first half of the thirteenth century) employs the square as a structural module. The maximum width of the plan is eight squares and that of its length is twelve, a ratio of 2:3. In counting the squares it may be seen that the ratio of 4:3 is used for the choir area, while for the whole transept it is 8:4. These proportions, which are echoed in musical theory, were to influence the architecture of the Renaissance as well. The Sistine Chapel, for example, seems inspired by the proportions of the biblical Temple of Solomon, as confirmed by a woodcut illustrating the commentary to the Book of Ezekiel published by Nicolaus de Lyra in 1485.

Bramante, too, adopted musical relationships in designing a cloister for the Roman church of Santa Maria della Pace, whose walls are proportioned in a 4:3 ratio. Palladio, in his treatise "Quattro Libri dell'Architettura" ("The Four Books of Architecture," 1485) recommends seven types of interiors, ranging, in decreasing order of perfection, from the circle to the square, to the square and a third (3:4), to the square and a half (2:3), to the double square (1:2).

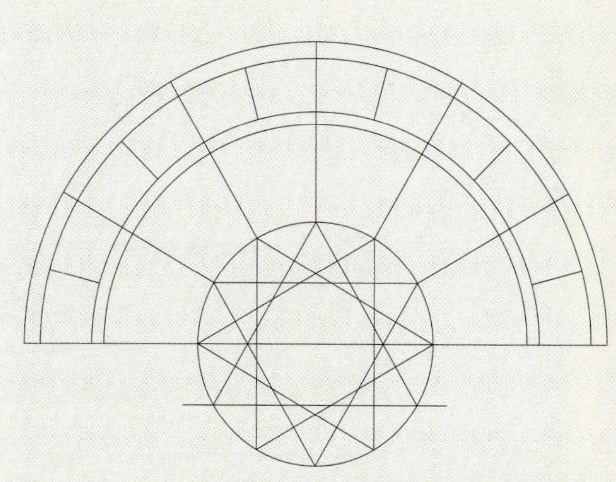

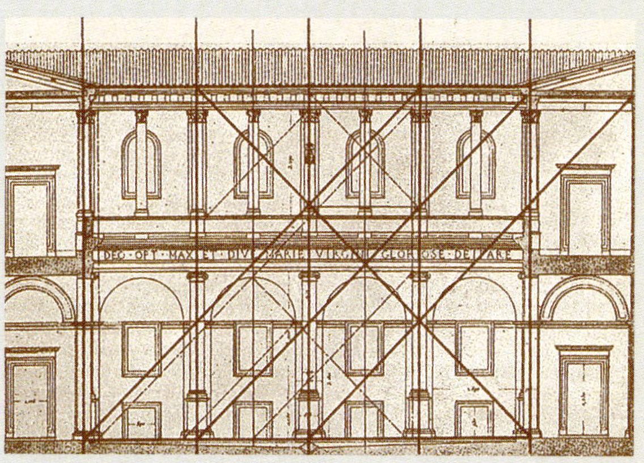

Top: *Diagram of the cavea of a theater according to Vitruvius.* The apexes of the triangles determine the division of tiered seats *(cunei)* into six sections.

Center: *Men wrestling and plan of a Cistercian church*, from the notebook of Villard de Honnecourt, *Livre de portraiture*, c. 1220–1235. Paris, National Library.

Above: *Proportional elevation diagram of the Church of Santa Maria della Pace in Rome by Donato Bramante*, 1500–1504, from a drawing by Paul-Marie Letarouilly.

● THE GOLDEN SECTION

Variously utilized by painters and architects, the "golden section" is defined in geometric terms as "that part of a line segment which represents the mean proportion between the entire segment and the remaining part." For the segment AB, the golden section AX thus derives from the proportion AB:AZ=AX:XB. This condition can be obtained through simple geometric calculations, which, in addition to segments, can be used to produce golden rectangles; these are particularly well suited to the design of temples and monuments. The Parthenon was constructed according to the rectangular golden ratio. The standard unit of measurement was the Attic foot (7.6 inches), which goes 160 times into the width and 360 times into the length of the stylobate (the base on which the columns rest, measuring approximately 100 x 227 feet), and 70 times into the height of the façade (just over 44 feet). The ratio of 360 to 160 is 2.25, or √5, the number that governs the ratios between the various harmonic rectangles. From Vitruvius we

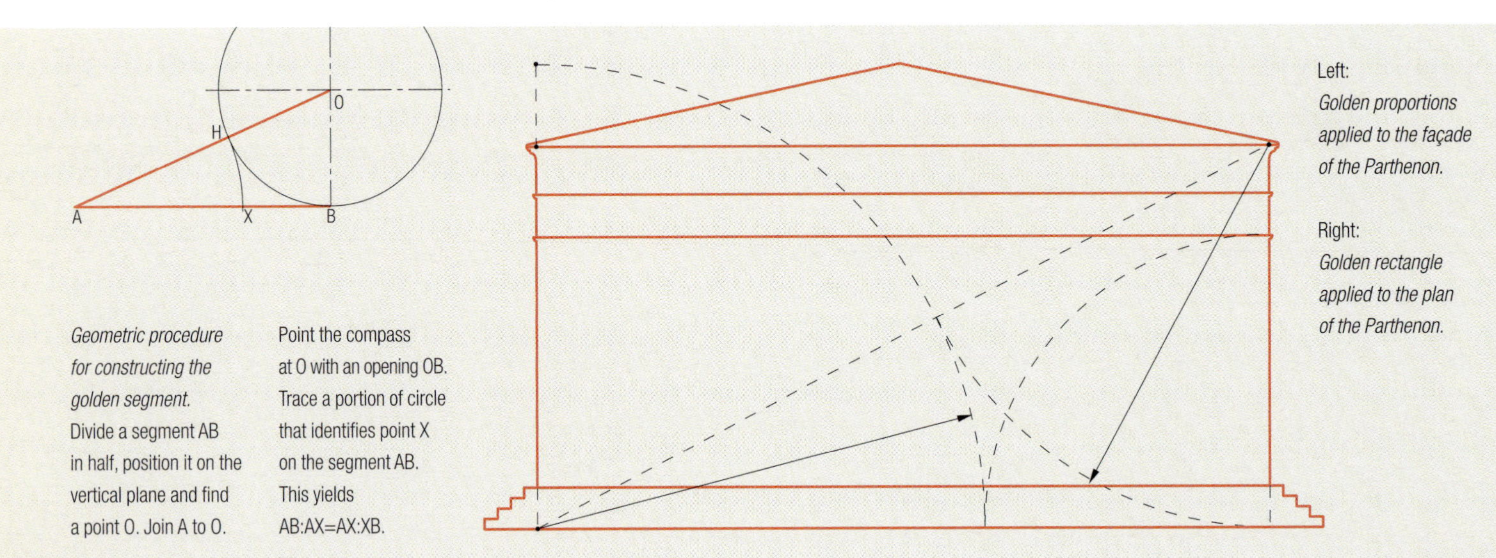

Geometric procedure for constructing the golden segment. Divide a segment AB in half, position it on the vertical plane and find a point O. Join A to O. Point the compass at O with an opening OB. Trace a portion of circle that identifies point X on the segment AB. This yields AB:AX=AX:XB.

Left: *Golden proportions applied to the façade of the Parthenon.*

Right: *Golden rectangle applied to the plan of the Parthenon.*

Charles Le Brun (attr.), *Design for the eastern façade of the Louvre*, after 1667. Paris, Louvre, Cabinet des Dessins.

know that architects competing for a building commission had to present an arithmetic drawing that listed measurements and proportional ratios, as well as a geometric drawing in which the surfaces were fully defined. This is exactly what Iktinos and Kallikrates had done in designing the Parthenon.

The architectural application of the golden section, imbued with symbolic and cosmological meaning, was revised during the Renaissance after the first printed edition of Vitruvius's work, edited by Cesare di Lorenzo Cesariano (1483–1543), a Milanese architect and writer who had been a pupil of Bramante. In France, the application of proportional rules is attributed to Claude Perrault (1613–1688), a physician and amateur architect who designed the eastern façade of the Louvre in collaboration with Le Vau and Le Brun. Strict application of these rules gradually declined in the eighteenth century, while the nineteenth saw a nostalgic revival of the architectural styles of the past. In the twentieth century, Le Corbusier was the first to reconsider the question of proportions and the application of the golden section.

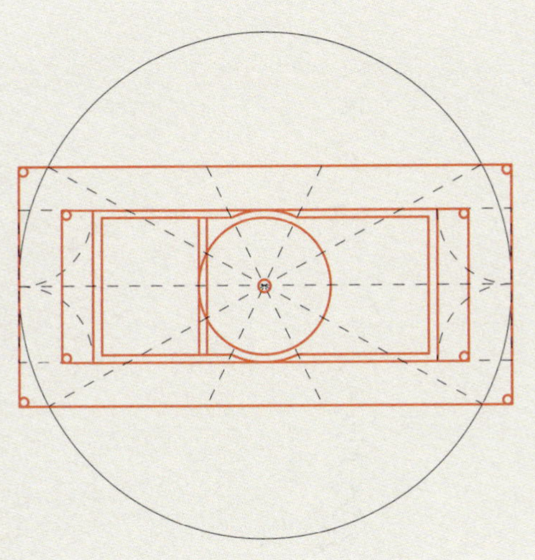

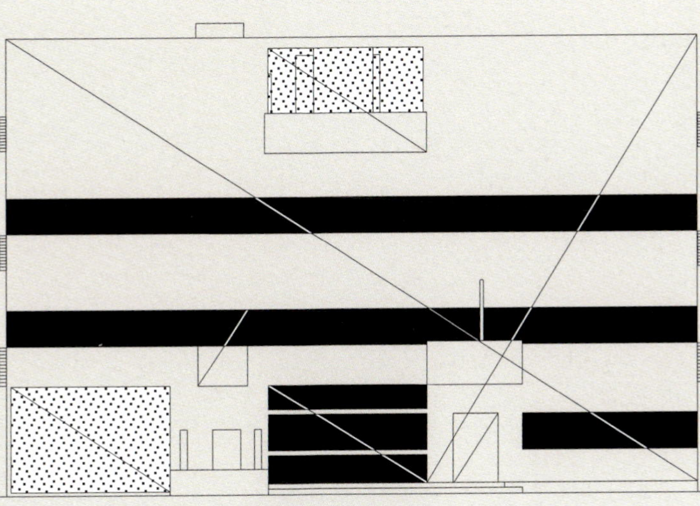

Le Corbusier and Pierre Jeanneret, *Proportional diagram of the façade of Villa Stein at Garches, France, based on golden rectangles*, 1927.

Architecture and Anthropomorphism

The relationship between cities, buildings, and people is not merely one of containers and contents. Buildings and cities are perhaps best understood as extensions and projections of human thought and of the role people seek in the world. And so it is only natural that, for symbolic reasons, towns and villages in certain cultures are laid out according to an anthropomorphic model, in which the architecture, too, shows structural analogies with the human body.

● MICROCOSM AND MACROCOSM

According to a simple concept found in a wide range of cultures, humans and the cosmos share the same form. Not by chance, humans are often held to be the highest expression of the created world. It is this identity of form that assures the "universal nature" of humanity, if not its immortality. It is not, however, "the image of the universe that 'cosmologizes' that of man," explains the orientalist Mariella Spagnoli Mariottini, but rather the image of man that 'anthropomorphizes' that of the universe. From this understanding comes the concept of the macranthropos, the cosmic man or divine essence—Purusha in India, P'an-Ku in China, and Tiamat in Mesopotamian civilization (who offers his body as building material for the universe)—a cosmos that assumes the shape of the human body, as in the case of the Polynesian god Tangaroa. And so the hairs of cosmic man become the forests of the world, his eyes the sun and the moon, and his breath the wind.

● PRIMITIVE AND ETHNOGRAPHIC CULTURES

In a Neolithic village, such as the South African kraal, an outer circle encloses a benevolent and favorable interior space, separating it from the hostile, dangerous outside world, symbolizing once again the relationship between the earth and the surrounding ocean. In the middle of the village stands a ritual pole, a phallic symbol representing the center of the world, while a hut symbolizes the womb, and its roof evokes the heavenly vault. The African cultures of the Fali (northern Cameroon) and the Dogon (Mali) are based on a distinctly anthropomorphic symbology. For the Fali, the layout of the village follows the image of the earth, with a head, upper and lower limbs, and a granary at the center representing the sex. The granary itself has a stylized human shape—a head, a body, and upper and lower limbs. In the cosmological symbolism of Dogon culture, an uncreated god, Amma, has coupled with the earth to generate both the universe and two primordial Nommo, negative and positive beings. From them descended

Left:
Wooden statue of Tangaroa from Rurutu, French Polynesia, before 1821. London, British Museum.
The body of the creator god Tangaroa is made up of the bodies of all men.

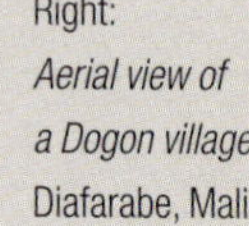

Right:
Aerial view of a Dogon village. Diafarabe, Mali.

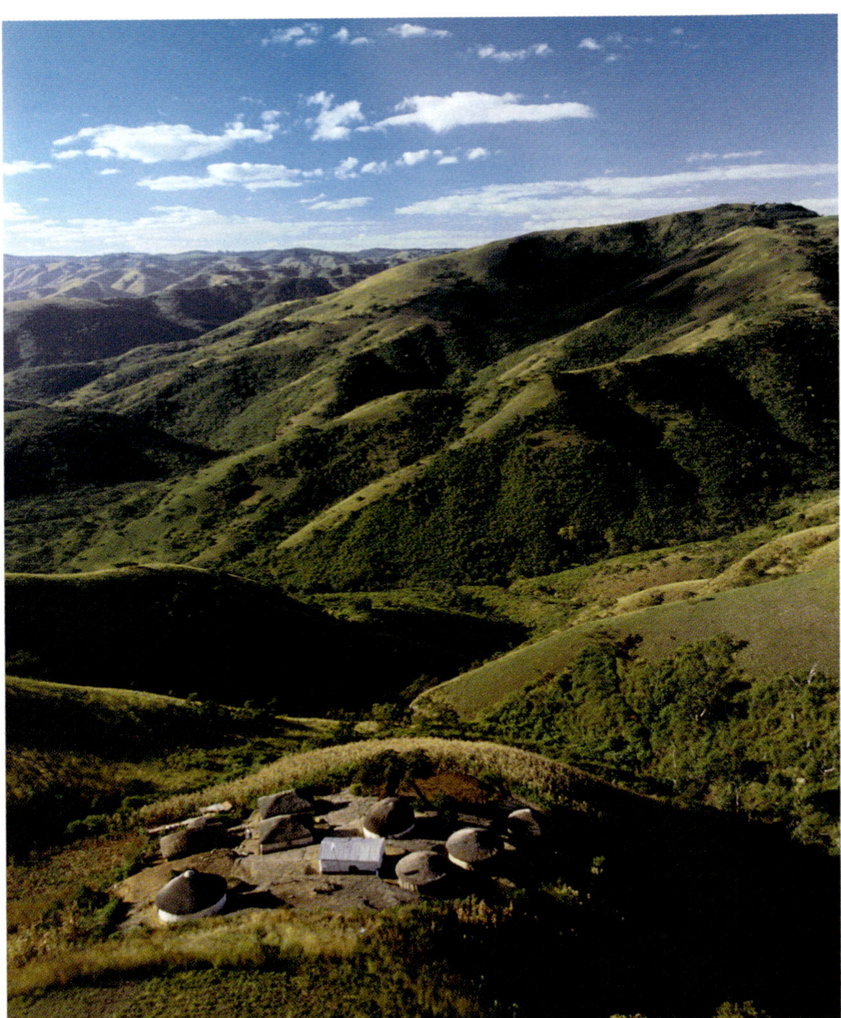

Aerial view of a Zulu kraal. Eshowe, Republic of South Africa. The *kraal* (from the Portuguese *corral*, enclosure for animals) consists of huts arranged in a circular or horseshoe shape, and is typical of the populations of southern Africa.

four male and four female ancestors who, through self-fecundation, gave birth to the ancestors of Dogon families, who became Nommo themselves. One of these is believed to have abandoned celestial life to organize the world and create humankind, to whom he gave eight joints. These correspond to the *dougué* stones (cosmic seeds of creation), the human soul, and the first ancestors. The two sets of shoulder and hip joints are regarded as male, while the two sets of elbow and knee joints are deemed female—like the families representing each. Marriage is allowed only between families of different sexes. The layout of the Dogon village reflects this scheme. The family houses occupy an area corresponding to the chest and abdomen. Communal areas are the feet; the houses for menstruating women are the upper limbs; and the council house (*toguna*) is the head. Even the individual huts are pervaded by anthropomorphic symbolism: the kitchen represents the head, the entranceway the sex, and the pantry the arms; the wooden pilasters for the roof of the *toguna* are human figures with upraised arms.

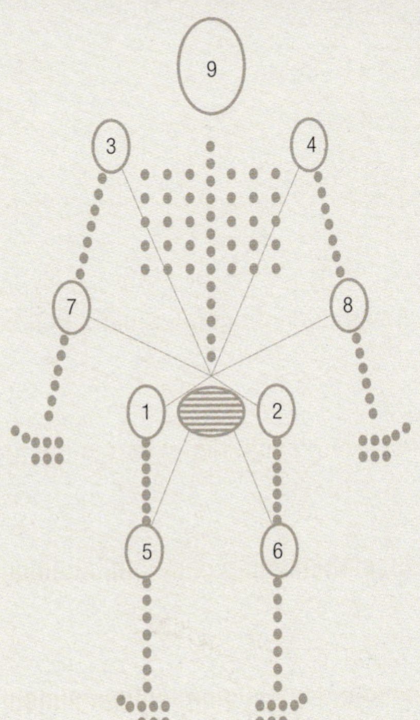

Diagram showing organization of Dogon tribes in anthropomorphic terms and according to the system of joints.

1, 2, 3, 4. The four primordial male ancestors (Nommo): hip joints (1, 2) and shoulder joints (3,4).

5, 6, 7, 8. The four primordial female ancestors: knee joints (5, 6) and elbow joints (7, 8).

9. Head: territorial order.

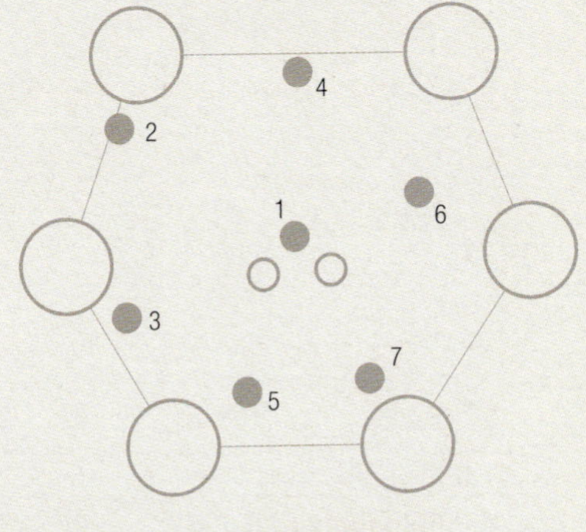

Diagram of central enclosure in a Fali village. Cameroon, West Africa.

1. Head (or sex)
2. Back
3. Right arm
4. Left arm
5. Right thigh
6. Left thigh
7. Right leg

Francesco di Giorgio Martini, *Diagram of anthropomorphic city*, from the *Trattato di architettura Civile e Militare*, c. 1485. Florence, Biblioteca Medicea Laurenziana.

FROM ANTIQUITY TO THE CHRISTIAN WORLD

The reluctance of Greek thought to accept an anthropomorphic concept of divinity, as expressed by Xenophanes (sixth century B.C.E.), produced even more subtle distinctions. In the *Timaeus*, Plato explains why the world is not anthropomorphic: in creating the universe, the demiurge "did not think he had to needlessly attach hands ... nor feet, nor, in general, anything necessary for walking," since the world neither walks nor grasps objects. Further in the dialogue, however, Plato employs the opposite argument to justify the fact that humans, created by the same demiurge, have feet and hands that are parts of a body in the service of the head "which is a most divine thing... dominating everything within us," and has the same spherical shape as the universe. An analogy is thus established between the world (which has an *omphalós*, a navel, situated at Delphi)

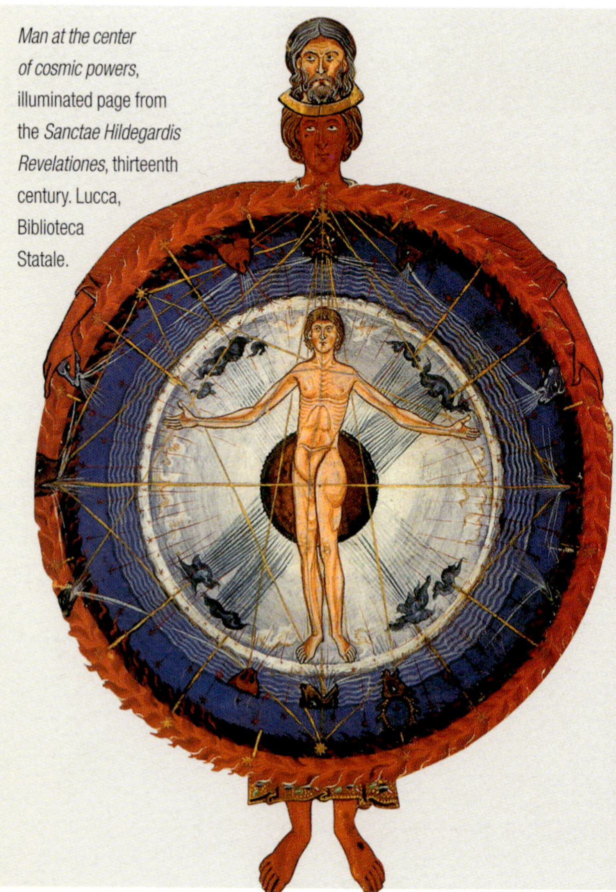

Man at the center of cosmic powers, illuminated page from the *Sanctae Hildegardis Revelationes*, thirteenth century. Lucca, Biblioteca Statale.

and humankind. But this relationship is based on the concept that the world is the highest example of human harmony, so that the temple, originally the mirror of the universe, inevitably mirrors the human form.

Christianity has shared this concept, since the created world is identified with Christ himself; humankind, Christ, and the universe overlap. The German mystic Hildegard of Bingen (1098–1179) states that the cosmos is as wide as it is high, exactly like a man standing with open arms. Christ had thus become the macranthropos of the new era, and churches had become the new model of the anthropomorphized, or humanized, universe.

● THE IDEAL CITY

The architects of the Renaissance also drew inspiration from the human body. According to Leon Battista Alberti (1404–1472), "As in the living being each member accords with the others, so in the building each part must harmonize with the others."

Francesco di Giorgio Martini (1439–1502) extended the relationship with the human body to the urban organism: "The city having the reason, measurements, and shape of the human body ... has all of the same partitions and members in perfect dimensions." The navel may be likened to a public square and the head to a fortified castle, cathedral, or lordly palace, according to need. But in the designs of architects and theorists such as Filarete (1400–1469), Bernardo Rossellino (1409–1469), and Bernardo Buontalenti (1536–1608), the city is linked to cosmic harmony through geometrically regular urban plans.

And it was on the basis of these concepts that Le Corbusier, in designing the city of Chandigarh in the Punjab region of India, chose the emblem of an open hand as a sort of mobile sculpture turning with the wind that blows from the Himalayas.

Left:
Bernardo Rossellino, *Piazza Pio II Piccolomini*, c. 1459–1462. Pienza, Siena, Italy.

Le Corbusier, *Study for monument to the open hand in Chandigarh*, 1951. Paris, Fondation Le Corbusier.

Left:
William Morris, *Pimpernel*, wallpaper, 1876. London, Victoria and Albert Museum.

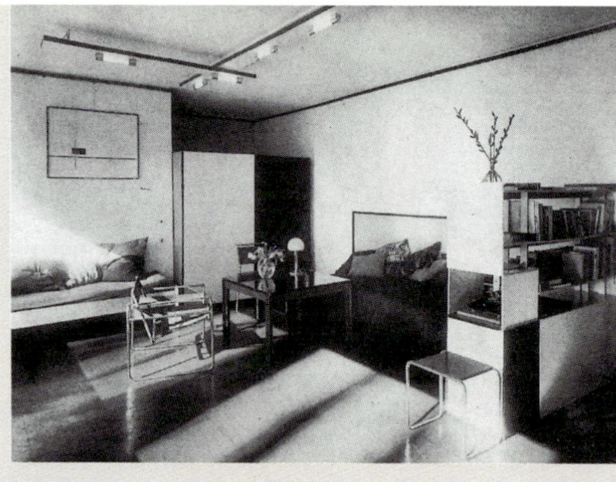

Above: *Living room of the Moholy-Nagy house at Dessau, Germany, in the 1920s.*

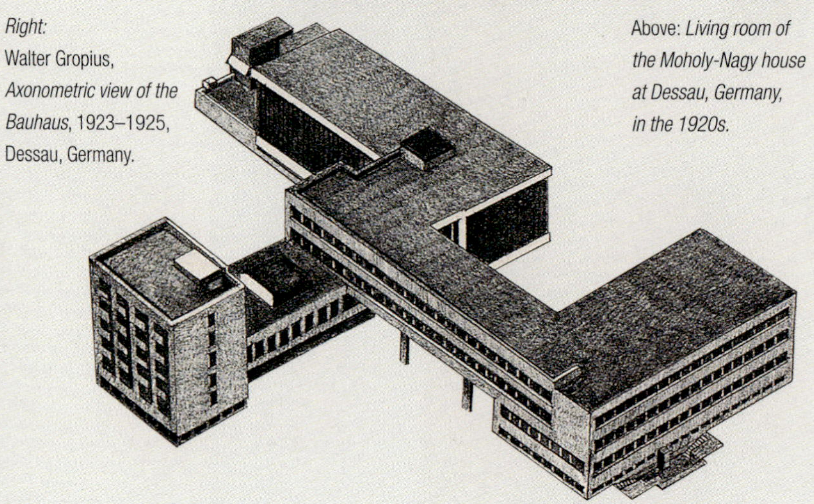

Right:
Walter Gropius, *Axonometric view of the Bauhaus*, 1923–1925, Dessau, Germany.

Architecture and Industrial Design

The concept of "design," as explained by Walter Gropius (1883–1969), "embraces in general the entire orbit of what surrounds us and derives from the hand of man, from simple domestic furnishings to the complex organization of an entire city." Starting with the Industrial Revolution, the mass production of architectural components has made it possible to construct buildings that are not only functional and accessible to a vast public, but also aesthetically satisfying. The object of design has thus become a work of art of sorts, reproducible but conceived with the care dedicated to the creation of a unique piece. In the literal sense, industrial design means "designing objects for mass production." The term is commonly used, however, to refer to human surroundings as a whole, "from the spoon to the city," in the phrase of Ernesto Nathan Rogers (1909–1969). In this sense, industrial design is like the last remaining fragment of the anthropocentric attitude that so strongly influenced earlier architecture.

● ORIGINS

The origins of industrial design date back to the Arts and Crafts movement in England, founded and promoted by William Morris (1834–1896). Influenced by the writings of the art critic John Ruskin (1819–1900), who acclaimed the craftsman's skill and the organization of work in the Middle Ages, Morris opposed art to industry, artistic creation to mass production. In 1861 he founded a company that manufactured furniture, household utensils, wallpaper, fabrics, tapestries, and stained glass, all combining functionality with high aesthetic quality. These concepts were to be developed later by Walter Crane and Lewis Day, the latter generally regarded as "the first designer." The new ideas were also to exert a strong influence on Henry van de Velde (1863–1957), architect and theoretician of the Art Nouveau movement, who in 1903 was already thinking about a "logical structure of products" in which the decoration of buildings and objects would be fused with their functionality. In a wide range of utilitarian objects

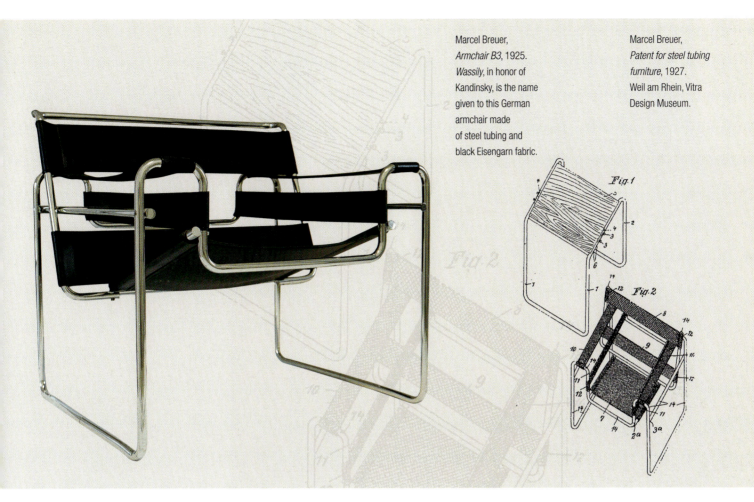

Marcel Breuer, *Armchair B3*, 1925. *Wassily*, in honor of Kandinsky, is the name given to this German armchair made of steel tubing and black Eisengarn fabric.

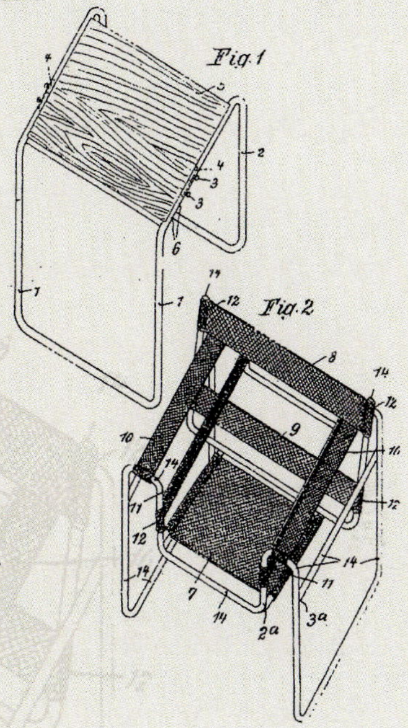

Marcel Breuer, *Patent for steel tubing furniture*, 1927. Weil am Rhein, Vitra Design Museum.

and furnishings, functionality was combined with decorative elegance and sweeping curved lines. The spread of Art Nouveau throughout Europe promoted a new integration between art and industrial production. In this climate, the German painter and designer Peter Behrens (1868–1940), architect and consultant to the Electric Power Company of Berlin (AEG), found himself engaged in 1907 in the design of factories, shops, and even stationery.

● THE BAUHAUS

The Bauhaus ("building house"), a vital force in the birth of industrial design, took its name from the Institute of Arts and Crafts founded by Walter Gropius in 1919, after the reorganization of the Weimar School of Applied Arts. The school's main objective was to design objects that could be mass-produced. A central aspect of this work was experimenting with new materials, including steel and curved plywood, thanks to the collaboration of artists and architects such as Hannes Meyer and Mies van der Rohe, who succeeded Gropius as director of the school. The Bauhaus was closed by the Nazi government in 1932, but several of its designers, among them László Moholy-Nagy and Marcel Breuer, continued their creative experiments in the United States.

● ERGONOMICS

The last frontier of industrial design, whose products are exhibited in museums as works of art, is ergonomics, the field of technology that considers physical capabilities, work processes, and environments in the design of machines and everyday implements, drawing on such other disciplines as industrial medicine and physiology.

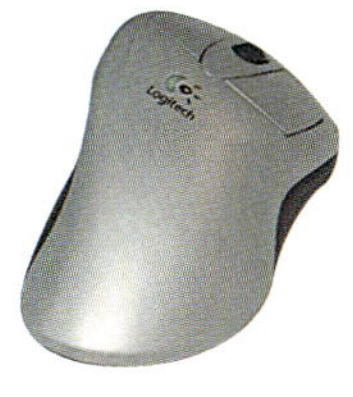

Ergonomic keyboard and mouse, 2001. The primary objective of ergonomics is to improve the relationship between humans, machines, and the environment. Striking examples may be seen in the continual modifications, not aesthetic alone, in the design of the keyboard and mouse for personal computers, a true symbol of the modern age.

Architecture and Decoration

Above:
Maori culture, *Whare Runanga (meeting house)*. Waitangi, New Zealand.

A building is decorated to make it more beautiful. The Latin words *decor* and *decus*, from which come "decoration" (the same root in English, Italian, and French), mean "beautiful, elegant" or "illustrious, dignified." While to decorate means to adorn with paint, friezes, hangings, or other embellishments, the technical and stylistic possibilities, both sculptural and pictorial, introduced over the centuries have been innumerable.

● ORIGINS

The tendency to decorate has distant origins. The most ancient examples of habitat decoration are rock paintings that date from more than 20,000 years ago. These cannot be considered architectural decoration in the strict sense, however, since they were painted in caves left almost in the natural state. As noted by the anthropologist André Leroi-Gourhan, "no truly identical decorated grottoes have been found," although the animals in these paintings are frequently grouped in hierarchies (horses, bison, or aurochs at the center, surrounded by less important animals such as wild goats, mammoths, and deer). Some idea of the decorations used on wooden buildings in Neolithic times is provided by examples from contemporary ethnographic cultures. In New Guinea, façades on the "houses of the spirits" near the Sepik river bear masks with human features (protecting spirits), while the typical Maori meeting house in New Zealand is decorated with panels bearing anthropomorphic sculptures and thresholds built of wood and mother-of-pearl adorned with stylized human figures covered with tattoos.

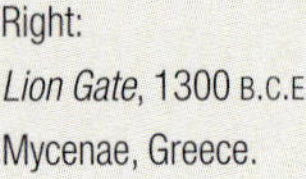

Right:
Lion Gate, 1300 B.C.E. Mycenae, Greece.

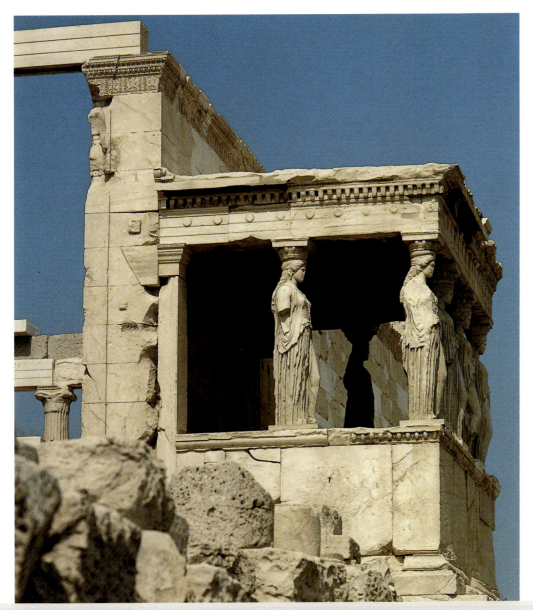

Loggia of the Caryatids, 422 B.C.E. Southern side of the Erechtheion. Athens, Acropolis.

● ANTIQUITY

The famous Lion Gate at Mycenae is one of the first examples of sculptural architecture in the Western world, anticipating an element that was to become fundamental to the Greek temple: decoration of the tympanum. This was an architectural problem, since a complex scene—linked to the dedication of the building and therefore crucial to its function—had to be inserted in a triangular space. To maintain thematic unity, the early architects employed monstrous, snakelike figures to fill the acute angles. Starting in the middle of the sixth century B.C.E., the figures were placed in "narrative cells," according to the space available and arranged as naturally as possible. Up to that time, however, the decorations were superimposed on the structure of the building. The column-statues of the Loggia of the Caryatids in Athens are the oldest known example of sculptural decoration with a structural function in the building, a theme that

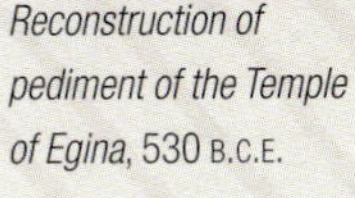

Reconstruction of pediment of the Temple of Egina, 530 B.C.E.

Greek and Roman decorative motifs.

1. Meander
2. Palmettes and lotus flowers
3. Egg-and-dart motif
4. *Cyma recta* with Roman ornament and fusarole

was to be further developed in the Middle Ages. In Romanesque portals, the column-statues decorate the embrasure or the central pilasters (*trumeaux*) that support the tympanum.

● THE MIDDLE AGES

In medieval architecture, the relationship between design and painted decoration was as important as the relationship between sculpture and building structure. Decoration often served to accentuate surfaces with varying or contrasting colors, creating a pictorial affect, as in the façade of Palazzo Ducale in Venice. In this case, the desired effect is produced not by painting, as in the brightly colored churches of Moldavia (on the Balkan peninsula), but by multicolored bricks and marble. The lucid geometry of the façade of San Miniato al Monte in Florence is one of the finest examples of the use of polychrome in medieval Western architecture. This technique has found its highest expression, however, in the decorations of the Islamic world, which employed such varied materials as majolica, stucco, glass, and marble. In the Far East, the wooden structures of temples and palaces are often embellished with gilded decorations. Late Byzantine churches in Europe, instead, are distinguished by facings made of bricks arranged in particular patterns. Sculptural decoration can coincide with a structural function (as in the case of the column-statues described above); they can also accompany, emphasize, and transfigure the structural lines of arches and vaults; or they can be superimposed on the underlying structure.

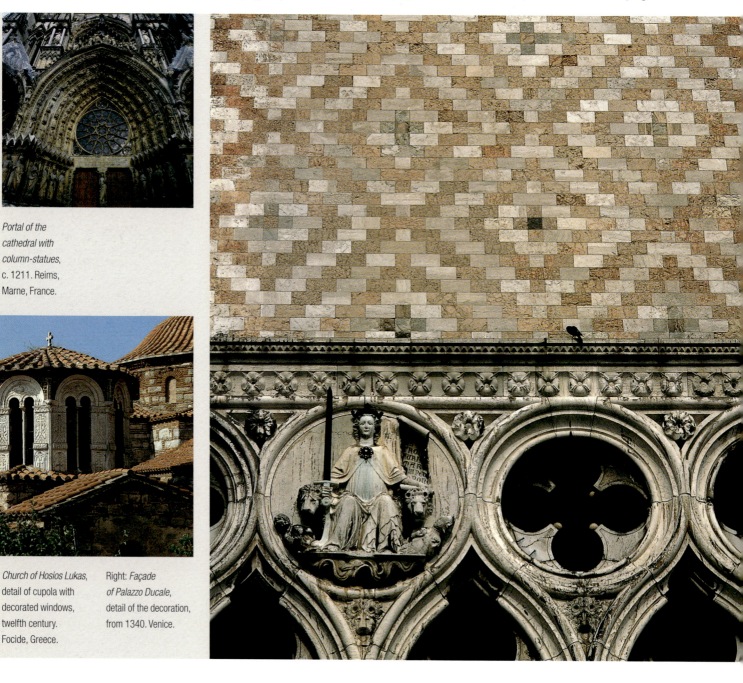

Portal of the cathedral with column-statues, c. 1211. Reims, Marne, France.

Church of Hosios Lukas, detail of cupola with decorated windows, twelfth century. Focide, Greece.

Right: *Façade of Palazzo Ducale,* detail of the decoration, from 1340. Venice.

View of the Monastery of Voronet, decorated with wall paintings in 1547. Northern Moldavia, Bucovina, Romania.

● FROM THE RENAISSANCE TO TODAY

In the Europe of princely courts, the decorative sobriety of the early Renaissance, whose architecture was distinguished by equilibrium and purity of form, gradually gave way to ornamentation that was increasingly more refined and sumptuous, as if to emphasize the status of buildings.

Decorative richness and variety were to be even further accentuated in the Mannerist style, and then to proliferate in Baroque and Rococo. In the late nineteenth and early twentieth centuries, with Art Nouveau and Liberty Style, the building itself became decorative. In the period after World War II, decoration was for the most part "reabsorbed" by structure, with the notable exceptions of an era marked by experimentation and returns to the past—as exemplified by the immense mosaic that covers the Central Library building at the University of Mexico, decorated with pre-Columbian motifs interpreted in a modern style.

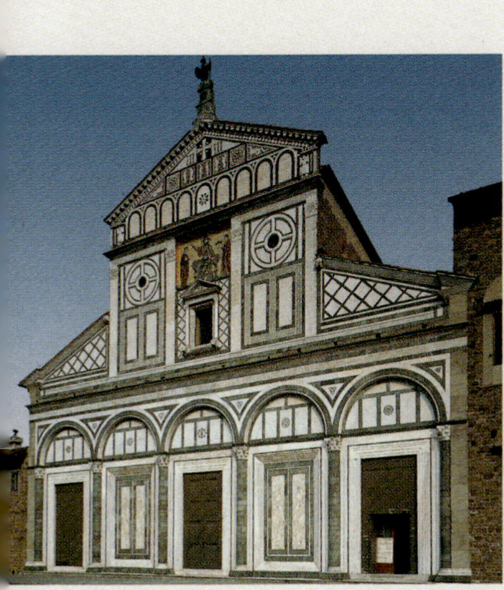

Above:
Façade of the Basilica of San Miniato al Monte, eleventh to thirteenth centuries. Florence.

Juan O'Gorman, *Central Library of the Universidad Autonoma de Mexico*, 1952–1953. Mexico City.

Architecture and Nature

A window in one of the houses built of wood typical of Arctic regions. Ilulissat, northwestern Greenland.

Left:
Andrea Palladio, *La Rotonda*, c. 1550, Vicenza. In his *Four Books of Architecture,* Palladio describes the site of La Rotonda as "pleasant and delightful ... situated atop a hillock very easy to climb." Since the villa overlooks "splendid views ... loggias have been provided on all four sides."

Nature can be seen either as a challenge or as a source of inspiration. In the dialectical relationship between architecture and nature, the design of a building, village, city, park, or garden may be either integrated with, or contrasted to, natural or artificial elements. In this sense, the garden represents the most significant example of human efforts to adapt nature to common needs. In recent decades the figure of the gardener-architect has assumed the profile of a true and respected professional: the landscape architect.

● THE LOCATION OF BUILDINGS

To decide where to found a city, the Ancient Greeks consulted an oracle; in the Middle Ages and Renaissance as well, astrologers were sometimes brought in to help choose the site, and elaborate rituals were carried out before work started on an important building. In parallel to the various astrological traditions, more concrete theories were also developed to establish the orientation of a building. Such theories took into account a variety of factors essential to improving the quality of life and the environmental setting. Vitruvius was

A slate roof. Cônques, Aveyron, France.

Residence known as the "El Greco house," fourteenth century. Toledo, Spain. The broad terrace (*zaguan*), atrium, and small patio are all designed to provide relief from the heat.

among the first to establish guidelines and precepts toward those ends. His directives were to be interpreted for centuries, with variations and modifications by a host of treatise writers and architects.

● EXPOSURE TO THE SUN

The orientation of a residence or other building is obviously conditioned by the environment, except in the case of houses of worship (Christian churches usually face toward the west, Islamic mosques toward Mecca). Since early times, exposure to the sun has been one of the primary factors in choosing a building site. Depending on the climate, latitude, and other environmental factors, solutions that ensure the best lighting and temperature have been adopted. In many countries today, regulations governing the construction of school buildings specify that light should fall on students' desks from the left, that classrooms should have a minimum cubic volume in relation to the number of pupils, and that they should be well ventilated. In tropical countries, windows are frequently left unglazed; in drier climates, there are fewer windows and doors, thereby protecting the interior from excessive heat.

In Mediterranean countries, windows are typically protected by shutters, while in northern regions houses are built with large windows to let in as much light as possible.

● BUILDING MATERIALS

Ancient construction techniques emphasized local materials for the simple reason that they were more readily available. One example is slate, a freestone extracted in France and Great Britain and widely used in Northern Europe, especially for roofs, since it provides excellent insulation. The typical Mediterranean house, by contrast, has an almost flat roof covered with terracotta tiles to protect the interior against high temperatures. In Africa, raw earth and straw are frequently used.

● FENG SHUI

Feng shui (Chinese for "wind and water") is a discipline inspired by ancient tradition that has recently spread from the Far East to the West. According to the principles of feng shui, the world is pervaded by positive forces, which should be utilized with respect, and negative forces, which should remain undisturbed. To bring these forces into harmony, thereby avoiding negative influences, building techniques extending even to the arrangement of rooms and their furnishings are studied. Many prominent Western designers now draw inspiration from feng shui. One of the first to do so was the British architect Norman Foster, whose designs include the headquarters of the Hong Kong and Shanghai Bank (1979). Since living in harmonious conditions is beneficial not only to health but also to business, the real-estate developer Donald Trump based his gigantic Riverside South project in New York on the theories of feng shui.

Below: Foster Associates, *Hong Kong and Shanghai Banking Corporation*, 1979–1985. Hong Kong.

The Garden

The word "paradise" derives from the Greek *parádeisos*, which comes in turn from the Persian *pairi-daeza* ("enclosed place"), suggesting that the ancients were so content to dwell in these cool, green places that they hoped to spend eternity there. In the classical world, the garden was not the Eden of Mesopotamian culture, but a sacred area in the vicinity of a temple. In Ancient Rome, the *horti* were embellished with grapevines, fruit trees, ornamental plants, statues, and waterfalls and enlivened by animals of every species. While the gardens of the ancient Islamic world were enchanting, perfumed places of delight, those of Western medieval cities were small plots of land or orchards. The garden in a monastic cloister, adorned with medicinal plants, became a place of meditation, the *hortus conclusus*, symbolic mirror of the world. The Roman

Viridarium, wall painting from Livia's villa at Prima Porta, 30–20 B.C.E. Rome, Palazzo Massimo, Museo Nazionale Romano.

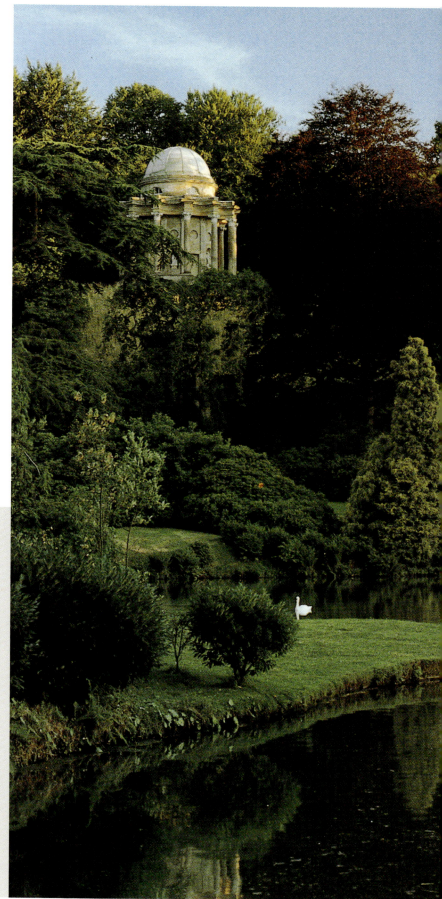

Left: *Temple of Apollo in Stourhead Park,* designed by Henry Flitcroft and Henry Hoare, 1744–1767. Wiltshire, England.

Garden with composition of stones, 1620–1647. Imperial Villa of Katsura, Kyoto, Japan.

tradition of patrician gardens was revived in the Renaissance, when it developed in monumental form in the so-called Italian garden, laid out in regular sections; the style then spread to France and Austria. In contrast to this geometric concept, the English landscape garden emphasized natural beauty and played an important role in the aesthetics of the sublime and the picturesque. The Romantic English park was widely imitated throughout Europe. Its origins dated back to the ideas of William Kent (1685–1748), the first architect "to leap over the fence and to see that all of nature is a garden." Later, the English and Italian styles were combined in the designs of Russel Page (1906–1985). Oriental gardens, too, boast ancient traditions; brooks, fountains, and grottoes are salient features. In Japanese gardens, influenced by Zen, abstraction and silence are served by meticulous designs of rocks and stones.

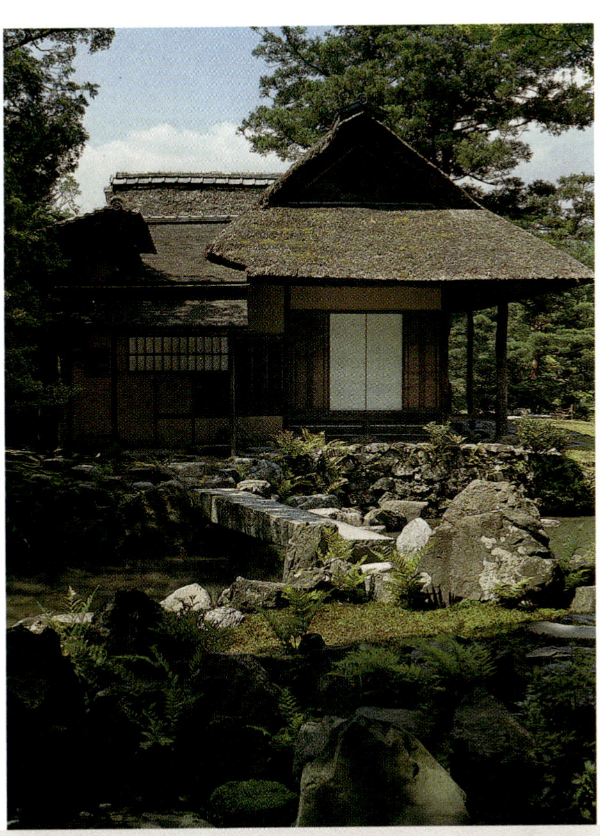

Layout of Boboli Gardens, Florence.

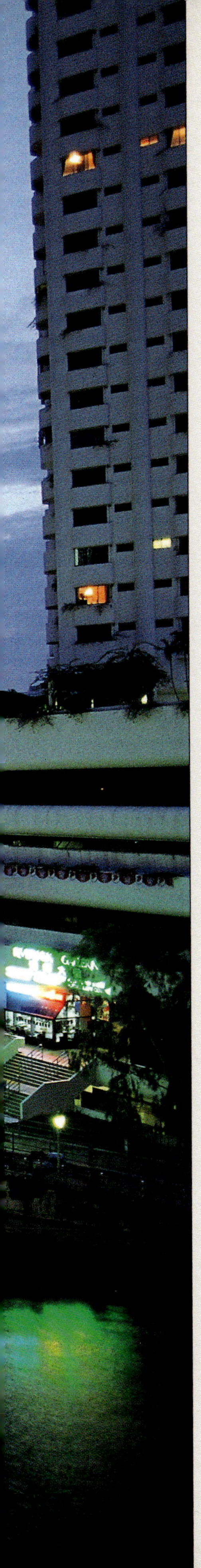

Buildings and Typologies

The word "building" is generally used to indicate a construction intended for habitation or other public or private human activity. Buildings, of course, are not all the same. They can differ not only in material but also in shape and structure, depending on the individual and collective requirements, which are in turn conditioned by the environmental, political, and social context.

Architectural styles also differ according to the prevailing tastes of different epochs and cultures. A first distinction may be made on the basis of functionality. According to this criterion, the pages that follow illustrate the most important building types—residential, religious, public, military, and collective; and for production, service, commerce, or burial.

Above: *Merchant-class home at 168 Herengracht, now site of the Theater Museum*, seventeenth century, restored in 1971. Amsterdam.

Remains of Temple of Hercules, sixth century B.C.E. Agrigento, Italy.

Left:
The business district of Singapore, with Elgin Bridge in the foreground.

Habitations

Paul Kane, *Indian encampment on Lake Huron*, 1845. Toronto, Art Gallery of Ontario. A *tepee* is a tent made of tanned leather stretched over poles converging at the top, traditionally used by North American Indians.

Since the remote past, the need for a habitation has been one of the primary requisites of humankind. The need for a shelter other than a simple cave is in fact common not only to settled populations but also to nomadic ones, which utilized (as they still do today) easily transportable tents or simple temporary structures, sheds often made of straw and branches.

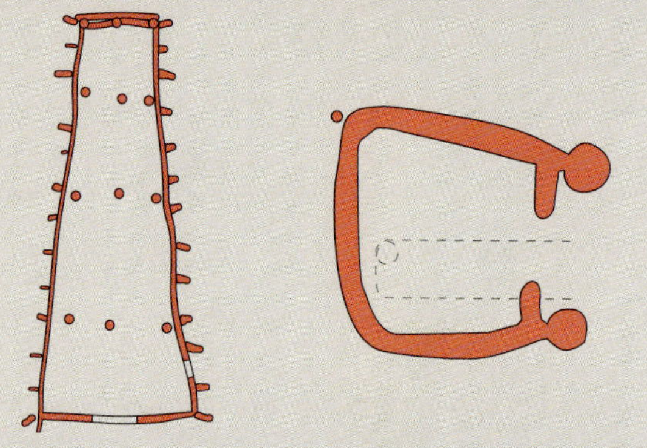

Plan of wedge-shaped hut, reconstruction based on excavations of dwelling places from the late Stone Age in Westphalia, Germany.

Section plan of stone hut, reconstruction based on excavations at Khinokitia, Cyprus, fifth millennium B.C.E.

● ORIGINS

The first stable dwelling places date from the Neolithic Age, when an agricultural economy began to take the place of hunting and gathering. Excavations in Poland, Germany, and Cyprus have enabled archaeologists to reconstruct the plans of Neolithic habitats. The buildings consisted of a single room (rectangular, round, or wedge-shaped). The circular huts excavated on the island of Cyprus are similar in structure to the *trulli* found in Apulia in southern Italy.

Roof of a trullo, Alberobello, Bari, Italy. The structure of the *trullo*, similar to the shelters used by shepherds in the Abruzzo region of Italy even today, recalls earthenware funerary urns from the Neolithic Age, in the shape of miniature houses.

Plan of a patrician home in Imperial Rome. 1. Vestibule. 2. Entrance. 3. Atrium. 4. Bedrooms. 5. Triclinium. 6. Room. 7. Studio. 8. Peristyle. 9. Bedrooms. 10. Kitchen. 11. Large triclinium. Surrounding the atrium, with an *impluvium* for collecting rainwater in the middle, were such other rooms as the triclinium (dining room with a bench, at times made of masonry, and marble table at the center). The more private rooms were entered from the peristyle, an open courtyard surrounded by a portico.

Right: *Peristyle of the Villa dei Misteri*, first century C.E. Pompeii.

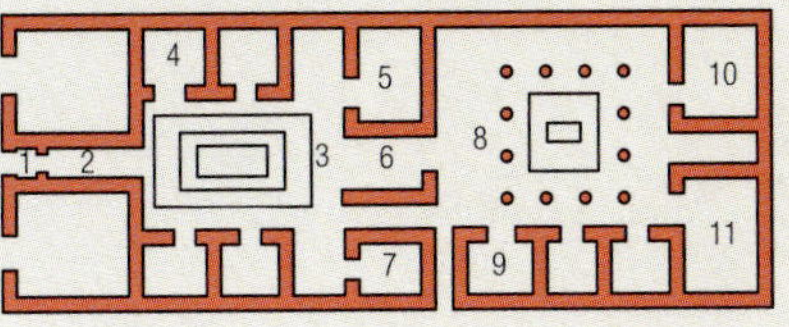

● ANTIQUITY

Already in Ancient Egypt there existed a sharp distinction among the dwellings of the upper class, middle class, and common people. The lordly mansion, surrounded by a wall that also enclosed a garden and servants' quarters, was a two-story construction with hypostyle halls (its roofs resting on columns) and a number of rooms. These houses were nearly fifty times larger than those of the middle class, which in turn differed from those of the common people, consisting mainly of huts made of unbaked brick. In Ancient Rome, the less well-to-do lived in multifamily complexes called *insulae*; its brick buildings were several stories high, with an entranceway, a main hall, and service facilities (latrines, wells, and cisterns for collecting rainwater) shared by several families. By contrast, the typical patrician residence (*domus*) was built on one floor only, with the entrance from the street flanked by two rooms often used as shops.

● THE MIDDLE AGES

In the medieval Western world, the variety of architectural solutions reflected a multiplicity of social and political contexts. In Rome, scattered with ruins, the remains of ancient buildings were reused for new constructions, which incorporated and transformed the great monuments of the past. In other cities, such as Venice, the local style was influenced by the Byzantine fashion of using precious materials for decoration. In Northern Europe, the buildings were frequently made of wood, with steep roofs and frames of exposed timber. In France and England, brick was commonly used. These materials have been utilized in a vast range of housing typologies in other cultures as well, from pre-Columbian America to China.

Aerial view of the medieval complex of Palazzo Caetani, adjacent to the ancient Tomb of Cecilia Metella. Capo Bove, Rome.

Model of Chinese house from the Han period (206 B.C.E.–220 C.E.). Henan, Provincial Museum, China.

Façade of an old house in the historic center of Strasbourg, France.

● THE RENAISSANCE PALACE

The Renaissance palace developed gradually, through the aggregation of medieval "courtyard houses." These were houses built around a courtyard that came to incorporate towers and other structures to form a unified whole; they often contained shops or storerooms on the ground floor and living quarters on the *piano nobile*. The purchase of these buildings by a single owner was often followed by a renovation of the structure and its surroundings, giving rise to the urban palace.

● THE MERCHANT-CLASS HOME

A new type of habitat that now began to develop was the elegant, refined merchant-class home. The first merchant-class residences are found in seventeenth-century Holland, where this social class was especially prosperous. The revival of Italian classical elements, fused with the Gothic style of traditional Dutch residences (a long floor plan and tall, narrow front), gave rise to highly original designs. In Amsterdam, a famous example of this style is located at number 168 on the Herengracht, the "gentlemen's canal" (p. 41). While retaining the dignity of the patrician home, bourgeois houses were practical and sober, in keeping with the style of the rising middle class.

Michelozzo, *Palazzo Medici*, completed in 1462, detail of courtyard. Florence. The inner courtyard of Cosimo the Elder's residence, considered the prototype of the Renaissance noble palace, reflects elements of both the Roman villa and the medieval "courtyard house."

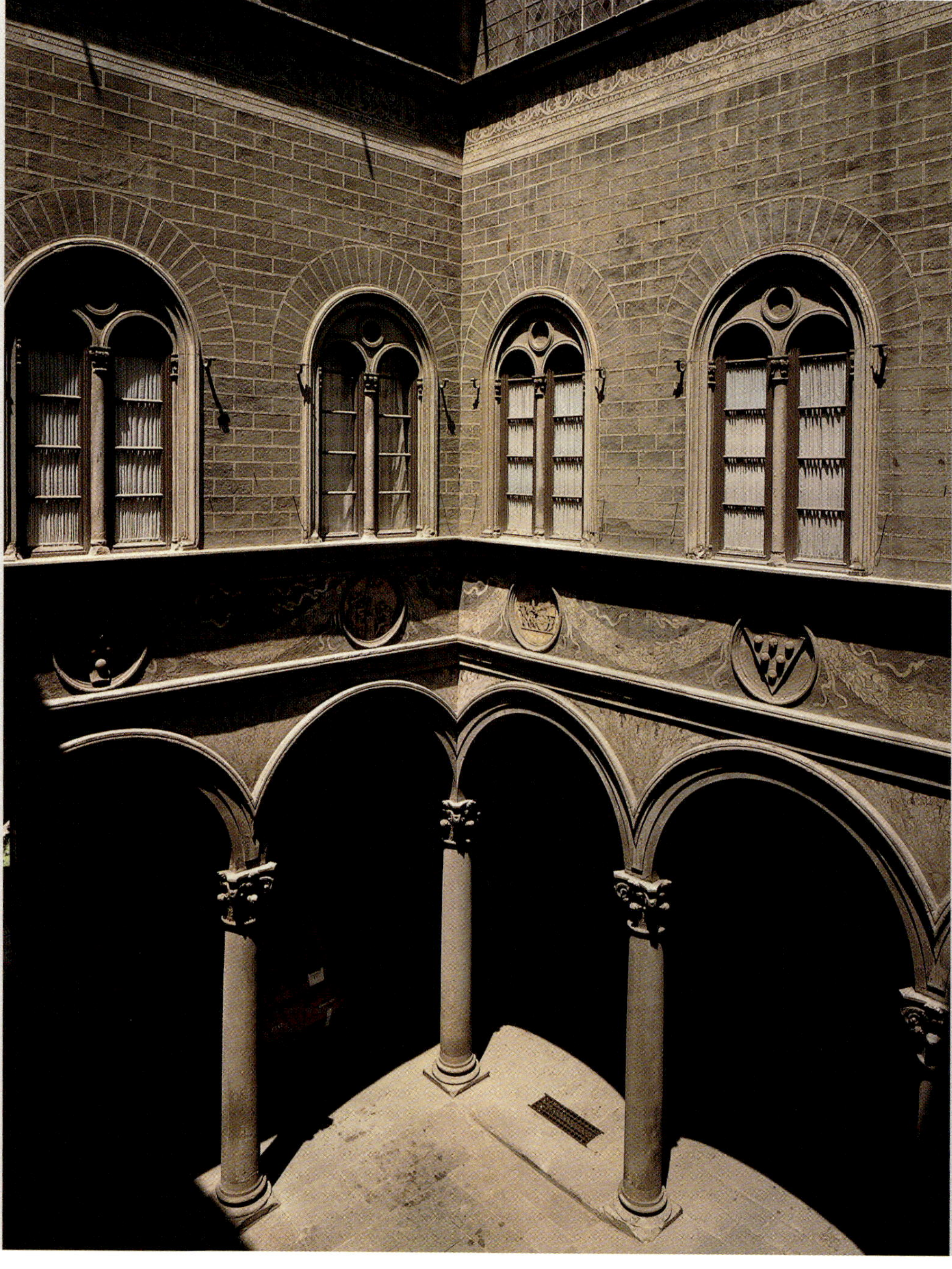

● THE APARTMENT BUILDING

The objective of reconciling elegance with low cost became increasingly evident in the eighteenth century. While the bourgeois house of the seventeenth-century accommodated a single family, in the eighteenth century the idea of an elegant building shared by several families became widely accepted. In this way, the various tenants could benefit from high-quality communal areas, such as an atrium, a garden, and terraces. Thus was born the concept of the apartment house, which was to influence residential construction for centuries to come.

● THE MODERN AGE

The most widespread residential structure in cities throughout the world today is the apartment building. This solution has undergone notable changes in recent decades, beginning with the experiments of the French architect Le Corbusier. The pressing need to reduce space, especially in big cities, has also led to the conversion of attics, mansards, and basements into residential units. It remains undeniable, however, that rooms filled with light are essential to a better quality of life. One solution, albeit reserved to the wealthier classes, is to "enlarge" living space by combining several rooms into one bigger one (as in a "loft," an apartment created in a renovated warehouse or abandoned factory). To escape pollution and noise, more and more apartment buildings are being built in the suburbs. The most attractive apartment buildings, even those designed for a great many families, have balconies, terraces, and communal lawns or gardens.

Le Corbusier, *Housing Unit*, 1947–1952. Marseilles.

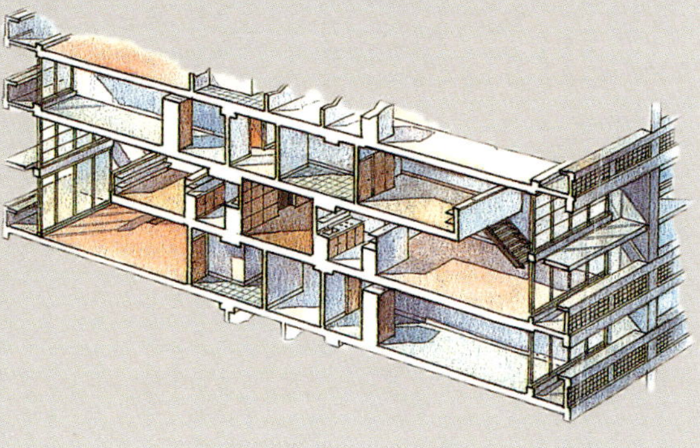

Reconstruction of a module of Le Corbusier's Housing Unit.

Religious Buildings

The structure of a religious building is a function of the faith itself. In the religious life of Ancient Greece, in some forms of Buddhism, in Hinduism, and in the rites of pre-Columbian America, the temple is a ritual structure extraneous to the people; lay worship takes place outside the building while observances inside are reserved to a priestly class. In the traditions of Judaism, Christianity, and Islam, by contrast, a religious building serves a communal purpose: synagogues, churches, and mosques are designed to hold masses of people.

● THE GREEK TEMPLE

The heart of the Greek temple is called the cella (*náos*, or "ship"), a windowless chamber that houses a statue of the divinity and could be entered only by priests. If it has no columns, the temple is defined as *astylar*. When the cella is preceded by a *pronaos* (vestibule) with two columns at the front, the style is called *in antis*. If the *antae* are repeated at the back, creating an *opisthodome* (adjoining porch), it is known as double *in antis*. The design is called *prostyle* if the antae are set behind a colonnaded vestibule at the front, and *amphiprostyle* when there is another colonnade at the back. The temple is termed *peripteral* when a colonnade runs around all four sides; *pseudo-peripteral* when the walls of the cella are lined with semicolumns; *dipteral* when the line of columns is double; and *pseudo-dipteral* when the inner colonnade is entirely lacking or is composed of semicolumns along the walls. A further classification indicates the number of columns on the front: a temple can be *tetrastyle, pentastyle, hexastyle, octastyle, decastyle, dodecastyle,* or *polystyle* (from four to twelve or more columns).

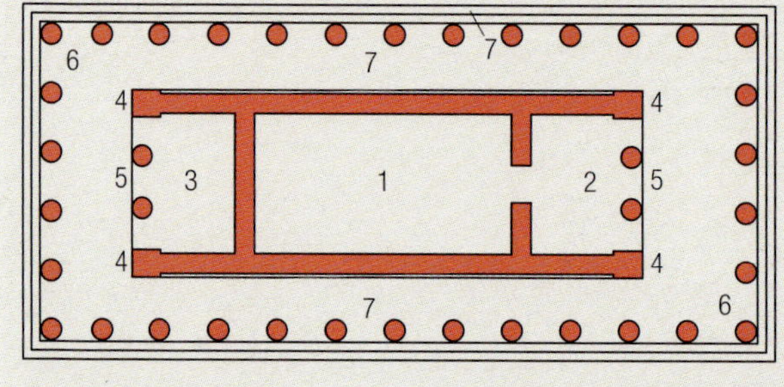

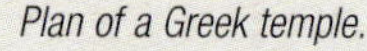
Plan of a Greek temple.

1. Cella or *náos*
2. Vestibule or *pronaos*
3. Opisthodome
4. Walls of anta
5. Columns *in antis*
6. Colonnade or peristyle
7. Stylobate

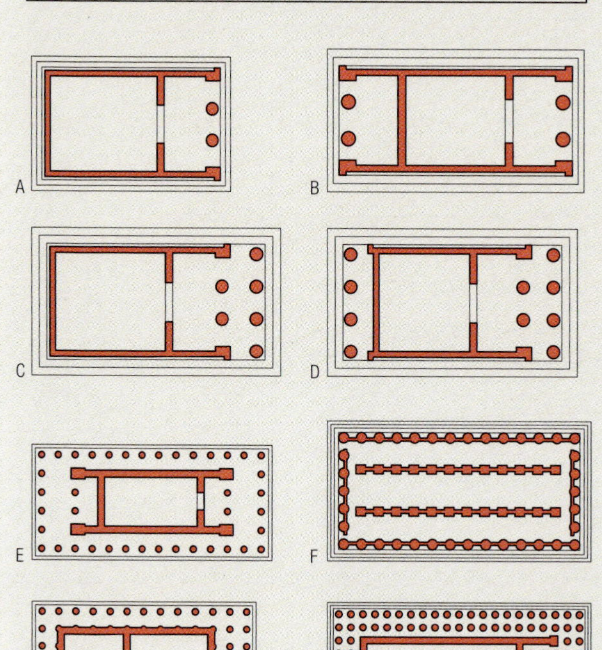

Plans and typologies of the Greek temple.

A. *In antis*
B. Double *in antis*
C. Prostyle
D. Amphiprostyle
E. Peripteral
F. Pseudo-peripteral
G. Pseudo-dipteral
H. Dipteral

Left: *Temple of Concord*, fifth century B.C.E. Agrigento, Italy. This temple, of the Doric order, is peripteral and hexastyle.

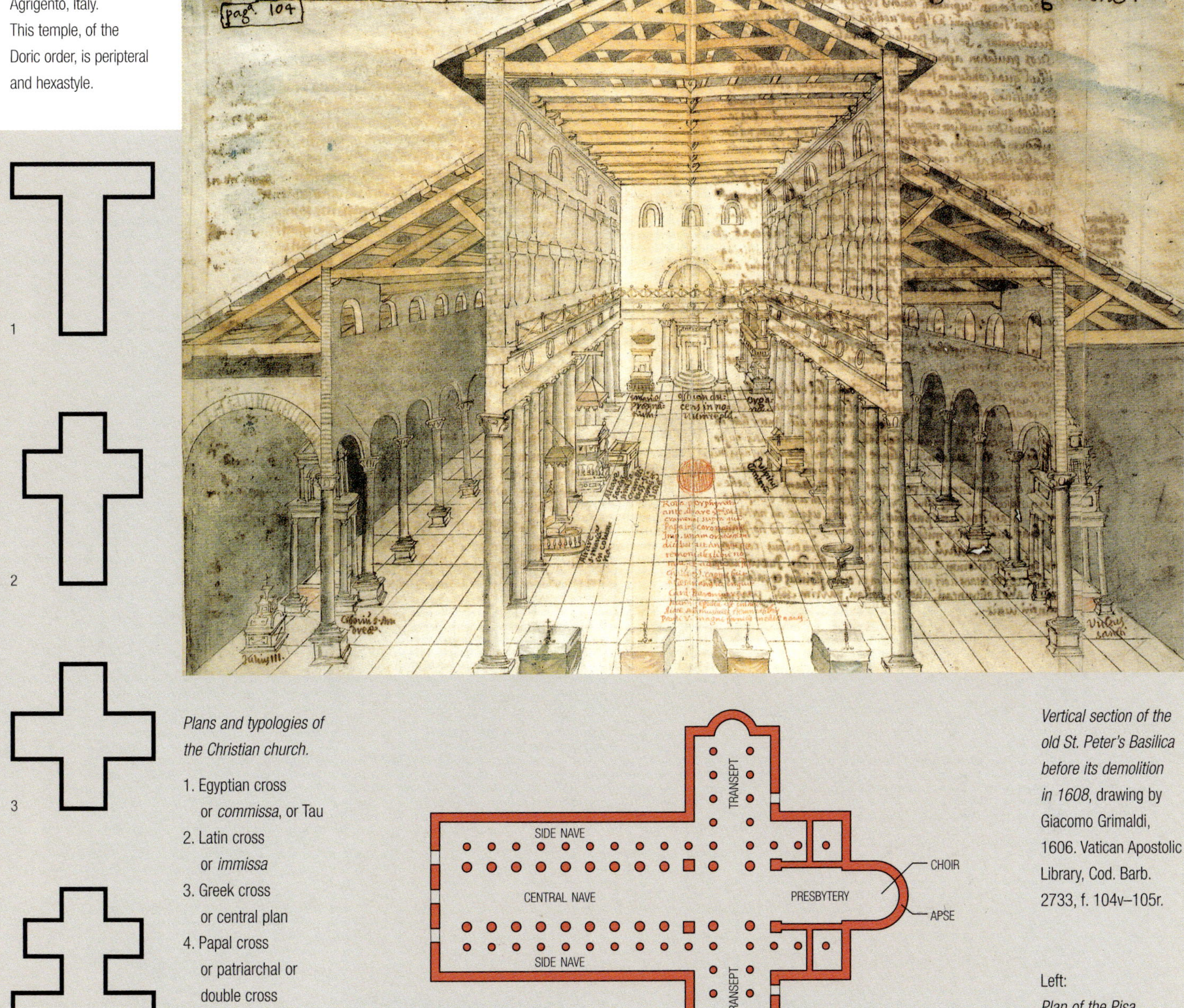

Vertical section of the old St. Peter's Basilica before its demolition in 1608, drawing by Giacomo Grimaldi, 1606. Vatican Apostolic Library, Cod. Barb. 2733, f. 104v–105r.

Plans and typologies of the Christian church.

1. Egyptian cross or *commissa*, or Tau
2. Latin cross or *immissa*
3. Greek cross or central plan
4. Papal cross or patriarchal or double cross

Left: *Plan of the Pisa Duomo*, first half of the twelfth century.

● CHURCHES AND CATHEDRALS

The church (from the Greek *ekklésia*, or "assembly") originated in the Christian world as place for the faithful to gather. The first church buildings reiterated the rectangular plan of the Roman basilica, which first served as a covered market and, during the Imperial Age, as a law court. Whereas in the Roman basilica the entrance was usually located on the long side of the building, the earliest Christian churches placed the entrance on the short side, with the presbytery concluding with an apse. A later development at this end of the church was the choir, with an altar and a *cathedra* (or bishop's chair, from which word "cathedral" derives). When the basilican hall (now called the nave) is crossed by a transept, the result is a *Latin cross plan*, an obvious symbol of Christ's crucifixion. Developing along with the Latin cross plan was another design, first used for secondary buildings such as votive chapels or baptisteries, and later for many churches and cathedrals. This was the *Greek cross plan*, or *central plan*, which could more easily be covered by a domed roof.

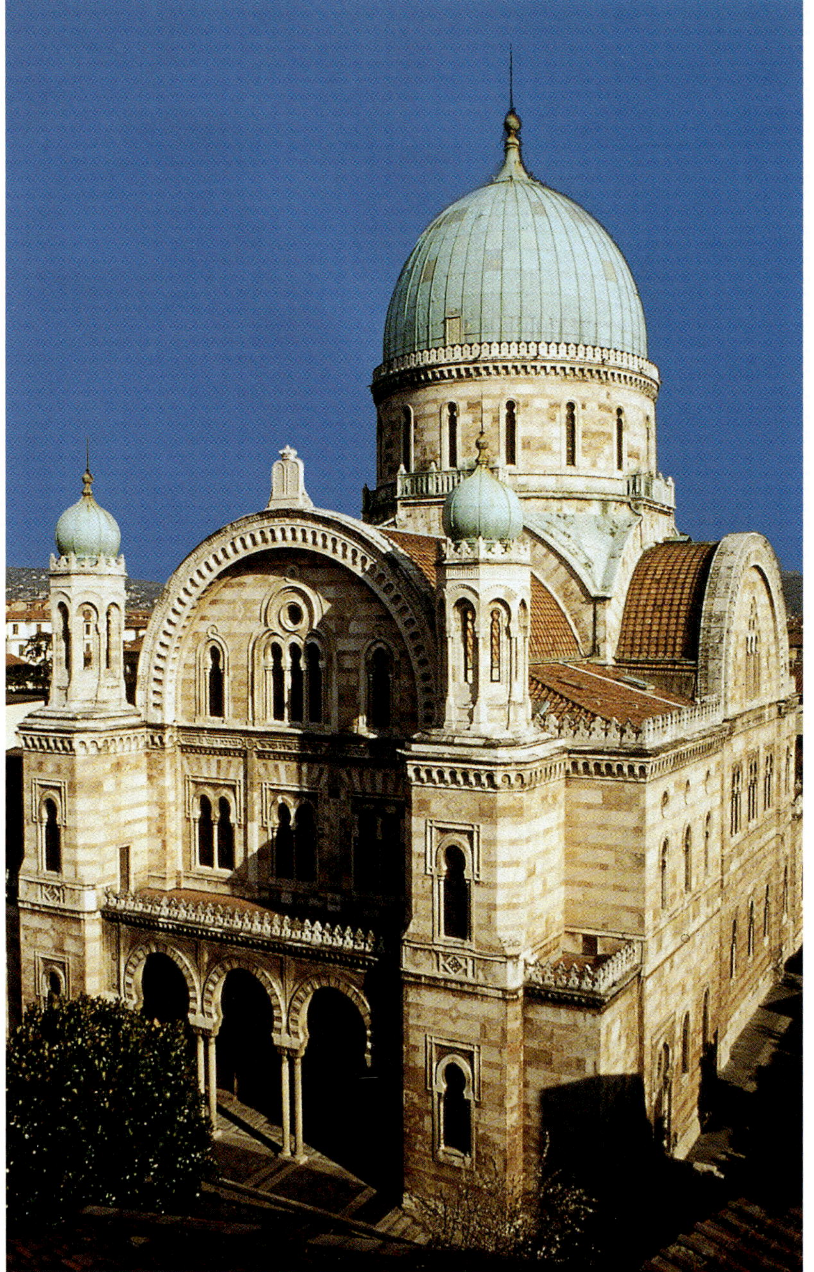

Marco Treves and Vincenzo Micheli, *Moorish style synagogue*, 1872–1874. Florence.

● THE SYNAGOGUE

Originally a building used for meetings and teaching (from the Greek *synagogé*, or "assembly"; in Hebrew *bet ha-knesset*), the Jewish synagogue took on a specifically religious function after the Temple of Jerusalem was destroyed by the Romans in 70 C.E. The original plan was basilican, oriented in the direction of Jerusalem. A niche in the eastern wall (*Aron ha-quodesh*) held the Scrolls of the Law (*Sepher Torah*). With the Jewish Diaspora, synagogues began to be built in different forms. The oldest surviving synagogue in Europe, located in Worms, Germany, is Romanesque in style, with elements dating to the twelfth century.

● THE MOSQUE

Originating as a meeting place for religious services as well as important decisions by the Muslim community, the mosque (in Arab *masjid*, or "place of prostration") was at first merely a plot of earth surrounded by a wall. It then developed into a hypostyle hall with a flat roof (*zulla*), similar to Egyptian buildings. A characteristic element of the mosque is the *quibla*, a windowless wall facing Mecca. Since the end of the seventh century, this wall has been adorned with a niche (*mihrab*), similar in shape to that of the synagogue. The plan of the Christian basilica also seems to have influenced the structure of the mosque,

Erich Mendelsohn, *Synagogue*, 1945. Cleveland, Ohio.

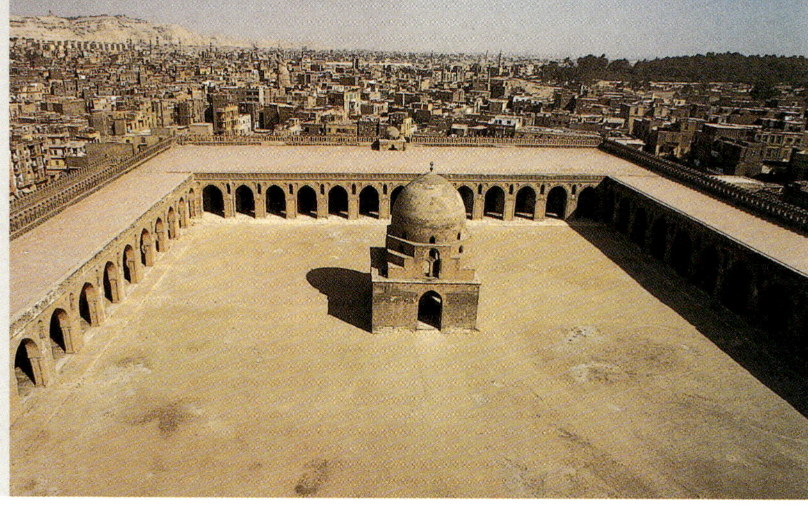

View of the courtyard of the Great Mosque of Ibn Tulun, ninth century. Fustat, Cairo.

which was later embellished, in a reflection of Syrian culture, by a courtyard surrounded by a portico (*sahn*), which opens into the hall of prayer (*haram*). From the eleventh century on, the courtyard was adorned with monumental portals (*iwan*) at the sides. The faithful are called to prayer from the high tower of the minaret (in Arab *minar*, or "place of fire").

● THE STUPA

The most ancient Buddhist monument is the *stupa*, a sanctuary with no interior space except for a small niche holding relics. In India, the stupa is a semispherical mound surmounted by discs. It is enclosed by a fence and accessible from four gates facing the cardinal points of the compass. Buddhists walk clockwise around the monument—an image of the cosmos and of the *parinirvana* (death of Buddha)—while offering prayers (*pradakshina*). A derivative structure is the pagoda, in which tiered roofs take the place of the discs symbolizing Buddhist heaven.

Types of pyramid.
1. With triple steps
2. Entirely without steps
3. With interior steps

1 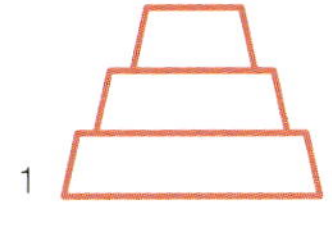

2 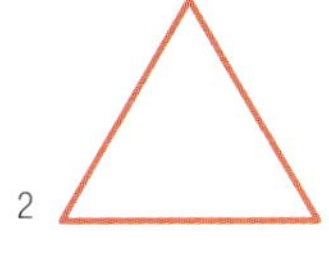

3 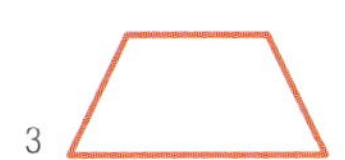

● THE PYRAMID TEMPLE

Common to various cultures and countries, ranging from the monuments of pre-Columbian America to the Babylonian *ziggurat* (from *zaquaru*, "to be tall"), temples in the shape of a truncated pyramid have an altar at the top and broad stairways leading to it on all sides.

Above: *One of the four entrance portals of a stupa*, first century B.C.E. Sanchi, India.

Below: *Shwezigon Pagoda*, begun in 1060. Pagan, Burma.

Pyramid of the Sun, third century C.E. Teotihuacán, Mexico.

Public Buildings

Detail of façade of Broletto, 1215. Como, Italy.

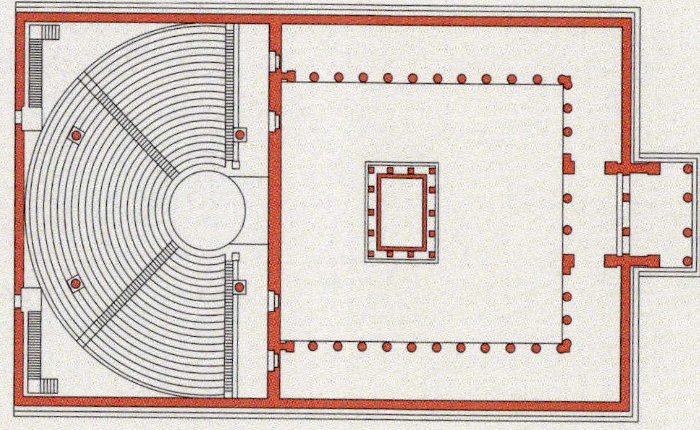

Plan of the bouleutérion of Miletus in Asia Minor. With a semicircular hall for the members of the council, a peristyle, and a prostyle, the *bouleutérion* was erected around 479 B.C.E. when the city, which had been destroyed by the Persians, was rebuilt according to the plan of Hippodamus of Miletus.

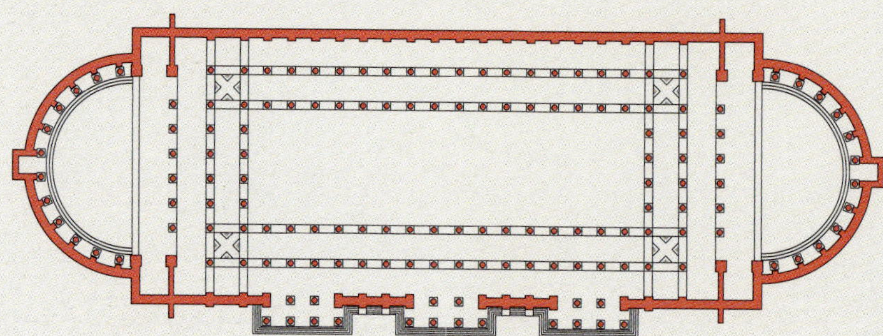

Plan of the Basilica Ulpia in Rome.

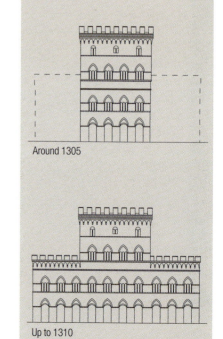

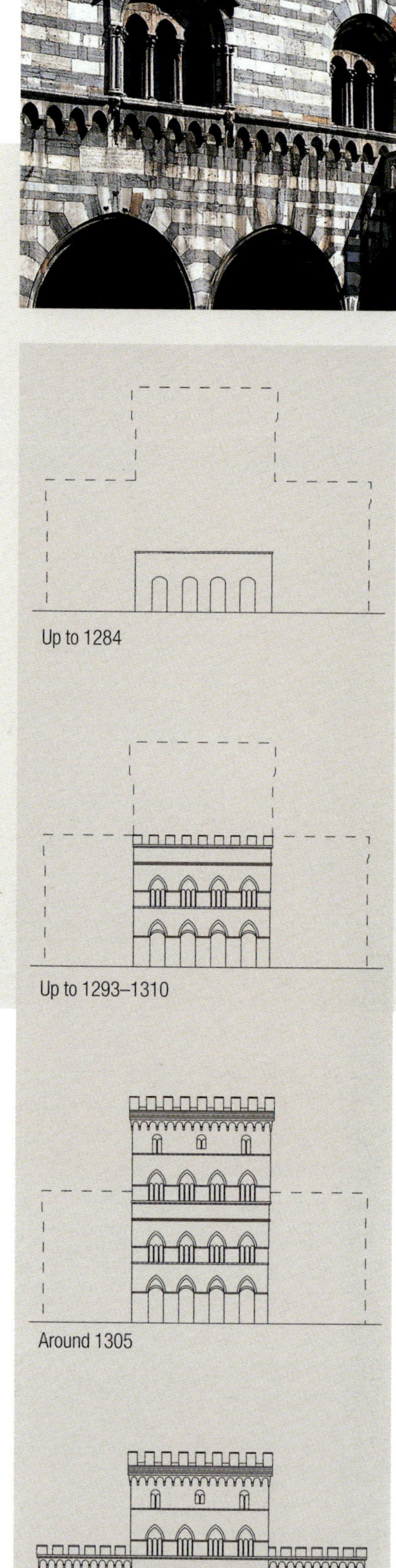

Right:
Diagram showing the stages of construction and enlargement of the Palazzo Pubblico in Siena, from 1284 to 1310.

These buildings are particularly important to the community, since they serve as the official sites of government and social activities.

● ANTIQUITY

With the reforms introduced by the Athenian statesman Cleisthenes (sixth century B.C.E.), a hall for public meetings called the *bouleutérion* (from *boulé*, council) was added to the *agorà*, the heart of the Greek city. The Ancient Roman counterpart to this supremely democratic edifice was the Curia, the home of the Senate. Erected by King Tullius Hostilius in the seventh century B.C.E. and rebuilt a number of times, the Curia in the Roman Forum was a single hall designed to hold, on three orders of tiers, some three hundred senators seated on wooden benches. The Roman basilica as well, a prototype for early Christian churches, was a rectangular hall with columns supporting the roof (hypostyle) and one or more apses (from the Greek *hapsís*, or "circle," a semicylindrical domed structure standing against a wall) where the judges sat.

● THE MIDDLE AGES

While before the seventh century municipal offices were usually housed in buildings destined to other functions, such as Bishop's seats, after the Peace of Konstanz (1183) and with the growing independ-

Mauritshuis, 1633–1635. The Hague. Designed by Jacob van Campen and Piet Post, the building was originally the headquarters of Governor Johan Maurits.

Below:
Mitchell, Giurgola, Thorp Studio, *View of the National Parliament complex*, 1979–1988. Canberra, Australia.

ence of the city-states, the need was felt for a building representative of the community as a whole. This gave rise, in central and northern Italy, to the *palatium novum*, or Palazzo della Ragione. The earliest type, the Lombard Broletto (a diminutive form of *brolo*, "enclosed orchard"), had a ground floor with portico and a first floor occupied by a hall with windows. From this simple plan the municipal palace was to evolve, hand in hand with economic development, into more complex structures with many rooms.

● THE MODERN AND CONTEMPORARY AGE

In sixteenth-century Europe, dominated by the absolute power of national governments and princely courts, only the Netherlands enjoyed a certain independence, which was reinforced between 1568 and 1648 by the establishment of a republic. It is from this period that the municipal palaces of Amsterdam and The Hague date. On the other side of the Atlantic, after the United States had won its independence (1783), the Capitol Building in Washington, D.C. (p. 157) became the model for city and town halls up and down the East Coast. From the nineteenth century to today, public buildings have been constructed all over the world in a vast range of types, from renovated old buildings to grandiose new complexes designed to house public institutions and international organizations.

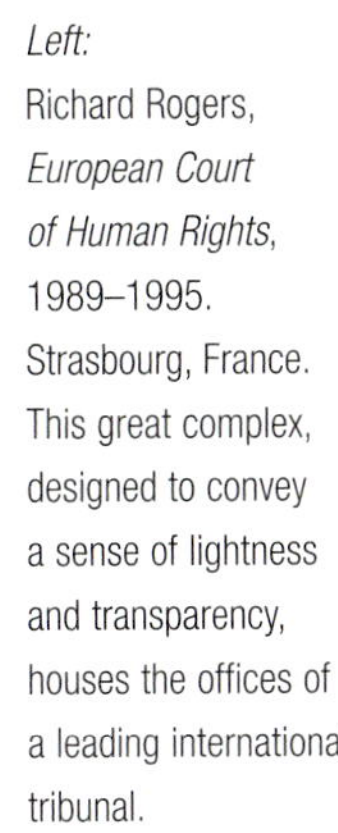

Left:
Richard Rogers, *European Court of Human Rights*, 1989–1995. Strasbourg, France. This great complex, designed to convey a sense of lightness and transparency, houses the offices of a leading international tribunal.

Military Construction

Construction for military purposes, which has developed hand in hand with human history, has consisted chiefly of fortified systems built to defend vast territories, cities, or even small villages.

DEFENSIVE WALLS

Ancient texts often mention city walls that were only apparently invulnerable: those of Jericho fell according to the will of Yahweh (*Joshua* 6:20), while the walls of Troy were penetrated through the expedient of the famous wooden horse suggested by Odysseus, the astute king of Ithaca whose feats were sung by Homer in the *Iliad* and *Odyssey*.

One of the world's most imposing defensive structures is the Great Wall of China, which snakes 3,750 miles through the countryside. In Chinese, the Great Wall is called *wan li*, or "ten thousand *li*" (a *li* is a unit of measurement equivalent to about 3.7 miles). A similar but less grandiose structure was Hadrian's Wall (first century C.E.), which marked the boundary between Scotland and England. Memorable among city walls were those built in Rome by the Emperor Marcus Aurelius (161–180 C.E.), which was stormed as late as 455 by the Vandals, and those erected by the Emperor Theodosius (347–395 C.E.) to protect Constantinople. Fronted by a moat 66 feet long and an embankment 46 feet wide, the Byzantine defense structure consisted of an outer wall 30 feet high and an inner one 36 feet high, with towers rising to a height of 75 feet. The introduction of heavy weapons necessitated significant innovations in the structural design of defensive walls, already studied during the Renaissance by such architects and scientists as Francesco di Giorgio Martini, Leonardo da Vinci, and Michelangelo.

Hadrian's Wall at Cuddy's Crag. Built under the Roman Emperor Hadrian around 122 C.E., the wall extends for 70 miles.

The Great Wall of China. The oldest sections of this fortification date from 395 to 284 B.C.E., while the portion standing today was built in the period between the fourteenth century, when the Mongols were driven out by the Ming Dynasty, and the sixteenth century.

A French medieval castle depicted by the Limbourg brothers for the Duke of Berry's Book of Hours, c. 1415. Chantilly, Musée Condé.

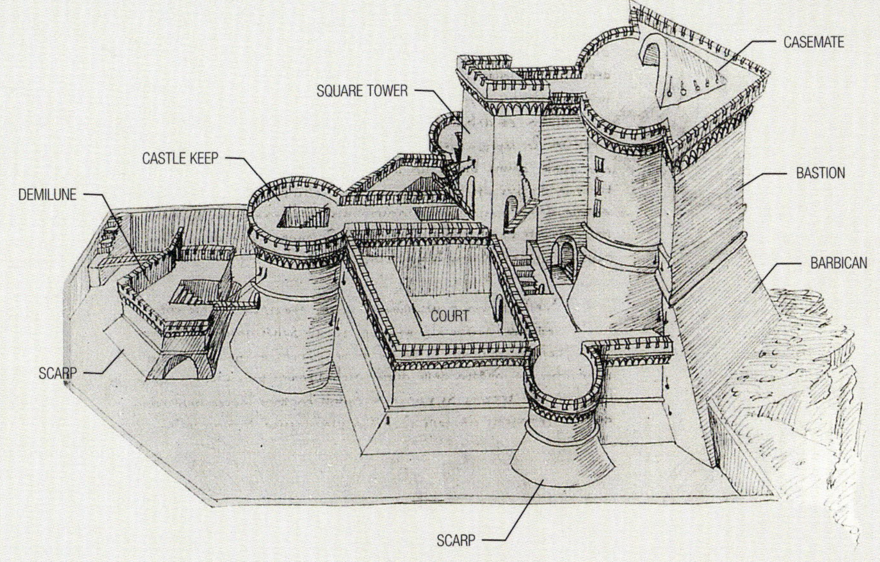

Elements of a fortress, reconstruction from a drawing by Francesco di Giorgio Martini for the plan of the Rocca Roveresca di Mondolfo (1483–1490, destroyed in the nineteenth century) built for Giovanni della Rovere. Florence, Biblioteca Nazionale, Codex Magliabechiano, II.I.141, f. 79r.

Leonardo da Vinci, *Trajectories of bombardments,* 1503–1504. Milan, Biblioteca Ambrosiana, Codex Atlanticus, f. 72v. Cannonballs were projected over the defensive walls, landing in the stronghold. To defend against this kind of attack, walls with reinforcing escarpments were used in later military architecture.

● FORTIFIED LINE

The modern version of the defensive wall is the fortified line, which appeared at the end of the nineteenth century. While the line protecting Amsterdam (1883–1920) was equipped with hydraulic systems that could flood the area in the event of danger, other defensive systems featured heavy fortifications and gun emplacements, both on the surface and underground. The Maginot Line, built in 1930 to prevent a German invasion across the eastern border of France, consisted of reinforced concrete structures connected by tunnels and underground passageways. The Siegfried Line, built by Germany in World War I, was restored between 1937 and 1939.

● FROM ACROPOLIS TO FORTRESS

The "high city" (acropolis), a settlement built on natural heights, was common to ancient cities around the Mediterranean, from Athens to Rome. With the decline of the Roman Empire and the territorial uncertainties that followed, armed expansion was limited by encircling walls and fortifications. The first castles (diminutive of *castrum*, or "fortress") were built at this time; these hard-to-reach structures often stood on hilltops or, when located on a plain, were surrounded by a moat. In medieval times, the castle walls were perfectly vertical to keep invaders from scaling the face. Military devices were used to hurl heavy stones or pour boiling oil on enemy soldiers, while the castle walls were topped by sentry rounds and watchtowers, usually placed at the corners. The inner tower (donjon), the point of last defense, could also be used for living quarters. With the development of artillery, significant changes were made in castle design. The fortress walls were no longer vertical but sloped (called escarpments), with a stone outwork (barbican). Storerooms were built for artillery (casemates) and for munitions (arsenals). The corner bastions became triangular or polygonal in shape.

Towers, Skyscrapers, and Lighthouses

A symbol of power and prestige, the vertically thrusting medieval tower-house can be regarded as a precursor of the modern skyscraper.

● FROM FORTIFICATIONS TO TOWER-HOUSES

While Byzantine fortifications (*kleisúrai*) had been built according to a general plan of imperial defense, the initiative in the medieval West was left to local lords. This gave rise, beginning in the ninth century, to the phenomenon of *incastellamento*, the gradual expansion of castles into villages. The process was mandated in an edict issued by King Ludovico II (r. 855–875), who ordered the population to live in fortified villages even during peacetime. The phenomenon spread throughout Europe, and some castles developed into large towns. The "knoll" castle, on the other hand, was developed to protect isolated territories. Originally it was a wooden tower (built of masonry from the eleventh century on) rising on an embankment. Isolated buildings of this kind, serving as both habitations and defensive towers, developed in elaborate forms, especially in England and France. In medieval Italy, even the houses in towns and cities took on a defensive character. Tower-houses, which could be inhabited on every level, became a means of controlling territory and symbols of power for noble families and political factions.

● SKYSCRAPERS

The term "skyscraper" was coined around 1880 in reference to an office building in New York that rose more than 150 feet. Already by 1854, one of the fundamental problems of tall multistory buildings—needed for living space in rapidly growing American cities—had been solved with the invention of the elevator by Elisha Otis. The skyscraper represented an extraordinary architectural challenge. Between 1883 and 1885, the military engineer William Le Baron Jenney (1832–1907) built the Home Insurance Building in Chicago with piers and lintels made of iron. With this material it

Above:
Medieval tower-houses.
San Gimignano, Siena.
This Sienese town is known the world over for its ancient towers, many of them still standing today.

Below:
View of the citadel.
Carcassonne, Aude, France. Built in several stages from the thirteenth to the sixteenth centuries, it was restored by Viollet-le-Duc in neo-Gothic style.

Sherve, Lamb & Harmon Studio,
Empire State Building,
1930–1931. New York.

became possible to erect even taller buildings. Those designed by Louis Henry Sullivan (1856–1924) and other members of the Chicago School introduced such innovative construction technologies as iron and steel frames, light masonry, and elevators.

Until the 1930s, the most imposing skyscraper was the Woolworth Building in New York, designed in 1913 by Cass Gilbert (1859–1934); at 525 feet, it combined a sense of modernity conferred by its height and a Gothic-inspired style. Since then, taller and taller buildings have been erected all over the world, from New York's Empire State Building (1931; 1,250 feet) to the Petronas Towers (1998; 1,483 feet) in Kuala Lumpur, Malaysia.

● THE LIGHTHOUSE

In use since ancient times, the lighthouse is a tower that identifies a coastline or port as a navigational point of reference for ships at sea. The lighthouse in Alexandria, Egypt, one of the Seven Wonders of the Ancient World, stood 350 feet tall and had a live fire at the top; others were lit with lanterns. Today, 2,000-watt lamps are commonly used, throwing a beam of light as far as 35 miles.

Left:
Minoru Yamazaki,
The twin towers of the World Trade Center in New York (1970–1973), destroyed in the terrorist attack of September 11, 2001.

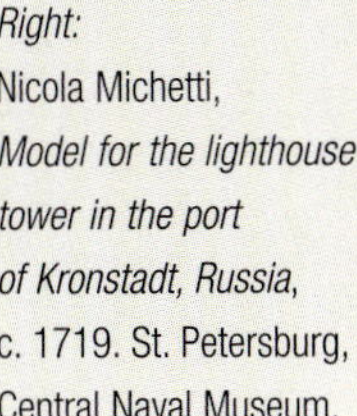

Right:
Nicola Michetti,
Model for the lighthouse tower in the port of Kronstadt, Russia,
c. 1719. St. Petersburg, Central Naval Museum.

Above:
Cesar Pelli & Associates,
Petronas Towers, 1998.
Kuala Lumpur, Malaysia.

Below:
View of Hong Kong.

Collective Architecture

Playing field for the game of tachtli. Yagul, Oaxaca Valley, Mexico. The game consisted of throwing a ball into a ring made of stone or wood located at the center of a rectangular field surrounded by a wall.

The innate human tendency to establish and maintain social relations has led over the centuries to the construction of a wide range of buildings designed to hold great crowds, ranging from sports stadiums and theaters to health-care facilities, libraries, and museums.

● THE STADIUM

The Ancient Roman circus, or "stadium," evolved from the U-shaped hippodrome, or racetrack, that curved along the slopes of a hillside. The stadium track, or arena, first used for chariot races, was surrounded on three sides by tiers of seats. Among the most famous structures of this type were the Circus Maximus in Rome, which could hold up to 300,000 spectators, and a stadium of identical design in Constantinople. The playing fields of pre-Columbian civilization were of a different kind altogether. Still surviving in Mexico today are the ruins of architectural structures built for *tachtli*, a ritual ball game played in Central

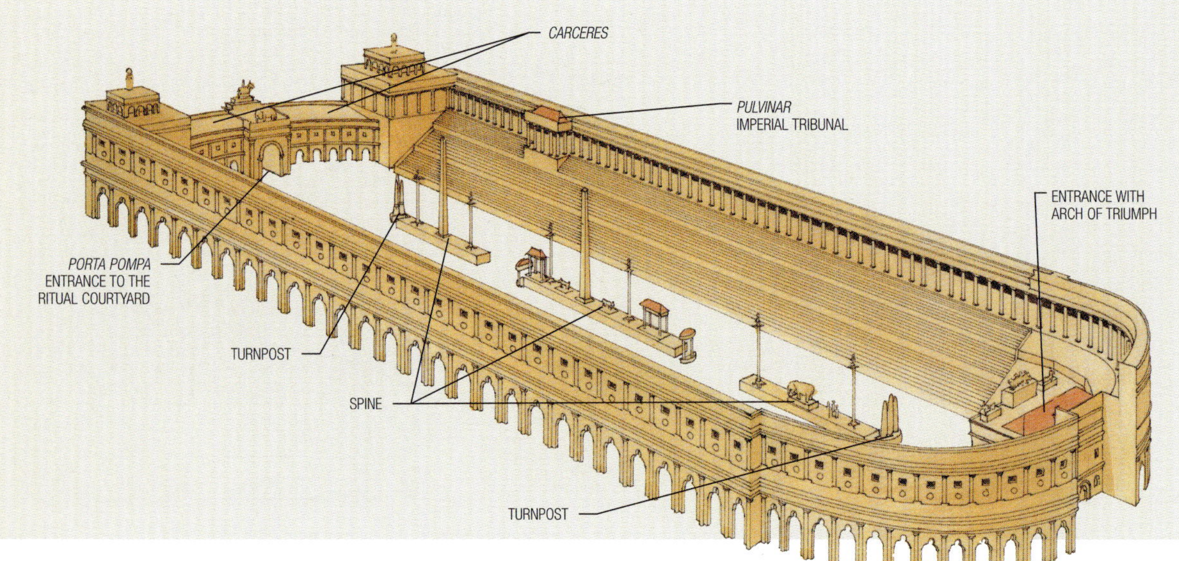

Reconstruction of the Circus Maximus in Rome. Built in stages from the fourth century B.C.E. to the first century C.E., the stadium was 2,100 feet long and 590 feet wide. The *carceres,* stalls in which the chariots were kept before the race started, were made of marble.

Below and at right: Pier Luigi Nervi, *Municipal Stadium*, detail of the tower and the ramps leading to the grandstand, 1929–1932. Florence, Italy.

America from the eleventh to the fifteenth century. In design and purpose, the modern stadium most closely resembles the classical amphitheater, where wild game hunts, gladiator fights, and naval battles were held. The amphitheater was elliptical in shape, with two or four levels and tiered seats around the circumference. In the twentieth century, the popularity of international sporting events such as the Olympics and World Cup soccer tournament have afforded architects a chance to design innovative and elaborate facilities around the world—from so-called Rationalist designs (such as Pier Luigi Nervi's reinforced-concrete Florence Stadium, 1929–1932) to experiments with the relationship between architecture and the surrounding environment (Bari Stadium in Italy, by Renzo Piano, 1989; the Sant Jordi Sports Palace in Barcelona, by Arata Isozaki, 1992) to highly original roofed structures (the National Gymnasium of Tokyo, by Kenzo Tange, 1961–1964; Hamar Olympic Hall in Norway, by Niels Torp AS Arkitekter Mnal, 1992; and Utopia Pavilion in Lisbon, by S.O.M. and Regino Cruz 1998).

Arata Isozaki, *Sant Jordi Sports Palace*, 1992. Montjuic, Barcelona, Spain.

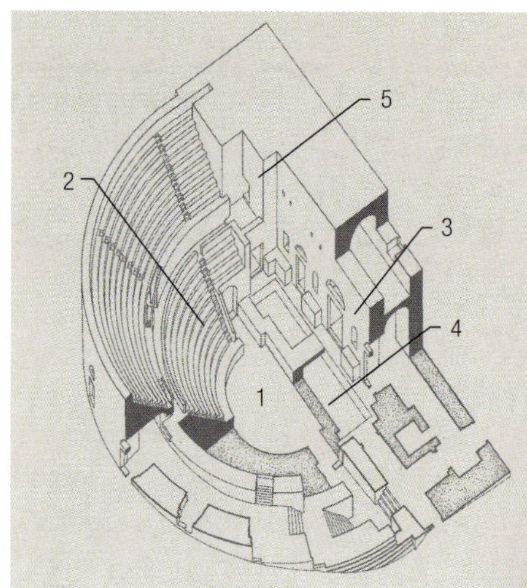

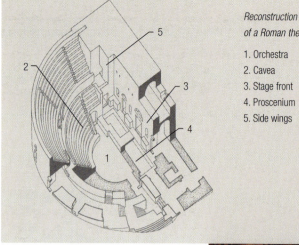

Reconstruction of a Roman theater.

1. Orchestra
2. Cavea
3. Stage front
4. Proscenium
5. Side wings

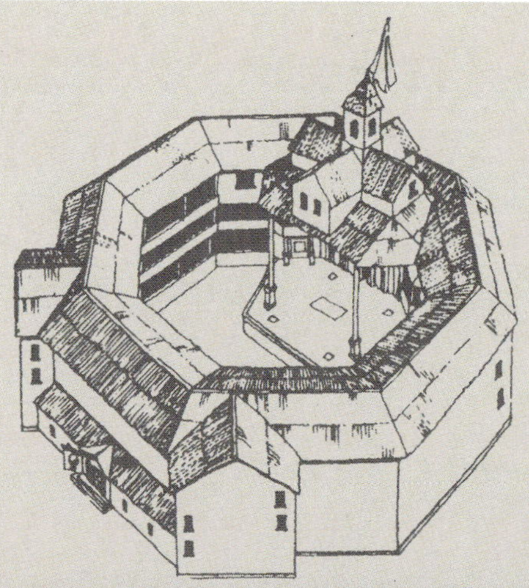

Reconstruction of Shakespeare's Globe Theater (1599).

● THEATER AND CINEMA

The modern theater type derives from that of Ancient Greece, through the mediation of the Roman model. In the Roman theater, tiers of seats were ranged in a semicircle in front of the proscenium, the stage where the performance was held, backed by a large decorated wall (*scenae frons*, or "backdrop"). In medieval times, religious plays were typically held in church courtyards, often with the whole town participating. In the fifteenth century, performances were given for smaller, select audiences in the courtyards of noble palaces.

Little remains today of early Renaissance theaters, which were built of wood and often itinerant; Shakespeare's famous Globe Theater outside London (1599) was the first permanent playhouse in England. One of the earliest examples of a modern theater—notable for the addition of a roof—was the splendid Olympic Theater in Vicenza, Italy, designed by Palladio for the Accademia Olimpica (1580–1583); the design featured a large orchestra section and classically inspired tiered seating. The evolution of this plan is evidenced in the Teatro Farnese in Parma, Italy, the prototype of theaters with a courtyard surrounded by a loggia, a design that became popular in the seventeenth and eighteenth centuries in so-called "Italian-style" theaters: the San Carlo in Naples (1737), the oldest in Europe, and La

Above:
Giovan Battista Aleotti, *Cavea of Teatro Farnese*, 1618–1628. Parma. Rows of boxes are superimposed around the outer circumference of Greco-Roman tiered seating.

Right:
Denys Lasdun, *Royal National Theatre*, 1967–1976. London, Embankment.

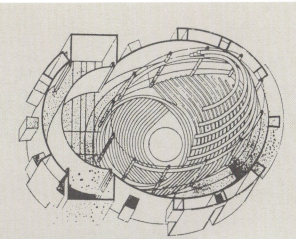

Left:
Walter Gropius, *Project for the Totaltheater,* 1926.
The project, never built, was designed to allow interaction between the audience and the actors. The orchestra could be rotated 180 degrees to any position, including the center.

Scala in Milan (1776–1778). In the nineteenth century, loggia and amphitheater features were combined to create a new theater design, in which the orchestra seats were separated from those of the gallery, and the stage was equipped with technologically sophisticated equipment (interchangeable backdrops and wings). Further design innovations, especially in the wings and stage, were made in the early twentieth century to accommodate the experiments of avant-garde dramatists. Prominent modern designs include Gropius's Totaltheater for the Berlin Philharmonic (1926, never built); the multipurpose Royal National Theater in London (1967–1977), consisting of three great halls, the Lyttleton Theatre, the Olivier Theatre, and the Cottesloe Theatre; and the spectacular Sydney Opera House (1973), one of the most recognizable buildings in the world.

Deriving from stage theaters and music halls, the modern cinema house required special features from the very beginning (1890s): rows of seats facing the screen and, behind the audience, a motion picture projector (later placed in a room of its own). Among the first examples was the Universum Cinema in Berlin, designed in 1928 by Erich Mendelsohn (1887–1953). During the era of silent pictures (up to 1927), a live orchestra was located in a pit or floor space in front of the screen. Many theaters today, like some stage complexes, include several or many halls.

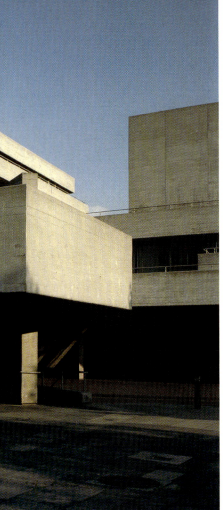

Top:
Hans Scharoun, *Philharmonie,* 1956–1963. Berlin.
The orchestra section and the gallery converge at the stage, the musical and architectural focal point of the hall.

Above:
Hans Poelzig, *Grosses Schauspielhaus,* 1918–1919. Berlin.
After surviving two world wars intact, the theater was demolished in the 1970s.

Josef Kaiser and Rhode Kellermann Wawrowsky, *Kosmos Cinema,* 1962–1997. Berlin.
A semicircular arrangement of underground movie theaters, connected by an elliptical corridor with a skylight, was added to the original central hall.

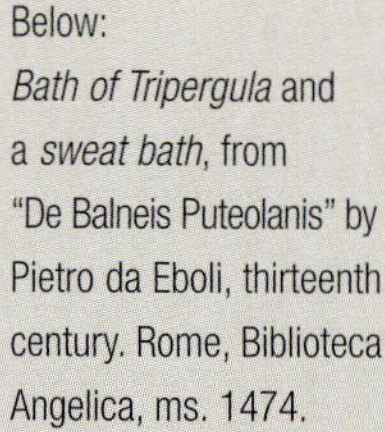

Left:
Eugène-Emmanuel Viollet-le-Duc, *Reconstruction of Roman baths for pupils of the Ecole Spéciale d'Architecture*, 1867.

Below:
Bath of Tripergula and a *sweat bath*, from "De Balneis Puteolanis" by Pietro da Eboli, thirteenth century. Rome, Biblioteca Angelica, ms. 1474.

● THERMAL SPAS AND PUBLIC BATHS

The origins of what can be called "Roman baths" date to about the third century B.C.E., when such facilities were privately owned and managed. It was near the end of the second century B.C.E. that the first public baths were inaugurated. Although thermal spas were already known in Pompeii, the first documented sites in Rome date only to 19 B.C.E. (The first thermal spas free to the public were those of Agrippa.) Frequenting public baths became a socially important activity in Imperial Rome, and the practice, regarded as a sign of civility, spread throughout the empire.

The most celebrated facilities in Rome were the Baths of Titus, of Caracalla, and of Diocletian. The layout reflected the custom of passing from the cold bath (*frigidarium*) to the hot one (*calidarium*) through the *tepidarium*. These great buildings also contained service areas, dressing rooms, gymnasiums, and libraries. The practice of bathing continued in medieval times. In a thirteenth-century poem extolling the waters at Pozzuoli and Baia in Italy, Pietro da Eboli deemed them healthy and even therapeutic. Thermal establishments were to remain highly popular, both for bathing and as meeting places for men and women, for many years, as reported in 1415 by the Tuscan humanist Poggio Bracciolini, who visited the Baths of Baden in Germany. It is in Islamic culture, however, that one finds the most striking examples of bath architecture. Among these are the great hypostyle hall of the Umayyad residential complex at Khirbat al-Mafjar in Palestine, destroyed in 747 (p. 249), and the Mameluk baths in Damascus, Syria, dating to the fifteenth century. Still popular today in Muslim countries is the *hammam,* consisting of a domed, circular main hall and adjoining domed rooms with saunas and baths.

The Temple of Asclepius on Rome's Tiberina Island, in a nineteenth-century engraving. Annexed to the temple, erected in 294 B.C.E., were the hospital facilities.

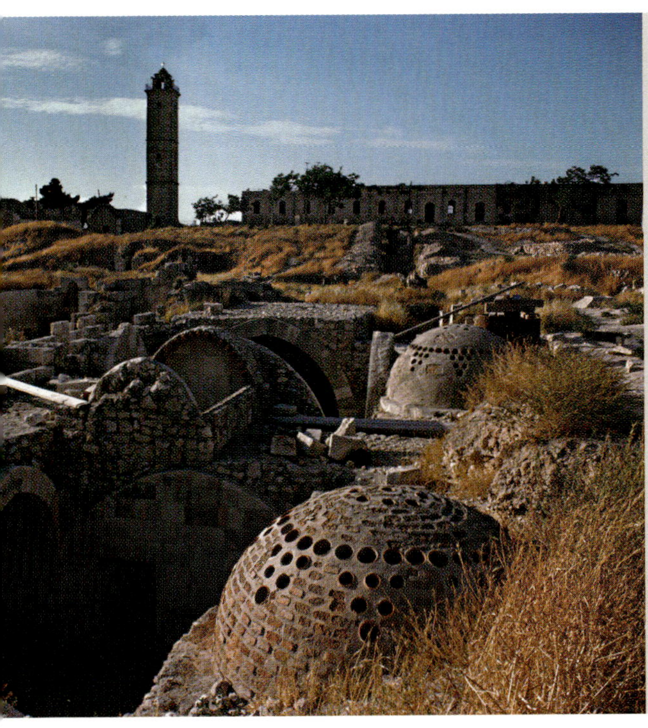

Left:
Remains of a Turkish bath. Aleppo, Syria.

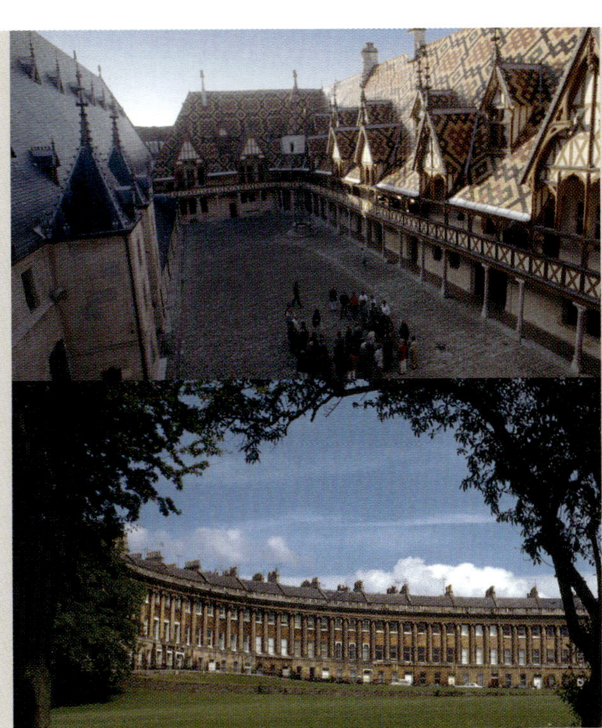

Courtyard of the Hôtel-Dieu, fifteenth century. Beaune, Burgundy, France.

John Wood the Younger, *Royal Crescent,* eighteenth century, Bath, England. The architecture of the Royal Circle and the Royal Crescent was inspired by the Baths of Diocletian.

In Europe, the architecture of thermal establishments has yielded some especially original solutions since the eighteenth century. In at least one case, that of Bath, England, the layout of the entire city revolves around the baths. Other cities too, such as Salsomaggiore and Montecatini in Italy, have been profoundly influenced by the presence of thermal establishments.

HOSPITALS

In Ancient Greece and Rome, religious complexes dedicated to the gods of health, such as the Temple of Asclepius on an island in Rome's Tiber River, served as hospitals. In medieval Europe, the hospital (from the Latin *hospitium*, which means "hospitality" as well as a lodging place for pilgrims) offered shelter to travelers, with separate quarters for men and women. From the tenth century on, therapeutic activity became the chief function of the hospitals, commonly known as God Houses (*Hôtel-Dieu* in French, *Godshuis* in German). The fourteenth and fifteenth centuries saw the rise of such great hospital institutions as Santa Maria della Scala in Siena, the Ospedale Maggiore in Milan, and the Hôtel-Dieu at Beaune in Burgundy, built at the initiative of Chancellor Rolin in 1443. This last structure, now a museum, rises around a central courtyard and retains the original arrangement of wards. Other such structures founded in the past have been transformed over the course of the centuries but still serve their original purpose. Such is the case with two hospitals in Florence: the Spedale di San Giovanni di Dio, founded in the late fourteenth century by the Vespucci family and rebuilt during the Baroque age; and Santa Maria Nuova, erected in the fifteenth century by the Portinari family and still the most important public hospital in the city's center. Noteworthy among hospitals of the eighteenth century is San Gallicano in Rome, designed by Filippo Raguzzini (1680–1771), with two wings of wards converging on a church at the center. In the twentieth century, the Finnish architectect Alvar Aalto introduced major changes in hospital design. In 1929, Aalto won the competition for a hospital in Paimio, Finland, with an architectural plan that aimed to be "functional from the human point of view." The building is distinguished by special lighting techniques and pastel color schemes for the ceilings, whose surfaces would be viewed by patients for many hours in the day.

Above:
Alvar Aalto, *Sanatorium,* 1929–1933. Paimio, Finland.

Below:
Alvar Aalto, *A room in the sanatorium,* 1929–1933. Paimio, Finland.

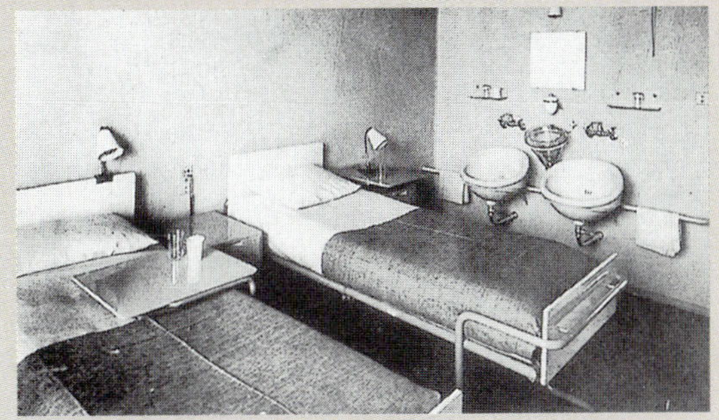

Right: Michelozzo, *Biblioteca Medicea (Medicean Library)*, 1454. Florence, San Marco. Known as the Sala Latina, the library, consisting of a long hall with three naves separated by elegant Ionic columns, was built for Cosimo the Elder de' Medici, who commissioned many of the codexes still kept in cabinets in the adjacent Greek Room.

Below: *Hall of Sixtus V*, 1587–1589. Rome, Vatican Palaces. Founded in the fifteenth century by the humanist Pope Nicholas V, the grandiose Vatican Library was moved by Sixtus V (1585–1590) to the rooms that still form part of the museum today.

Michelangelo Buonarroti, *Monumental stairway*, 1526. Florence, Biblioteca Medicea Laurenziana (Medicean Laurentian Library), San Lorenzo.

● LIBRARIES

If the oldest known library was the one in the Sumerian city of Lagash (2100 B.C.E.), the most famous in antiquity were those of Alexandria and Pergamum, both said to have been destroyed by fire. Citizens of Imperial Rome had access to many libraries (the Ulpia in Trajan's Forum being the most important), with reading rooms, conversation areas, and separate collections of Latin and Greek texts. Beginning in the early Middle Ages, the principal "place of knowledge" shifted to the monastery, where the library was often annexed to the *scriptorium*, a busy workshop in which manuscripts were copied and illuminated. The modern library began to develop during the Renaissance. The first collections of manuscripts and codexes, already accessible to scholars (beginning with the library founded by Cosimo the Elder in Florence's Monastery of San Marco) were followed in the sixteenth century by libraries founded by princes and popes. Among these was the Medici's Laurentian Library in Florence, with a monumental staircase designed by Michelangelo; another was that of Pope Sixtus V (1590–1595) in Rome. University and national libraries specifically intended for public use began to appear in the seventeenth century. Today, special attention is focused on the correct lighting of reading rooms and the functionality of all library space, which must be both welcoming and conducive to concentration. To provide the best service, special technology is employed for climate control and conservation, electronic cataloguing, and the transporting of books. Many libraries are multifunctional, having not only reading rooms but also auditoriums, conference rooms, and cafeterias, with architectural solutions often on a monumental scale.

● MUSEUMS

The essential purposes of the museum (from the Greek *muséion*, or "place of the Muses") are conservation, documentation, and education. The museum as a public institution, however, developed only over the course of the eighteenth century. Up to that time, collections of art and other precious objects were privately owned and chosen strictly on the basis of personal taste. A prime example was the great collection of France's Cardinal Richelieu (1585–1642), later passed on to the Louvre. By the late seventeenth century, some collections could

Left and below: Frank Lloyd Wright, *Solomon R. Guggenheim Museum*, 1943–1959. New York. Wright designed an immense continuous spiral, topped by a transparent dome.

be visited upon request, such as the Tribune in Florence's Uffizi, designed by Bernardo Buontalenti and organized according to true museum principles. Guidebooks of the time already discussed the advantages of good lighting and the need to protect works of art subject to deterioration outdoors.

One of the first places in Italy designed to conserve works of art was the Clementine Museum in the Vatican Palaces (1771–1794), commissioned by Pope Clement XIV to the architects Alessandro Dori and Michelangelo Simonetti. In London, the classical-style British Museum (1823–1847) was designed by Robert Smirke to house the museum's original acquisitions in 1753 (the scientific collection of Sir Hans Sloane), sculptures from the Parthenon, and other antiquities. Such world-famous museums as the Hermitage in St. Petersburg and the Louvre in Paris were established in existing buildings, which were duly enlarged and renovated.

In modern times, the restoration of existing museums and the design of new ones have presented special challenges and opportunities for the world's great architects, among them Gae Aulenti, Mario Botta, Frank O. Gehry, Hans Hollein, Arata Isozaki, I.M. Pei, Renzo Piano, and James Stirling. Museum science, which deals with the arrangement of a museum's rooms and collections, has become a serious and respected discipline in its own right. Many modern museums function as dynamic cultural centers, offering activities and resources beyond mere exhibition; the museum is no longer a mere container of art for passive public viewing, but a place of shared experience, community engagement, and active learning.

Left:
Lantern of the Tribune in the Uffizi, detail, 1584. Florence.
In the octagonal Tribune, designed by Bernardo Buontalenti for Francesco I de' Medici, natural light flowed in from the skylight to illuminate the most unusual pieces in the Medicean collections. The Tribune is located on the first floor of the Uffizi, the great building with two wings designed by Giorgio Vasari to house the administrative and judicial *uffizi*, or offices, of the Grand Duchy of Tuscany. The museum was officially opened to the public in 1765.

Above:
Sverre Fehn, *Museum of the Glaciers*, 1989–1991. Fjærland, Norway. Situated at the edge of a glacier, the museum overlooks the most important piece in the "collection," the glacier itself. The interior is lit by natural sunlight flooding in from skylights.

Manufacturing Facilities

Buildings erected specifically for manufacturing purposes, with architectural features designed to meet such needs, began to be systematically built after the Industrial Revolution of the nineteenth century. Buildings of this kind, however, had existed as early as the Middle Ages.

Claude Monet, *The Brook at Orbec*, 1872. Paris, Musée d'Orsay. In the background of this painting rise the smokestacks of a French factory.

● ANTIQUITY

In the cities of the ancient world, furnaces and brick factories, in which the wealthy classes often invested, were especially common. In Rome, preindustrial activities of this type were located, not by chance, around Campo di Marzio, in the vicinity of the Temple of Vulcan, the god of fire. This was one of the first forms of mass production, existing alongside more traditional activities such as weaving and coin-minting. The processes were purely those of the craftsman, however, and the real "factory" remained the workshop.

● THE MIDDLE AGES

During the Middle Ages most of the buildings in Europe associated with production were devoted to agricultural activities. In the monasteries, an

Left:
Peter Behrens and Karl Bernhard, *AEG turbine factory,* 1908–1909. Berlin. The German electricity company commissioned Behrens not only to design five buildings but also to supervise every aspect of production, including advertising.

Below:
Walter Gropius and Adolf Meyer, *Fagus Works*, 1911–1914. Alfeld-an-der-Leine, Lower Saxony, Germany.

important role was assigned to the grange (from the Medieval Latin *granica*), a building with the structure of a simple cabin: on the outside, a single roof with two slopes, on the inside, a rectangular nave with a ceiling made of wooden beams. High and roomy, the grange could be used for many purposes—not merely for storing grain and other cereals, but also for grinding corn, making wine, curing hams, and aging cheese.

The building that most strongly anticipated those of the industrial age was the arsenal (from the Arab *dar al-shina'a*, "house of work" or "workshop"). At its peak, the arsenal of the Republic of Venice employed 16,000 carpenters, who could build a galley in a single day.

● THE MODERN AGE

With the Industrial Revolution, starting from the 1830s, great industrial sheds were built to house the new machinery, often with smokestacks to dispose of waste deriving from the combustion of coal. The design of these factories, the province of engineers up to the first years of the twentieth century, was increasingly entrusted to architects.

In Germany, a decisive step in this direction was taken by the AEG turbine factory in Berlin (1908–1909) and by the gas production works at Frankfurt-on-Main (1911), designed by Peter Behrens. Here the functional arrangement of space was combined with a monumental approach to design and new aesthetic values. The factory building was designed to represent the grandeur of production and at the same time to alleviate the monotony of mechanical work. Walter Gropius also designed new industrial facilities in Germany, such as the Fagus Works (1911–1914), whose structures were lightened by the use of iron and glass and whose designs were diversified in form and function.

The great revolution in factory typology, however, occurred in the United States, where the theories regarding machine productivity formulated by the engineer Frederick Winslow Taylor (1856–1915) had, among other things, led to the adoption of the assembly line and the systematic organization of work.

Henry Ford (1863–1947) was the first to apply Taylor's principles. By the early 1900s, the famous industrialist was able to mass-produce the first automobiles at low cost. His various production facilities, such as the Ford glass factory at Dearborn, Michigan, designed by Albert Kahn in 1942, were great spaces traversed by extremely long conveyor belts.

In Europe, the birth of the automotive industry led to such innovative architectural structures as the Lingotto in Turin (Giacomo Matté-Trucco, 1924–1926), inspired by Rationalist principles. From the postwar years to the present, design and experimentation in a wide range of industrial fields have produced buildings in which human labor is increasingly replaced by automated systems.

Above: Albert Kahn, *Ford Glass Works*, 1924. Dearborn, Michigan. Four great furnaces for manufacturing sheets of glass are connected to a long, shed-like structure with large windows that can be opened to discharge heat.

Right: Eliel and Eero Saarinen, *Interior of the General Motors Technical Center*, 1949–1956. Warren, Michigan.

Frank O. Gehry, *Herman Miller Furniture Factory*, 1989. Rocklin, California.

Service Facilities

The old Port of Messina (Italy) in a Renaissance miniature in the National Library of Rome.

Falling under this architectural category are facilities designed for urban infrastructures: ports, railway stations, and airports.

● PORTS

Undoubtedly the most ancient of the categories considered here is the maritime port. Its importance, both commercial and military, has been confirmed over the centuries by the testimony of writers, such as Pliny; by the plans of famous architects and engineers, such as Bramante and Leonardo da Vinci; and by an abundant iconography.

Modern seaport facilities center around a harbor office, headquarters of the port authority. Types include small boat harbors, mercantile ports (often located beside a railway), and landing-stages for the oil industry. Facilities include mooring wharves, warehouses and packing sheds, oil tanks, and pollution barriers.

● RAILWAY STATIONS

The first railway stations have been called "cathedrals of steam," honoring the god (steam) who revolutionized travel and ways of life. The Milan Station, one of the oldest in Italy, was built in 1862 by the engineer Bouchot for the Paris-Lyon-Mediterranée railway company, in imitation of the Tuileries Station in Paris. Beginning in 1913, the Milan structure was redesigned in Art Nouveau style by Ulisse Stacchini (1871–1947) with the same sense of monumentality as New York's Pennsylvania Station, erected a few years earlier. In succeeding decades, Italian station design generally followed Rationalist principles, emphasizing clean-cut simplicity

Alessandro Mendini, *Streetcar stop on Kurt-Schumacher Strasse*, 1994. Hanover, Germany.

Above: McKim, Meade & Whithe Studio, *Pennsylvania Station*, 1902–1912. New York.

Below: Ulisse Stacchini, *Plan for the Milan Central Station*, 1913–1931.

Right: Giovanni Michelucci (with Italo Gamberini, Pier Niccolò Berardi, Nello Baroni, Sarre Guarnieri, and Leonardo Lusanna), *The Santa Maria Novella Station in a pre-World War II photograph*, 1933–1936. Florence, Italy.

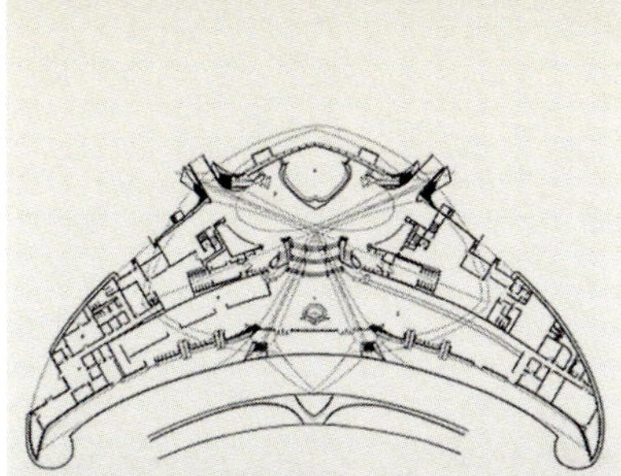

Left and below:
Eero Saarinen,
TWA terminal at the John F. Kennedy Airport (Idlewild), 1956–1962.
New York.

Paul Andreu and Jean Marie Duthilleul,
Connecting corridor at the Charles de Gaulle Airport, 1994. Paris.

rather than monumental effect. Exemplary in this regard is the Santa Maria Novella Station in Florence (Gruppo Toscano, 1933–1936).

Oriented along the same lines, although employing different materials and techniques, are more recent achievements, such as the Waterloo International Terminal in London (Nicholas Grimshaw, 1988–1993) and the TVG station at Lyon Satolas Airport in France (Santiago Calatrava, 1996).

● AIRPORTS

A major municipal airport generally covers an area of three to five square miles and is equipped with facilities for the parking, maintenance, and refueling of aircraft (hangars); warehouses for cargo; and buildings for passenger transit (terminals). The taxiway is the longest element in an airport, extending for one to three miles. Until the 1970s, airports generally followed a linear design, so that passengers had to be transported to their aircraft in shuttle buses. More modern airports adopt a "satellite" or "star-shaped" layout, allowing passengers to reach their departure gates more directly and to enter the aircraft through an enclosed corridor. One of the first major projects of the postwar period was the TWA Airlines terminal at Kennedy Airport in New York (Eero Saarinen, 1956–1962). The enormous importance assumed by airports in recent decades is confirmed by the plans proposed by some of the greatest architects of the time, which take into account a complex host of factors, including geomorphologic and meteorological characteristics, integration with the surrounding environment, and connections with other infrastructures.

Nicholas Grimshaw,
Waterloo International Terminal for Eurostar trains, 1988–1993.
London.

Transportation Infrastructures

Bridges, roads, highways, parking lots, railways, and subways facilitate transportation and provide connections to otherwise inaccessible areas, thereby improving the quality of life.

● BRIDGES

Bridge or bridge-like structures serve the function of spanning obstacles, such as rivers, valleys (viaducts), rail lines or roadways (overpasses), or even the sea (boat decks, utilized in military operations since ancient times). Bridge foundations typically consist of pylons (or intermediate piles), which can be connected by arches or a roadway. When the latter is suspended, trestles are used instead of pylons. The arched bridge (with a single or multiple span) also has "shoulders" (the abutments at either end that withstand the thrust from the embankment). Bridges come in an almost infinite variety of materials and designs. Over the course of time, bridges have evolved from simple wooden crossings to sturdy, imposing structures made of stone, iron, cast iron, steel, and reinforced concrete.

Bridges may be classified according to the following types: mobile, truss (with the bearing structure formed by straight girders resting on abutments or intermediate piers), arch, and suspension. In a suspension bridge, a pair of steel cables is supported by high pylons and anchored to the abutments; the framework is suspended from the abutments, fixed in place with vertical tie rods. Bridges of this type provide the longest spans, with the greatest distance between piers.

The first bridges were used to connect pile-dwellings to the land. Preeminent among ancient bridge builders were the Romans, who applied the principle of the round arch to erect imposing structures in wood and stone—from spans across the Tiber to monumental aqueducts. In the Middle Ages and the Renaissance, covered bridges provided shelter and housed shops, as exemplified by the Rialto in Venice and the Ponte Vecchio in Florence. During periods of recurrent warfare, they could be furnished with fortified towers, as on the famous Charles Bridge in Prague. Beginning in the nine-

Left:
Venice's Rialto Bridge, in an eighteenth-century veduta.

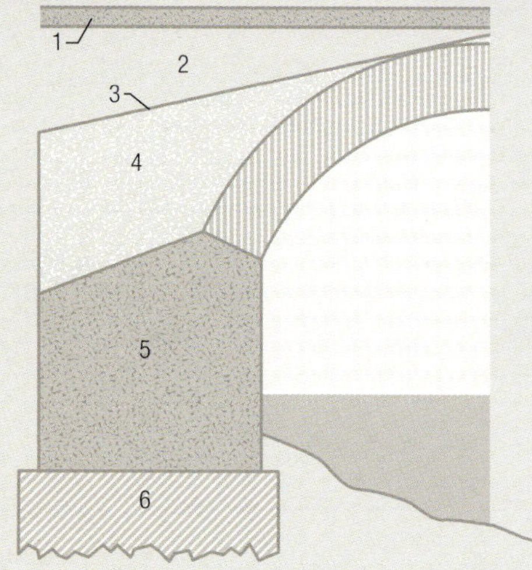

Right:
Longitudinal section of a masonry bridge.
1. Roadbed
2. Road fill
3. Coping
4. Reinforcement
5. Abutment
6. Foundation

teenth century, bridge design and construction were driven by the needs of the industrial society. Thanks to new engineering techniques and the utilization of iron and reinforced concrete, significantly longer and stronger spans could be constructed. Among the first of these were Robert Stephenson's iron railway bridges, built with tubular girders, which soon spread from Britain to Germany and throughout Europe. In the United States, suspension bridges became increasingly prominent, beginning with those of John Augustus Roebling in the late nineteenth century. Bridges in Switzerland designed by Robert Maillart between 1901 and 1940—using reinforced concrete for the structure itself, rather just the pylons—were also revolutionary. Recent years have seen a steady stream of imposing new bridge projects, requiring innovative construction methods. The new typologies, many of them sophisticated variations of the suspension bridge, have been designed with the help of computers and built with special materials appropriate to the terrain. Examples include a variety of bridges in the Far East, striking for their length, and the highly original pedestrian bridges in some European cities. Among the new generation of engineer-architects engaged in futuristic bridge design, the name of Santiago Calatrava is prominent.

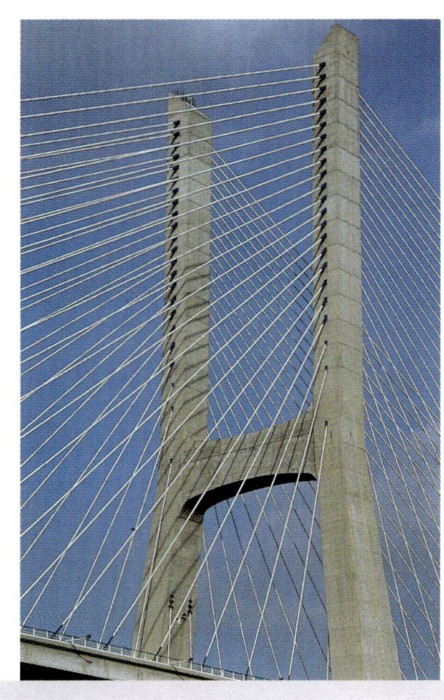

Michel Virlogeux, *Vasco de Gama Bridge*, detail, 1995–1998. Lisbon.

Above:
John Augustus Roebling, *Brooklyn Bridge*, 1869–1883. New York. Revolutionary in design and daring in execution, this was the first great suspension bridge in the United States with cables formed from parallel steel wires spun in place.

Left:
Joseph B. Strauss, *Golden Gate Bridge*, 1937. San Francisco, California.

● ROADS, HIGHWAYS, AND PARKING LOTS

The first great road-builders were the Romans, whose military power depended to a large extent on their road system. An efficient network of roads, in fact, ensured control of the empire. Roman roads were wide enough for two carriages to pass side-by-side and were for the most part straight. Paved with stones, they were easy to travel and resistant to weather without requiring special maintenance.

In medieval times, many of the old Roman roads in Europe were refurbished, extended, or adapted to current needs.

Among the most important of these was the Via Francigena, which led from Santiago de Compostela in Spain to Rome, continuing from there along the Via Appia to Brindisi, where pilgrims could embark for Jerusalem.

Road construction and modes of travel remained relatively unchanged until the early nineteenth century, when macadam (from the name of its inventor, the Scottish engineer John L. McAdam, 1756–1836) was first introduced. Macadam is a paving material made of gravel bound with sand, water, and fragmented stone, and flattened on the roadbed by a steamroller. Later, a calcareous and bituminous rock material called asphalt was applied to make roads impermeable. The most modern roads are usually composed of a reinforced-concrete roadbed topped with asphalt.

In the last two centuries, new means of transportation and ever-increasing travel for commerce and personal reasons have brought about a revolution in the infrastructure.

Urban planners, engineers, and architects have redesigned cities and entire regions in an effort to strike a balance between the construction of new facilities and the safeguarding of the natural, historic, and artistic heritage of the respective country.

The greatest innovation in twentieth-century road construction has been the superhighway, along with accompanying interchanges, service areas, rest stops, eating establishments, and commuter parking areas. Urban parking lots, increasingly constructed underground or in elevated tiers, may be ramped, managed with elevators, or even automated.

● RAILWAYS AND SUBWAYS

Transportation by rail began even before the train was invented, introduced in Germany in 1649 to ease the effort of horses transporting material from mines. The first wooden tracks were replaced with iron plates in England; the first iron rails per se date from 1767.

A major breakthrough in railroad transportation came with the invention by George Stephenson (1781– 1848) of a steam locomotive (called *Locomotion*) that could pull a passenger train. He also helped build the Stockton & Darling Railway, named for the first towns linked by rail in September 1825.

View of the Via Appia Antica in Rome. This "Queen of Roads" was built in 312 B.C.E. under the Censor Appius Claudius. Linking Rome to Brindisi, it was constructed in different layers: from the bottom, the *statumen,* a rough stone roadbed; the *ruderatio,* a conglomerate of stones and lime; the *nucleus,* composed of coarse gravel; and the *pavimentum,* a mixture of fine gravel and bits of stone in which large slabs of smooth stone (*silex*) were sunk for strength and durability. The surface was curved, allowing rainwater to drain off.

Below:
Vertical section of a Roman road

1. *Statumen*
2. *Ruderatio*
3. *Nucleus*
4. *Pavimentum*

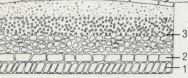

The first regular rail service, from Liverpool to Manchester, was inaugurated four years later. Railroad lines soon spread throughout Europe, the United States, and the rest of the world.

By the early 1900s, electric locomotives began to replace steam-driven engines, bringing major improvements in efficiency, speed, and comfort. Third-rail systems and cogwheel trains were used in high mountains (rack railway), and funiculars (cable railways) provided access to Alpine peaks.

Electrically operated rail lines became widespread in cities, first as trams running on the surface, then on elevated tracks, and finally underground.

The first subways were built in London (1863), Vienna (1894–1897), and Paris (1899–1904). Today they are found in major metropolises throughout the world, from New York to Beijing, from Moscow to Mexico City.

Some cities, such as Tokyo and Seattle, boast elevated monorail systems, in which the train runs on a single electrified rail.

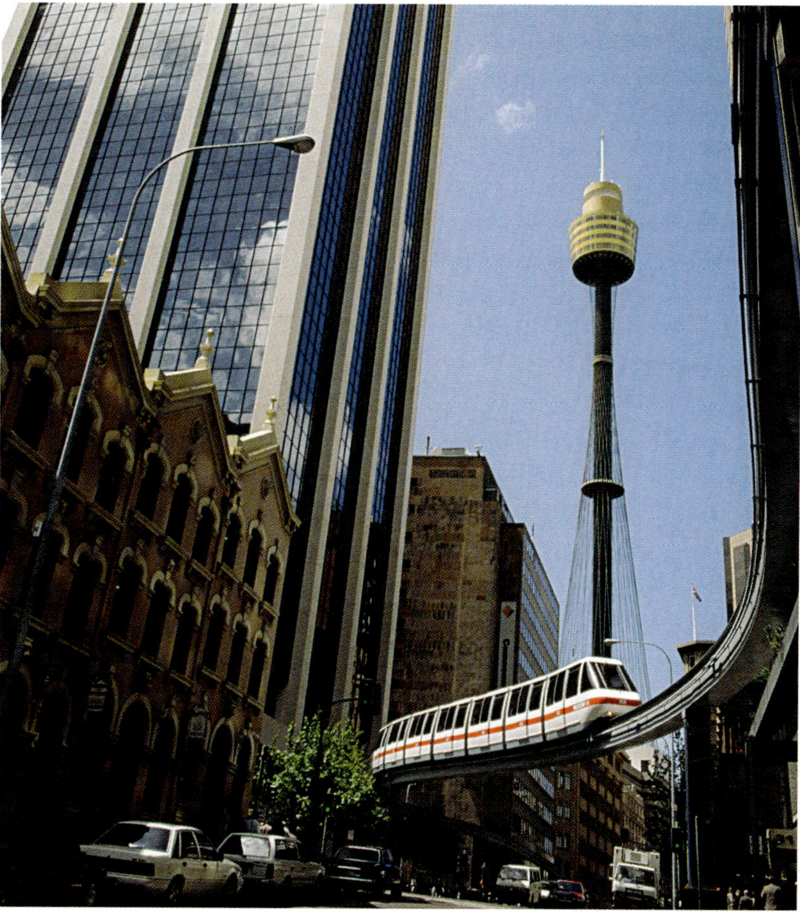

Monorail and, in the background, the AMP Tower, 1984. Sydney.

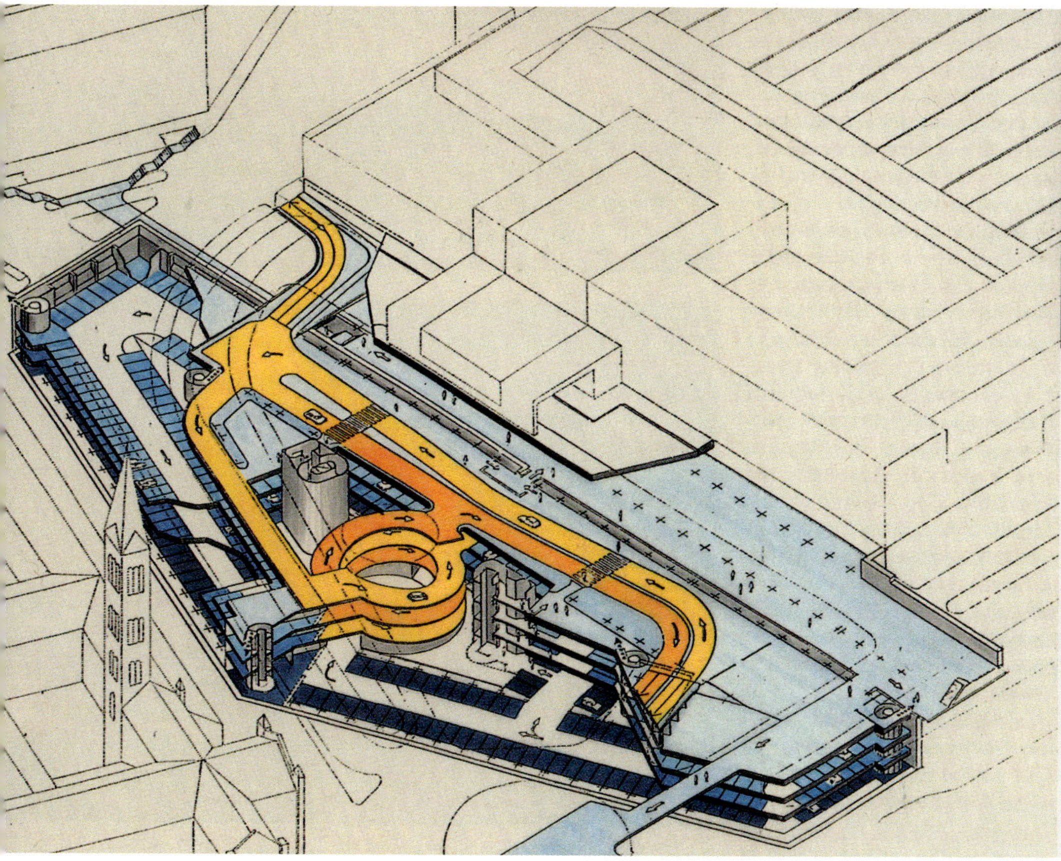

Left:
Axonometric drawing of the underground parking facilities at Piazza Stazione, 1989–1992 (designed by Paolo Felli, Pier Lodovico Rupi, and Enzo Giusti). Florence, Italy.

Aerial view of the clover-leaf between highway Routes 4 and 17 west of the George Washington Bridge. Bergen County, New Jersey. The highway has no level crossings, but bridges and ramps (clover-leafs) allow vehicles to change direction without interrupting the flow of traffic.

Commercial Buildings

Map of Athens' port of Piraeus, built under the direction of Hippodamus of Miletus, c. 470 B.C.E.

1. Emporium
2. Agorà and sanctuaries
3. Military port

Commerce, an activity fundamental to the economy of all civilizations, requires not only structures for transporting and storing goods (ports, railway stations, and airports), but also places where the merchandise arrives at its final destination, the customer.

● ANTIQUITY

The public square has always been a nerve center for commerce, as in the case of the Greek *agorà*. In many cities, the presence of temples dedicated to protective gods helped make an area suitable for commerce. At times, the place where goods were sold was in the vicinity of a port, as at Piraeus, the port of Athens, where the "general markets" (*empórion*) were located—the grain market, the stock market, and five great porticoes under which vendors sold their wares.

The most famous marketplace of antiquity was the great Trajan's Market in Rome, designed by Apollodorus of Damascus, which for centuries was the center of commercial as well as religious and judicial life in the city.

● THE MIDDLE AGES

The medieval world continued to utilize the meeting places of antiquity, with some important changes: the streets were much wider and they were lined

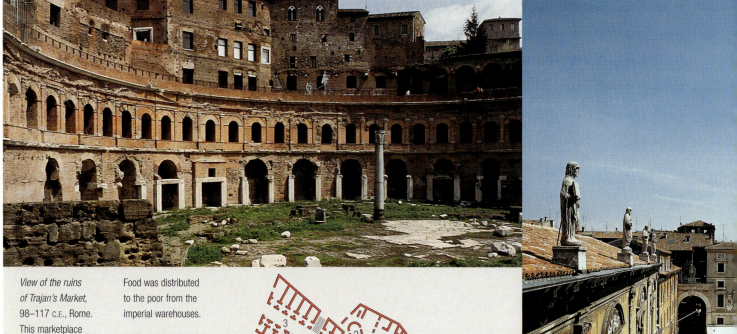

View of the ruins of Trajan's Market, 98–117 C.E., Rome. This marketplace consisted of about 150 shops, with vendors selling goods of all kinds. An important structure was the great hall, entered from Via Biberatica; the hall apparently served as bargaining or exchange center. Food was distributed to the poor from the imperial warehouses.

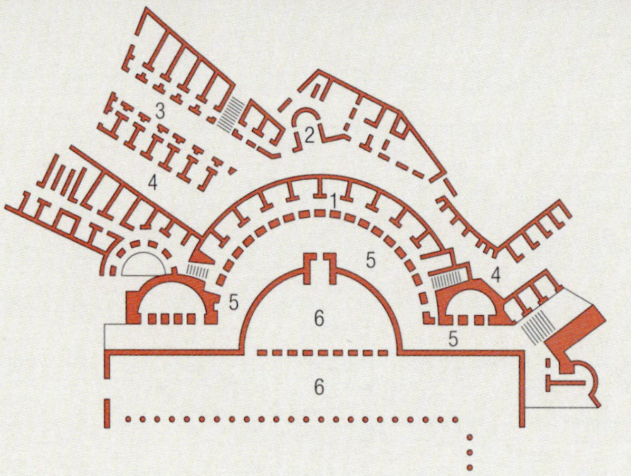

Plan of Trajan's Market in Rome

1. Exedra
2. Apse-like hall
3. Floors of shops: 1st, 2nd, and 3rd floor and great hall
4. Via Biberatica
5. Cobbled street
6. Trajan's Forum

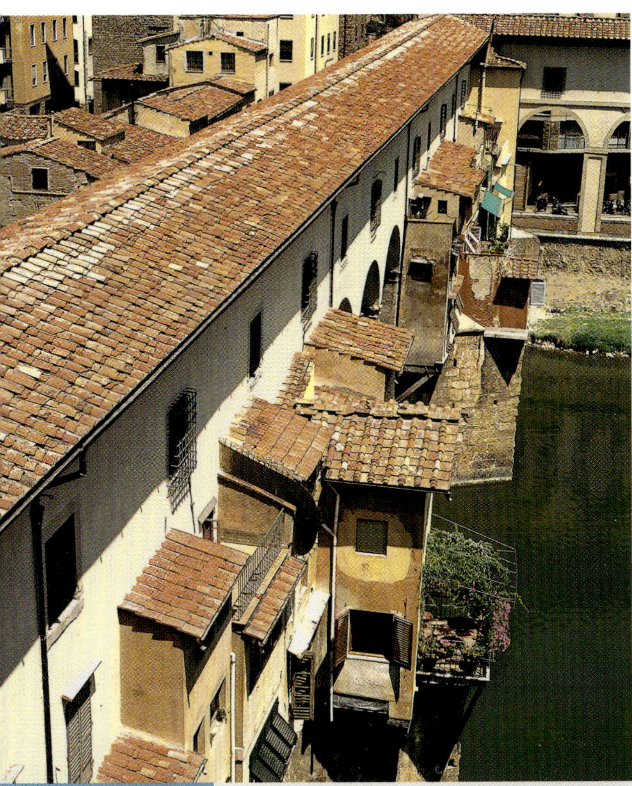

with porticoes under which stood the shops. Public squares were frequently occupied by markets. It was at this time that multiple public squares, such as those in Verona and Bologna, Italy, were built.

Similar types are found in Bruges, Belgium, and Lubeck, Germany, where the market squares open out before the cathedral and the *beffroi* (town hall). Another development was the bridge lined with shops.

Enormously important in the Islamic world is the bazaar (*suk* in Arabic), a quarter often located near the main mosque in the business district of a city. The *suk* is a labyrinth of narrow streets lined with stands, usually roofed, with many side passageways. Divided into commercial sectors, it may also contain mosques, caravansaries (inns), and fountains.

● THE MODERN AGE

The most striking changes occurred at the turn of the last century, with the innovation of large department stores such as Marshall Field & Co. in Chicago, Harrod's in London, and the Galleries Lafayette in Paris. Today, supermarkets, malls, and shopping centers have profoundly altered the face of urban centers, and of suburbs even more. This is the case of the Triangle des Gares Euralille (Jean Nouvel, 1994), an enormous shopping center containing not only stores but also hotels and offices, located at the meeting point of several high-speed train lines linking Paris to London and Brussels. These new "cathedrals of spare time," where consumption becomes recreation, are distinguished by their multiplicity of services and monumental aspect.

Ponte Vecchio, fourteenth–seventeenth centuries. Florence. The oldest bridge in Florence, originally a defensive structure, it was rebuilt after the flood of 1333 with three spans and shops lining both sides. In 1564 Cosimo I de' Medici had the Vasari Corridor built above the shops on the eastern side, while in the seventeenth century the characteristic wooden balconies, which now serve as back rooms for the goldsmith shops, were added.

Piazza dei Signori, thirteenth–fifteenth centuries. Verona. This square leads into the Piazza delle Erbe, also the site of a market.

Top: Gerrit Berckheide, *The Market Square in Haarlem*, 1693. Florence, Uffizi Gallery.

Above: Hans Hollein, *Detail of the Haas House*, 1989. Vienna.

Right: E.H. Zeidler, *Eaton Center*, 1970. Toronto. This multilevel shopping center, with long corridors and plazas covered by plexiglas domes, has the aspect of a futuristic city.

Tombs and Cemeteries

According to the urban historian Lewis Mumford, "The burial of the dead in tombs marked by a mound, a tree, or a big stone [probably represented] the first permanent meeting place for the living." As such, it was the "embryo of a city," he said. "The first 'cities,' the only complete ones, built of enduring materials, are the 'cities of the dead'." One of these was Saqqara, Egypt, which developed from 2700 to 2650 B.C.E. around Djoser's step pyramid.

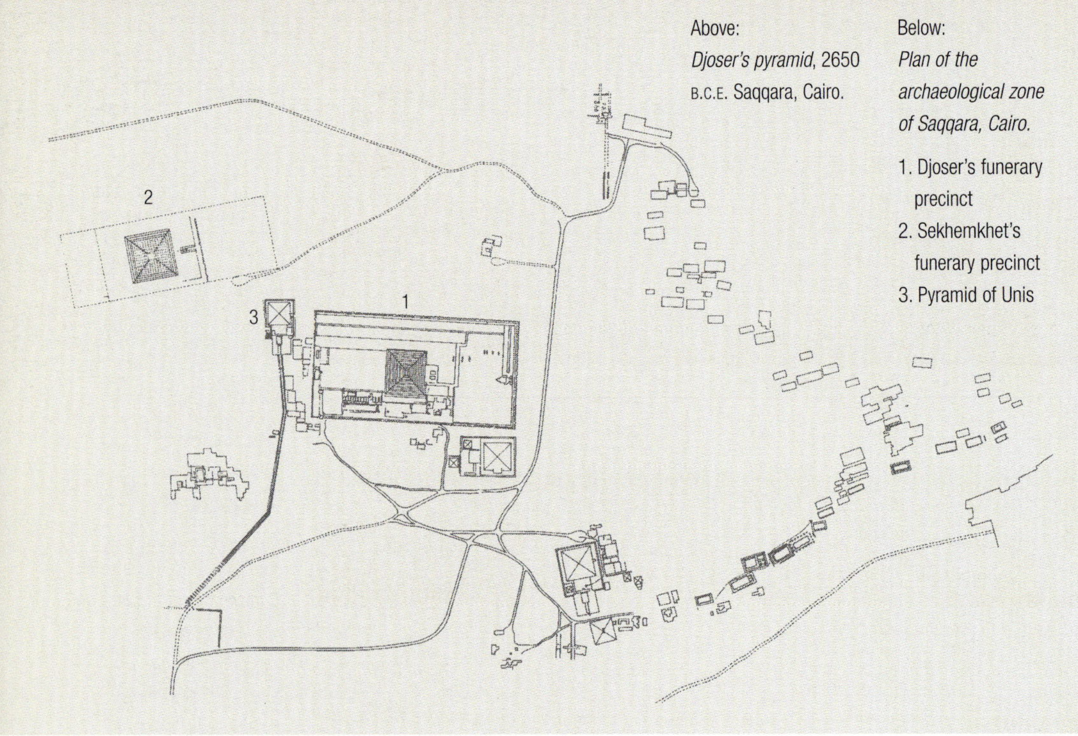

Above:
Djoser's pyramid, 2650 B.C.E. Saqqara, Cairo.

Below:
Plan of the archaeological zone of Saqqara, Cairo.

1. Djoser's funerary precinct
2. Sekhemkhet's funerary precinct
3. Pyramid of Unis

● ANTIQUITY

In ancient civilizations, the world beyond the tomb was considered as important as life on earth, if not more. Death was understood as the attainment of a condition of stability far removed from mortal suffering. Various structures were designed to conserve the remains of the dead and perpetuate their memory, but also as a "house" in which the deceased could rest serenely. Such was the case of the Egyptian *mastaba*, the private tomb of the Ancient Kingdom that was to evolve into the monumental form of the step pyramid. Inside the

View of an Etruscan circular tomb, seventh–sixth centuries B.C.E. Cerveteri, Banditaccia Necropolis, Viterbo, Italy.

mastaba, a rectangular mound built of stone or terracotta with oblique sides, were placed many portraits of the deceased, so that the *ka*, the spirit-double, could recognize its home and inhabit it. Even richer were the Etruscan tombs, excavated in soft rock and divided into chambers, with the cells connected by corridors to form a necropolis. The walls were sometimes decorated with frescoes or stucco bas-reliefs portraying household objects and implements of everyday use. In addition to *tholos* tombs, the Greeks elaborated the Eastern forms of the "tower" and "mansion" tombs. The greatest of these, on a truly monumental scale, was the Mausoleum of Harlicarnassus in Ionia, (p. 219), one of the Seven Wonders of the Ancient World. Roman tombs, many of which reiterate the Etruscan circular plan, were usually located outside the sacred enclosure of the city and subjected to strict state control, as in the case of the monumental tombs of Aquileia. In addition, actual funeral roads were built, such as the Appian Way. With the Imperial Age, personal tombs of increasing splendor, commemorating the cult of a personality, were erected. The coming of Christianity brought a revolution in this field. The clandestine nature of the new faith led to the construction of underground catacombs and the return of the cult of the dead inside city walls. Christian churches came to be built over the tombs or relics of saints and martyrs, as in the case of St. Peter's in Rome and the great cathedrals throughout Europe.

● THE MIDDLE AGES AND THE MODERN ERA

With the establishment of Christianity, churches themselves or the land immediately surrounding them (as with many Anglo-Saxon cemeteries) became burial sites. Beginning in the fourteenth century, because of the great plague epidemics and the growth of true cities, cemeteries were built increasingly farther away from urban centers. This characteristic, typical of the modern cemetery, was to become standard practice during the Enlightenment of the eighteenth century. Burial in churches was prohibited in the Hapsburg Empire (1743) and the Kingdom of Spain (1787); in Paris, the Cemetery of the Innocents was closed (1785). The Napoleonic Edict of Saint Cloud (1804) extended the regulations to the Italian provinces, where it was also required that all tombstones be of the same shape and size. These regulations gave rise to the monumental cemeteries of the nineteenth century, such as the Kensal Green Cemetery in London (1838), the first modern cemetery and a model for many others in London; and the Père-Lachaise cemetery in Paris, filled with neo-Gothic monuments. In contemporary society, cemeteries, relegated to the outskirts of cities, tend toward sobriety and minimalism, with structures often repeated in series.

Aldo Rossi and Giovanni Braghieri, *Cemetery of San Cataldo*, 1971–1984. Modena, Italy. The architect combines basic geometric elements, imbuing them with strong historical and symbolic connotations, in an "architecture of shadows" distinguished by a play of light that "marks the hour and the passing of the seasons."

Tomb of the baker M. Virgil Eurisace, 30 B.C.E. Rome. Although dating from the end of the Republican Age, this monument anticipates the individual experimentation that was to be typical of the Augustan Age (as exemplified by the Pyramid of Gaius Cestius in Rome). The tomb confers a monumental air on ordinary vases used to bake dough in ovens, and is decorated with scenes illustrating the bread-making process.

Camposanto, 1278–1283. Pisa. According to the fourteenth-century *Chronicle of Pisa*, the Camposanto was built by Giovanni di Simone, who filled the area with tons of soil "conquered" by Pisa in the Holy Land.

Techniques, Materials, and Structures

If an architectural work, as defined by the dictionary, is "the artistic elaboration of structural, functional, and aesthetic elements," then the purpose of the various techniques is to produce stable, long-lasting buildings that can withstand the elements, stress, and physical impact. Fundamental to this purpose is the material, employed in different ways depending on a variety of factors. The pages that follow analyze these uses and factors in relation to the most common building types: architecture in wood, stone, brick, reinforced concrete, steel, and glass. The section then proceeds to a discussion of the elements that make up a building's architectural "fabric" (column, capital, arch, and so on), codified in classical treatises as a kind of alphabet.

From above:
Great stupa, fifteenth century. Gyantse, Tibet.

Schmidt, Hammer & Lassen K/S, *Katuaq Greenland's Cultural Centre*, 1997. Nuuk, Greenland. This great multifunctional structure is distinguished by a long, undulating façade made of wood and glass. Erected in the world's smallest capital city, the Katuaq (Inuit for "drum player") houses temporary exhibitions, a large cinema, a theater, and restaurants.

Left:
The dome of the Pisa Cathedral viewed from the Camposanto.

Building with Wood

One of the most ancient human construction materials, wood—light and adaptable, particularly well suited for roofing—has been used not only alone but also in combination with mud, straw, bricks, and stone. Complemented with such other materials as steel and glass, wood has made a striking return in contemporary architecture.

● ANTIQUITY

In the ancient world, wood was used especially for beams, roofs, and doors. Early columns, triglyphs, and other structural elements were probably also made of wood, retaining the same shapes and forms when, at some later time, they were transposed into stone. According to this hypothesis, the Egyptian banded column derived from stalks of papyrus bound together, while the triglyphs on Greek temples may have derived from the gouged ends of wooden roof beams. Remains of Ancient Egyptian mud huts with roofs made of reeds supported by wooden beams (the houses of workers in the necropolis of Thebes) support the theory. In the Greco-Roman world as well, wood was used not only for the roofs of temples and basilicas but also for lower-class housing. (The fire that swept

Above:
Wooden funeral aedicule of Ika and his wife Imerit, IV Dynasty. Cairo, Archaeological Museum. The shape of these framed openings did not change when stone began to be used in place of wood.

Right:
Stav-Kirke at Borgund, c. 1150. Fagusnes, Norway. This church, supported by vertical interior posts, has eave decorations reminiscent of the rostrum on a Viking ship.

Left:
Trussed-beam ceiling, thirteenth century. Florence, Church of the Santi Apostoli.

Below: *Construction plan based on the balloon-frame system.* Utilized in the United States since 1833, balloon-frame construction is a building technique based on a skeletal wood frame; precut beams and piers are assembled by nailing rather than by jointing.

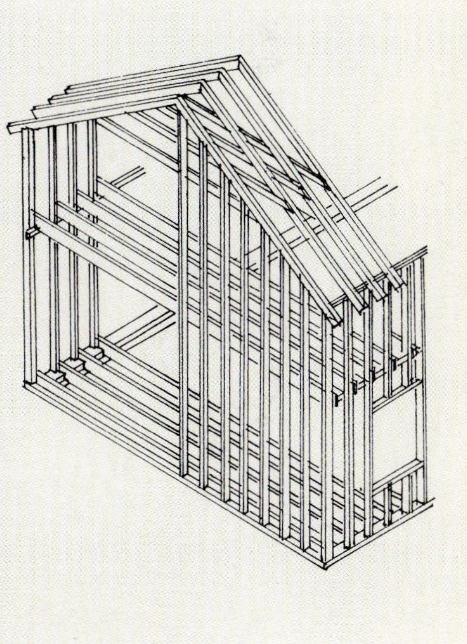

through Rome under Nero's reign in 64 C.E. is well documented.)

FROM THE MIDDLE AGES TO THE MODERN ERA

In substantial continuity with the model of the Roman basilica, the first Christian churches were covered with wooden roof-trusses called *capriata* (from *capra,* "truss" or "fixed joint"), an elastic structure composed of fixed beams, usually triangular in shape. The form resembles the overturned keel of a ship (thus the term "nave," the Italian word for "ship"). It is no coincidence that in medieval Norway the wooden structure of the Viking ships served as a model for the traditional *Stav-Kirke*, churches supported by bearing poles. Especially in the countries of central and northern Europe, both houses and granaries were usually made of wood. Crutch construction was quite common, with each corner bearing pier made of a single tree trunk, bent to form the contour of the roof. Over the centuries, masonry was increasingly used in place of wood as a roofing material. The wood roof survived only in the civil architecture of northern Europe until the seventeenth century. It was revived in the United States in the nineteenth century thanks to the balloon-frame construction system, which was widely applied from 1870 to 1890 in the so-called Stick and Shingle style. In the twentieth century, wood was used again in combination with other materials, often as an evocation of nature and the local landscape.

Building with Stone

Since ancient times, stone—more difficult to procure and work than wood, but much stronger—has been used especially for the most important buildings of a community.

● ORIGINS

Prehistoric megalithic monuments such as the *dolmen* (chamber tombs widely used from 4000 to 1000 B.C.E. in Europe and Asia) and the enigmatic complex of Stonehenge (p. 201) can be defined as triliths: two stones fixed vertically in the ground, surmounted by a horizontal slab that functions as an architrave.

Among the most ancient stone structures are cyclopean walls, made of enormous rough-hewn blocks laid without mortar. Walls and palaces from various ancient civilizations whose ruins can be seen today in Asia Minor (Hittite civilization), Greece (Tiryns and Mycenae), and Latin America (Cuzco) are called *opus poligonale* for their many-sided stone

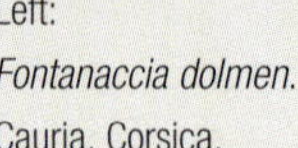

Left:
Fontanaccia dolmen.
Cauria, Corsica.

Above:
Outer wall with opus quadratum *structure,*
first century C.E.
Verona, Roman amphitheater.

Right:
Opus reticulatum *walls.*
Lucus Feroniae, Villa dei Volusii, Capena, Rome.

blocks. By contrast, *opus quadratum*, employed by the Romans starting from the fourth century B.C.E., is a wall system in which rectangular blocks are laid dry in regular rows. From Middle Eastern tradition, the Ancient Romans then derived one of the most important innovations in construction technology: the use of lime to bind the stones together and amalgam to fill the gaps in the walls. Depending on the shape of the hewn stone, the outer walls were termed *opus incertum* (irregular) or *opus reticulatum* (regular). Greek temples, instead, were constructed of large stone blocks, cut to form the various structural elements, such as columns and architraves.

● THE MIDDLE AGES AND THE MODERN ERA

In the metaphor of a contemporary chronicler, Europe after the year 1000 was covered with "a great white cloak of churches." More than 1,400 churches and monasteries were built in a matter of a few years, relying primarily on stone for the structural elements. Later, the widespread use of bricks favored the application of stone as facing. Used in this way, *bossage* (quadrangular stones hewn in relief) conferred a rustic, animated effect on external walls.

Above:
Detail of diamond-point bossage, sixteenth century. Lisbon, Casa dos Bicos.

Below:
Detail of rusticated bossage, c. 1440. Florence, Pitti Palace, façade.

Building with Brick

Masonry units made of hardened clay, bricks have been the most widely used construction material since ancient times. Employed according to traditional methods, brick offers the same advantages as stone, as well as greater versatility and rapidity of construction.

● ANTIQUITY AND THE MIDDLE AGES

The rise of the first civilizations on the banks of great rivers depended in part on the availability of clay, the raw material of brick. Made first of raw clay, bricks were later baked in state-owned workshops, fabricated in sizes established by decree, and marked with an official seal. In this sense they represented the first example of a state monopoly, as well as the most ancient form of industry. Bricks had to be shaped in such a way that they could be picked up with only one hand. This enabled workers to lay the bricks rapidly in long rows and layers, either directly superimposed on one another or in steps. Soon, however, other shapes came into use; for example, the unbaked bricks employed at Ebla, Syria, between 2400 and 2000 B.C.E. were square. Already in the third millennium B.C.E., the widespread use of baked bricks had permitted the construction of imposing buildings. The Romans used them to construct temples, defensive works, and aqueducts. Thanks to its versatility, brick could even be used to build solid, elegant columns, in imitation of the monolithic marbles but at a lower cost and with the certainty of an unlimited supply. For building arches, vaults, and roofing, Byzantine brickworks between the fourth and the sixth centuries produced square bricks about 2–3 inches thick and 16–18 inches wide, usually marked with an official seal and subject to periodic inspection. The ancient technique of brick construction was to remain virtually unchanged in Romanesque and Gothic architecture, effectively adapted to new stylistic and structural requirements.

Below:
Terra-cotta decoration, detail of the Ishtar Gate, according to the reconstruction carried out on site. Babylon, Iraq. The original door (580 B.C.E.), from the ancient site of Babylon, is now in the Pergamum Museum, Berlin.

Above:
Basilica of Maxentius, fourth century C.E. Rome, Via Sacra.

Remains of brick columns, 120 B.C.E. Pompeii, basilica. The fluting on the columns was created by laying pentagonal-shaped bricks around a cylindrical core. The column was then covered with stucco and painted to resemble marble.

Left:
Francesco Borromini, *Terra-cotta façade*, 1640. Rome, Oratorio dei Filippini.

Below:
Aldo Rossi, *Centro Torri*, 1988. Parma.

● THE MODERN AND CONTEMPORARY ERA

Among the boldest and most innovative of all brick structures is the great dome on the Florence cathedral, Santa Maria del Fiore (1429–1433), constructed by Filippo Brunelleschi with layers of self-supporting bricks in a fishbone pattern (p. 287).

In Baroque Rome, brick was put to striking use by Francesco Borromini, who exploited its every potential in works such as the façade of the Oratorio dei Filippini.

Since brick was regarded as a construction material of the poor, it was rarely exposed to open view during the eighteenth and nineteenth centuries, often covered with plaster or whitewash. In the twentieth century, the technique of brick building was essentially rediscovered, beginning with Walter Gropius (Fagus Works, p. 64) and evolving in the more recent projects of Aldo Rossi in Italy (Centro Torri in Parma, 1988) and the Netherlands (the Bonnefanten Museum in Maastricht, 1990–1994).

Reinforced Concrete and Prefabricated Buildings

Even in Roman times, concrete (from *calx*, "lime," and *struere*, "to amass") was used as a binding mortar for bricks or hewn stone. It is an artificial product formed of hydraulic lime (lime with a dicalcium silicate additive) or of cement and aggregate (sand or pozzuolana, gravel or crushed stone) mixed with water.

Today concrete is produced in various ways, such as by grinding clinker (from the Dutch *klinken*, "to resonate"), a mixture of clay and lime baked almost to the vitrification point for use in high-strength bricks. Portland cement, composed of natural marls and clays from the Portland quarries in Great Britain, is the most widely used of these products.

Above:
Le Corbusier, *Diagram of reinforced-concrete structure for an apartment building according to the Dom-Ino construction system*, 1914.

Right:
Auguste Perret, *House at 25 b, Rue Franklin*, 1903–1904. Paris. The reinforced-concrete structure is faced with terracotta and ceramic tiles.

● REINFORCED CONCRETE

To expand the uses of concrete—used almost exclusively until the mid-nineteenth century for bridge pylons, port facilities, piping, and sewage channels—it was necessary to increase the material's tensile strength. From 1852 to 1892, dozens of patents were granted for solutions to this problem; in the most successful of these, steel reinforcement bars were placed in the formwork before the concrete was poured. This was the origin of reinforced concrete, and today's technique for producing it is basically the same. It was a revolutionary discovery because, as noted by Pier Luigi Nervi, architects now were able to "create fused stones of any shape superior to natural ones in their capacity for withstanding stress." The advantages of low cost, versatility, and strength ensured the success of this new material, employed by Le Corbusier in designing the Maison Dom-Ino (1914), a prototype of the modular housing unit. In the early days, concrete was covered with more expensive materials or simply disguised with paint. Since the 1950s, however, it has been appreciated for its intrinsic beauty and has often been left exposed, in keeping with contemporary trends in the figurative arts.

● PREFABRICATED ELEMENTS

The concept of fabricating elements to be assembled on site is a recurrent theme in the long history of architecture. But it was only with the building techniques and materials of the twentieth century (reinforced concrete, iron, and glass) that it became possible to begin low-cost industrial production of modular elements and panels that could be easily assembled on site.

Building with Iron, Steel, and Glass

The systematic utilization of these materials dates from the nineteenth century, although iron had already been employed since the late seventeenth century to reinforce masonry or to support it during construction, and glass had been used for windows since Roman times. In the nineteenth century, engineers and architects began to understand that these elements could be combined and that doing so would allow building solutions that were otherwise unthinkable. Iron structures, in fact, resolved all problems of weight support and load dispersal, while glass panels filled spaces that, in theory, could remain empty since they no longer had to serve a support function. This led to the construction of greenhouses, railway stations, and later skyscrapers with exceptionally luminous interiors.

● FROM THE NINETEENTH CENTURY TO TODAY

At first iron was employed in public facilities such as bridges, railway stations, and subways. The use of iron conferred on these works an air of modernity, while the bare structures were embellished with decorative elements. This building technique, faster and more economical than traditional ones, called for the use of prefabricated section bars of various shapes, joined with rivets shot hot into holes drilled in the I-beams. With this type of connection, imposing structures such as the Eiffel Tower in Paris (pp. 332–333) could be erected, and it became the most widely employed technique in the nineteenth century; the same or better results, in fact, could be obtained by conventional bolting or electric welding (in which the steel is heated to 1300° C, its melting point). The quality of the ferrous material was also important. While cast iron (iron with a high percentage of carbon, making the structure more fragile) was used at first, smelting in blast furnaces was soon employed to produce steel, a purer, stronger, and more elastic material. Used for skyscrapers since the latter part of the nineteenth century, steel structures allow a freer distribution of space. This was demonstrated by Ludwig Mies van der Rohe in 1929 with a pier built of chrome-plated steel that joined translucent glass walls (Barcelona Expo, German Pavilion). Since then, steel has become the material of choice in high-tech architecture, especially after the spectacular steel trusses designed by Renzo Piano and Richard Rogers for the Pompidou Center (1977) in Paris.

Left:
Decimus Burton and Richard Turner, *Palm House at Kew Gardens*, 1844–1848. London.

Above:
Piano & Rogers, *Detail of bearing structure of the Pompidou Center*, 1971–1977. Paris.

Columns and Other Vertical Elements

Columns, piers (or pillars), pilasters, and lesenes are vertical elements codified in architectural styles. While columns and piers have undergone significant evolution and have been used in a vast range of applications, pilasters are the heritage of the classical world and the styles that hark back to it.

● COLUMNS

The column is an element of support, serving the structural function of joining the base of a building (the lower structures) to the top (upper elements). It normally consists of a cylindrical shaft that rests on a base and is topped by a capital. Columns may be monolithic or fashioned from rocks or bricks, appropriately shaped and finished. They are classified according to the morphology of the shaft, which may be tapered at the top or bottom, fluted, cabled (where the fluting is decorated with a motif—such as a braid, rod, or cord—covering the lower third), or else smooth. The columns typical of the Greco-Roman world were followed by those of the Middle Ages (twisted, knotted, Salomonic). The chief innovation of the late sixteenth century was the

Right:
Colonnade of Amenophis III, c. 1450 B.C.E. Luxor.

Below:
Coupled and knotted columns, thirteenth century. Chiaravalle della Colomba, Piacenza, cloister of the abbey.

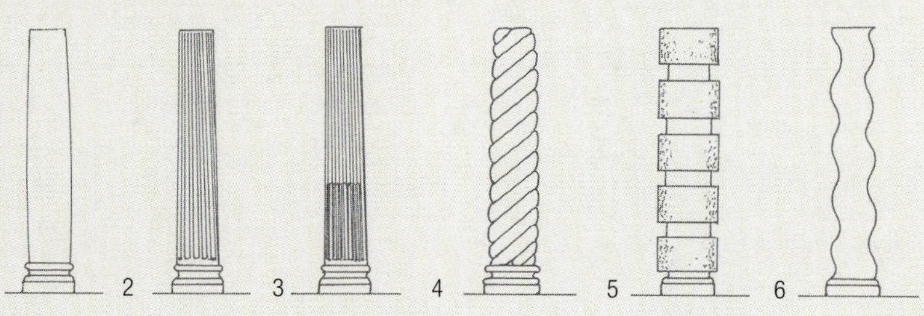

Diagram of a typical column

1. Base
2. Shaft
3. Capital

Diagram of a typical base and pedestal of a column

A. *Base*
1. Torus
2. Scotia
3. Plinth

B. *Pedestal*
4. Dado
5. Plinth

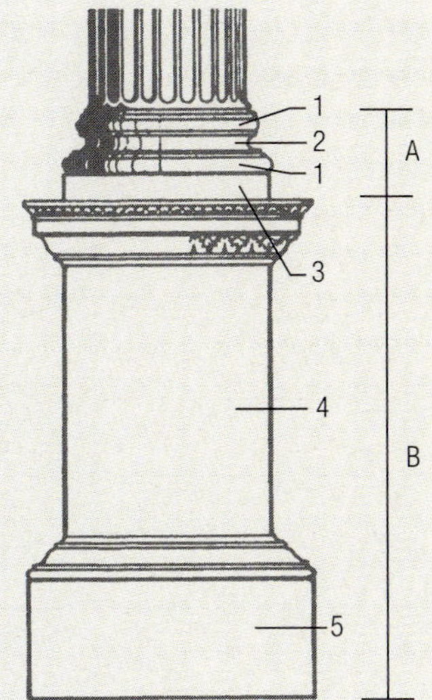

bossage column; that of the Baroque age was the tendril-covered column with grapevines winding around the shaft. Modern columns are built of steel and have no capital. Columns are also classified according to their positions: "coupled," in pairs; "corner," located at a corner of the building); "back-to-back," placed against a wall (but known as "half-columns" when partially embedded in the wall); and "flush," incorporated in a pier.

● PIERS

The pier, also known as a pillar, is a vertical structural element whose section is usually square, rectangular, polygonal, or composite. Since its function is that of supporting arches, ceilings, and lintels, it represents an evolution of the vertical component of the trilith. Built of stone or masonry, piers are sometimes decorated with figures or historical scenes, and are not classified under any architectural order. Among the many variations in type, the most important, dating from the Middle Ages, is the "bundle pillar" (called a pier when its structure is animated by the presence of half-columns standing against it). The reinforced-concrete "mushroom pillar," so-called because it ends at the top in a truncated cone or reversed pyramid, joins the base of the building to the overhead floor slab.

● PILASTERS AND LESENES

A pilaster is an upright rectangular member projecting in relief from a wall; it is structurally a pier, in that it supports weight, but it is treated architecturally as a column; a pillar strip has minimal projection and is purely decorative.

A lesene is a pilaster strip without a base or capital. Each can belong to different architectural orders.

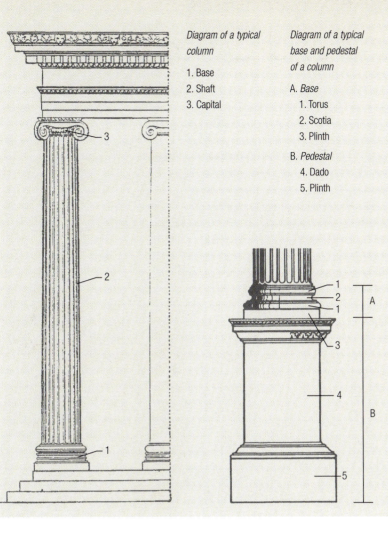

Pilasters in the Pazzi Chapel in Santa Croce, begun by Filippo Brunelleschi in 1433. Florence.

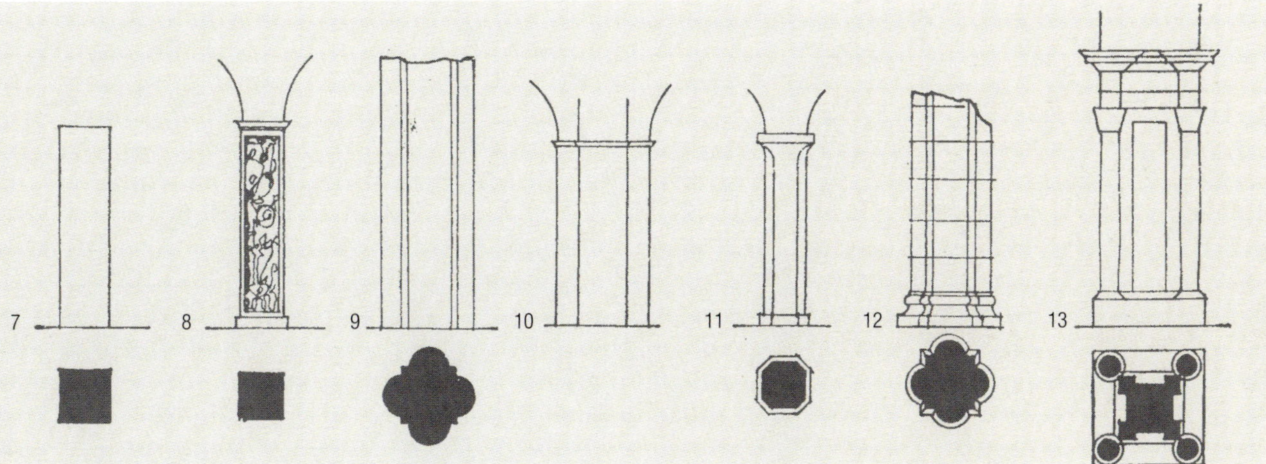

Types of columns and piers

1. Smooth
2. Fluted
3. Cabled
4. Twisting
5. Rustic
6. Salomonic
7. Square smooth
8. Decorated
9. Bundle
10. Roman
11. Romanesque
12. Gothic
13. Renaissance composite

Capitals

An integral part in the structure of a column or pier, the capital is the element upon which the classical architectural orders are based.

It tops a vertical member (column, pier, or pilaster), with which it may be connected by an echinus. Since it serves to broaden the base on which an architrave or an arch rests, it is a structural element of the building. The support may be reinforced by an intermediate device (an abacus, dado, or plinth), which in medieval times was destined to undergo a development equal to or even greater than that of the capital itself, becoming the "dosseret" or "pulvin."

Drawing of a typical capital.

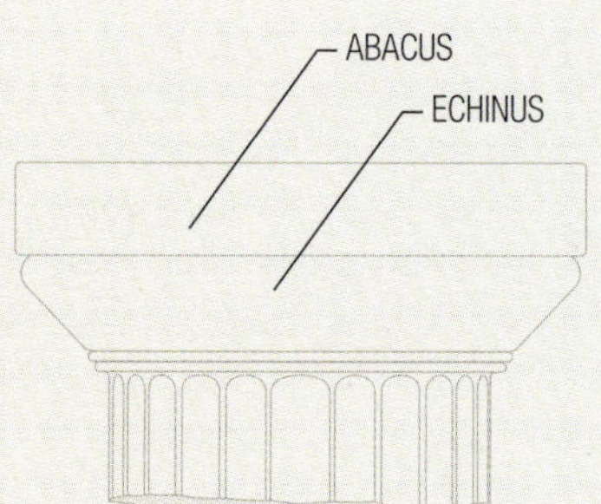

Below:
Capital decorated with human protomés in the hypostyle hall of Hator's chapel, c. 1500 B.C.E. Deir el-Bahari, Thebes.

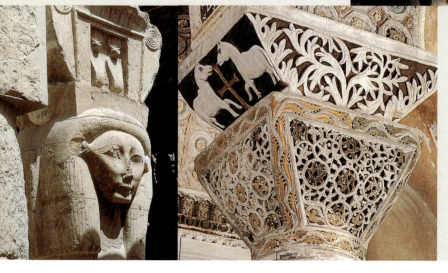

Left:
Byzantine capital with pulvin, sixth century C.E. Ravenna, San Vitale, Italy.

Above:
Capitals in the Medersa, c. 1340. Salé, Morocco.

Right:
Figured capital, detail of pulpit, end of twelfth century. Volterra, Duomo.

● ANTIQUITY

Different versions of the capital were already seen in the ancient world. Widely used in Egypt, capitals were inspired by the bell shape of papyrus clumps, decorated with human protomés (sculpted figurines), or shaped like a closed papyrus bud. In the highly refined Achaemenid Empire, capitals adorned with animal protomés, typically fork-shaped and either back-to-back or facing each other, were common. In the great palaces of the Minoan Age cushion capitals, with an abacus and an echinus already distinguished, were frequently used.

● FROM THE CLASSICAL ERA TO THE MIDDLE AGES

The most important capital types (Doric, Ionic, and Corinthian) are related to the architectural orders standardized in Greece. Throughout antiquity, the connection between capital and architrave was predominant. In Roman architecture, capitals are connected to piers by a stringcourse (horizontal band). In the great innovation of the Middle Ages, handed down from Byzantine culture, the capital was transformed into a support able to withstand the weight of the arches above it by enlarging the abacus, which then took the name of dosseret or pulvin (Latin *pulvinus*, "cushion"). The relief decorations on capitals were enriched by images linked to Christian iconography and by floral elements of classical inspiration.

● THE MODERN AGE

While the Renaissance faithfully reiterated the classical types, adapting them in new contexts, Baroque and late Baroque architecture displayed fanciful solutions inspired by ancient examples and invented new ones as well. Capitals were widely used until the end of the nineteenth century.

Above:
The Coliseum, 72–80 C.E. Rome. The half-columns on the outer wall support a stringcourse that resembles an architrave.

Below:
Capitals of the Pazzi Chapel in Santa Croce, begun by Filippo Brunelleschi in 1433. Florence.

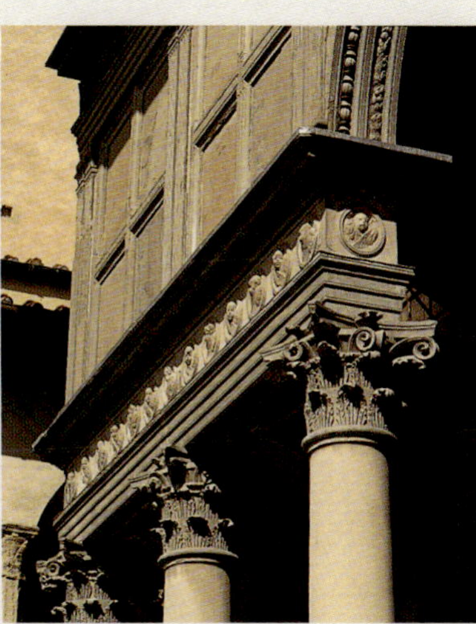

The Architrave and Other Horizontal Elements

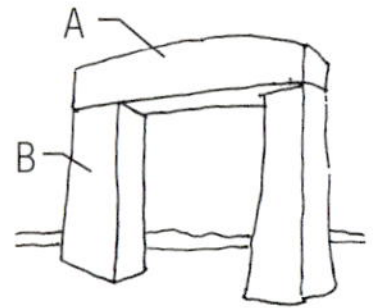

Diagram of a trilith

A. Architrave
B. Pillar

The horizontal elements in architecture are weight-bearing members that finish a structure at the top. In a trilith, the horizontal element is the architrave; in a classical temple, it is the trabeation or epistyle. Other horizontal elements include lintels over doors; projecting corbels that support wood beams; and ridgepoles, at which the sides of a roof peak and converge.

● THE ARCHITRAVE

The literal meaning of this term, of Renaissance origin, is "main beam." In antiquity it was called *epistylion* and in the Middle Ages *trabes*. It could be made of either stone or wood. Today the reinforced-concrete elements situated in the same position are also called architraves. In Greco-Roman architecture, especially that of temples, the architrave constituted the lower part of the trabeation, directly supported by the capitals. In the Middle Ages, the architrave was almost entirely replaced by arches, being used rarely and almost exclusively as an allusion to antiquity.

● THE TRABEATION

The trabeation, or entablature, is the horizontal weight-bearing system which, resting on columns, forms the base of the roof. It consists of the following elements, from bottom to top: architrave, frieze, and cornice. A frieze may be either continuous or made up

Above:
Architrave over the western portal of the Collegiate of San Giovanni Battista, twelfth century. San Quirico d'Orcia, Siena, Italy.

Trabeation of the Celso Library, after 107 C.E. Ephesus, Turkey. Above the two capitals is an architrave bearing an inscription in Greek, a frieze with plant volutes, and a cornice.

of alternating triglyphs and metopes, depending on the architectural order. In medieval architecture, as mentioned above, the rarely used trabeation was chiefly a reference to antiquity, especially from the fifteenth century on. The ancient model of the trabeation served as an inspiration for various other architectural features, such as the stringcourses on bell-towers and the façades of palaces.

● OTHER TYPES

Among the most important horizontal elements, both structurally and decoratively, are the platband over a door or window, which may be either monolithic or made of bricks; the corbel, an element projecting outward that can serve as support for wood or brick beams; and the roof-ridge beam (ridgepole) at the top of a sloping roof.

Leon Battista Alberti, *Palazzo Rucellai*, c. 1450. Florence. The stringcourses are inspired by the classical model of the trabeation.

Diagram of corbel on the Erechtheion Gate, fifth century B.C.E. Athens, Acropolis.

The Arch

Since an arch provides greater stability than a trabeation, it can be used to span wider spaces. The weight above the arch is distributed along its convex line and is shared equally by the two supporting walls.

An arch is not only an element designed to span voids and thereby create openings (ranging from doors to bridges), but it can also serve as support for a wall. A discharge arch, for example, inserted within a wall structure, serves to distribute excess weight and relieve stress on weak points. A flying buttress, on the other hand, shores up the wall from the outside, through an arched support that relieves horizontal thrust and discharges it to the ground. Arches, moreover, carry a multitude of symbolic meanings. Already in Roman times, the arch had become a monumental, commemorative emblem of the feats of military heroes and emperors (the triumphal arch), a usage that was to endure until the modern age.

● STRUCTURE AND TYPES

An arch starts from the top of abutments or piers that may be finished

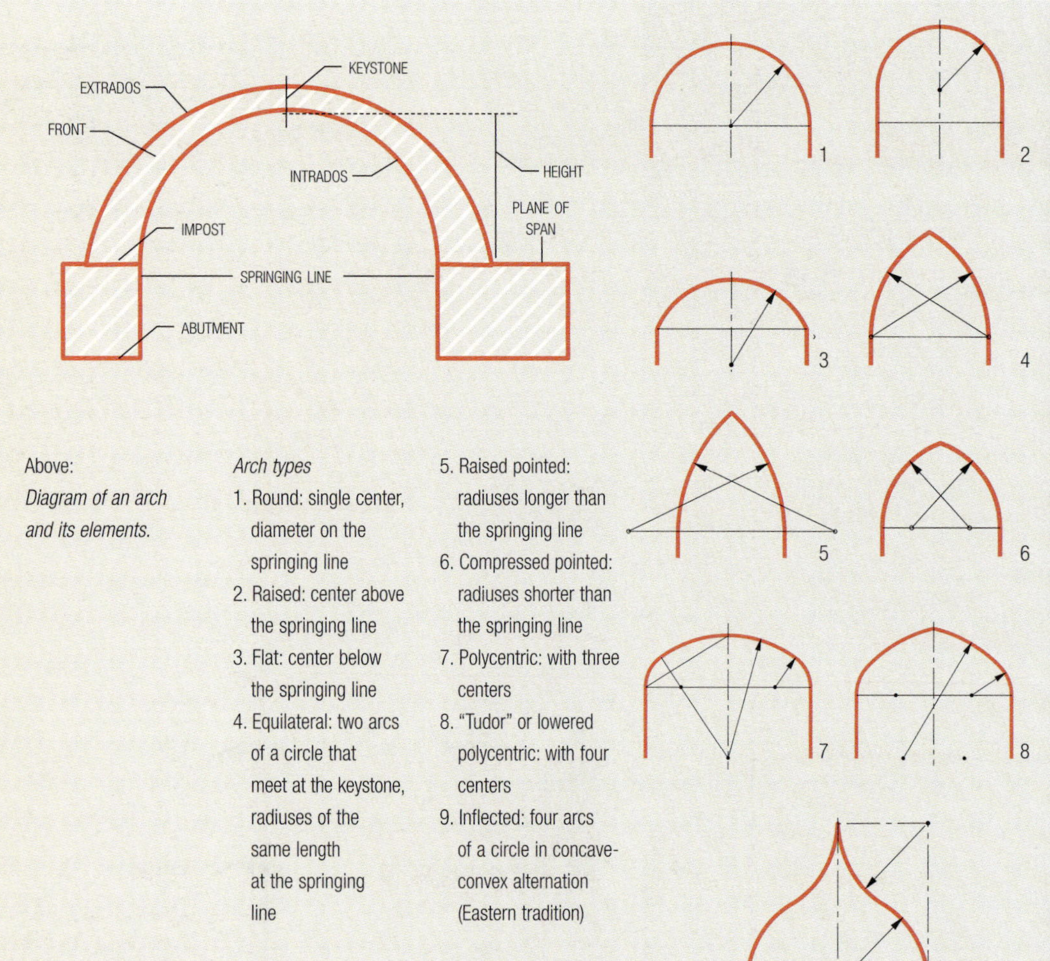

Above:
Diagram of an arch and its elements.

Arch types

1. Round: single center, diameter on the springing line
2. Raised: center above the springing line
3. Flat: center below the springing line
4. Equilateral: two arcs of a circle that meet at the keystone, radiuses of the same length at the springing line
5. Raised pointed: radiuses longer than the springing line
6. Compressed pointed: radiuses shorter than the springing line
7. Polycentric: with three centers
8. "Tudor" or lowered polycentric: with four centers
9. Inflected: four arcs of a circle in concave-convex alternation (Eastern tradition)

with brackets or corbels, on which rests the so-called springing line, where the curve begins. The round contour peaks at the center, or crown, where a wedge-shaped keystone locks the other pieces in place. The stone blocks used to construct an arch (voussoirs) are cut in the shape of a truncated pyramid and pieced together as if in an immense fan. The inner side of the arch proper, always exposed, is called the intrados; the upper side, usually encapsulated in a wall, is referred to as the extrados. The thickness of an arch is determined by the distance between intrados and extrados; the distance between the piers is called the span.

The various types of arch are classified according to the contour of the curve and the position of the center in relation to the springing line.

Left:
Composite arch (inflected and round) with Gothic coping, fourteenth century. Venice, St. Mark's Basilica, façade.

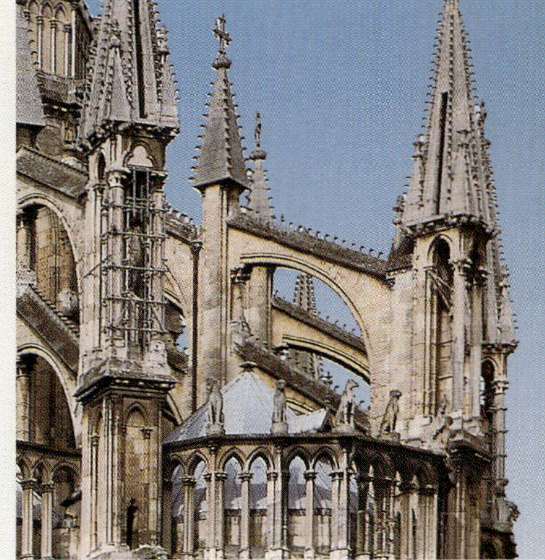

Right and below:
Gothic flying buttresses.

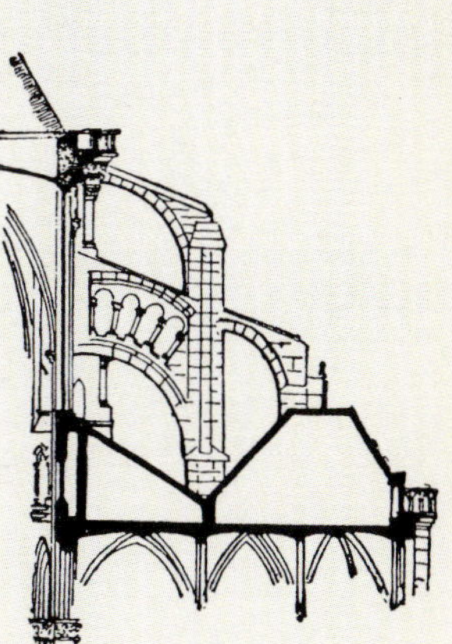

Vaults and Ceilings

A vault may be considered the translation of an arch (along a preferential convex line) or its rotation (around an axis). Like the arch, the vault has an extrados and an intrados, a springing line, and piers that support the whole. While an arch connects two points at a distance from each other, a vault serves the function of covering an interior.

In other words, while the arch is "linear" in nature, the vault constitutes a geometric surface. The structural behavior of these two elements is similar, considering that the vault disperses weight onto lateral arches and, like them, has a keystone.

The vault also has a symbolic meaning, often being compared to the sky and decorated to imitate the vault of heaven, viewed in biblical tradition (Psalms 104:2) and classical culture as a tent stretched out by the divinity.

Complex cross-vaulting with star-shaped intersections in the upper gallery of the Dos Jerónimos Cloister, early sixteenth century. Lisbon.

Diagrams of main types of vault

1. Barrel
2. Domical
3. Cross
4. Cloister (or tent)
5. Cavetto
6. Umbrella

● HISTORY AND TYPOLOGY

The most ancient examples of a pseudo-vault (rows of overhanging voussoirs laid one above another toward a peak and closed with a slab) may be seen in the Egyptian pyramid of Dahshur (2590–2570 B.C.E.) and the *tholos* tombs of the Minoan and Mycenaean civilizations (c. 1570 B.C.E.). In the West, vaults began to be used extensively in Roman times. More sophisticated, stronger types, based on the application of the pointed arch, were introduced in the Middle Ages. The basic vault typology thus was established.

The structure and designation of a vault are determined chiefly by the type of arch employed and by whether the vault is simple or composite. The most elementary form—consisting of the translation of a round or flat arch—is the barrel vault, a semi-cylindrical structure that rests on two end arches. The domical vault is a hemispherical *calotte* (concavity in the shape of a Catholic clerical skullcap) that discharges weight onto the lateral arches bounding a rectangular space, or span; the semidome corresponds to one quarter of a sphere. The ceiling is also known as a calotte, while the spaces between the arches are called spandrels, or pendentives. The cross-vault, a composite type, is formed by the intersection of two barrel vaults; it is a ribbed vault when the intersecting arches (vaulting ribs) are visible. The cloister vault is very similar, consisting of four segments that can also be adapted to rectangular spaces. When it is cut by a plane parallel to that of the impost, it is known as a cavetto vault. The lunette vault has groins (or segments) and lunettes at the sides. The umbrella vault, which covers a space that is polygonal (central) rather than rectangular, has multiple groins and lunettes around the center.

● CEILINGS

Modern materials and new technical solutions have led to the development of new ceiling forms that echo the effects of the vault. A striking example is the parabolic roof, utilized for the first time by Le Corbusier in the Philips Pavilion at the Brussels World's Fair held in 1958. It consists of a sort of membrane, even made of fabric, held in place by rigid bearing elements to form a parabola or parabolic arch.

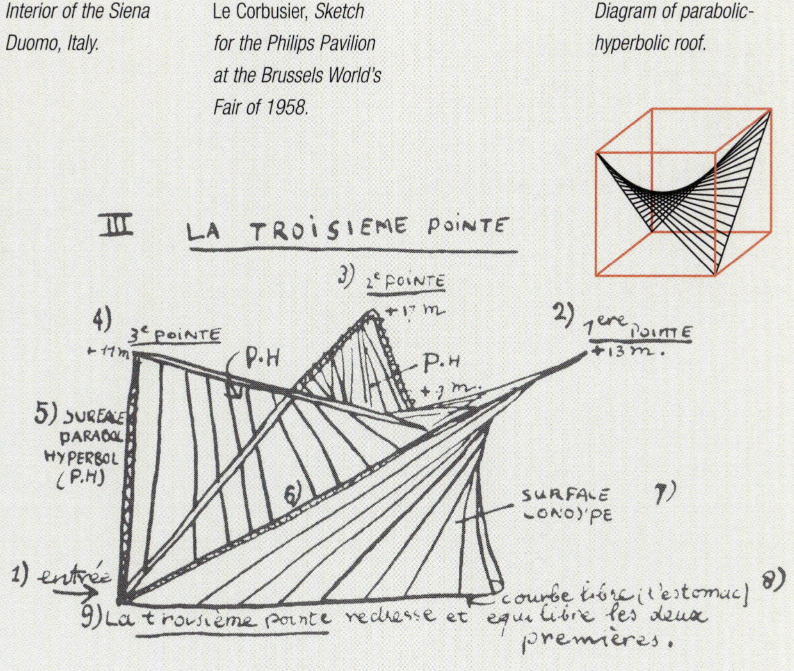

Interior of the Siena Duomo, Italy.

Le Corbusier, *Sketch for the Philips Pavilion at the Brussels World's Fair of 1958.*

Diagram of parabolic-hyperbolic roof.

The Dome

The dome, or cupola, can be considered a complex vaulted roof. The fulcrum of the building, a dome is of the extrados type when the surface is exposed to view; it can also be concealed by a prism-shaped structure called the lantern, topped by a roof.

In geometric terms, a dome is formed by the rotation of an arch around its own keystone. In this sense, the dome resembles the domical vault, from which it differs in having no dispersing arches tangent to its perimeter. On the contrary, it often rises above a domical vault whose true calotte has been cut off. This produces corner elements called (as in the domical vault) pendentives or spandrels—portions of a sphere that create a transition from the

Diagram of a dome and its elements

1. Dome with pendentives
2. Dome with tambour inserted on the pendentives
3. Corner squinches

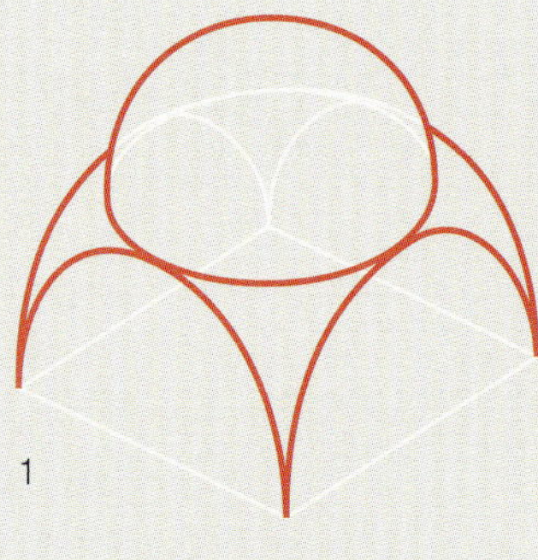

1

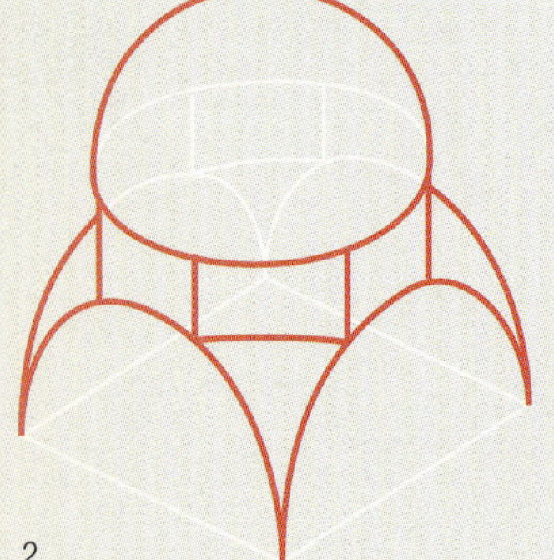

2

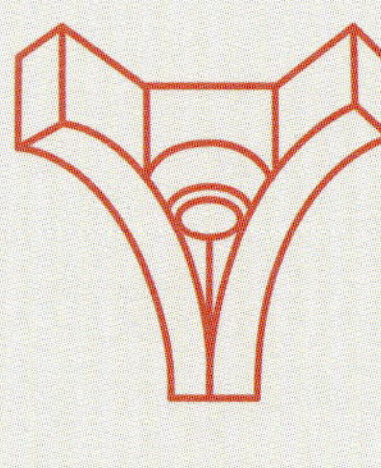

3

Above:
Central dome of the Jami Masjid mosque, 1644–1658. New Delhi.

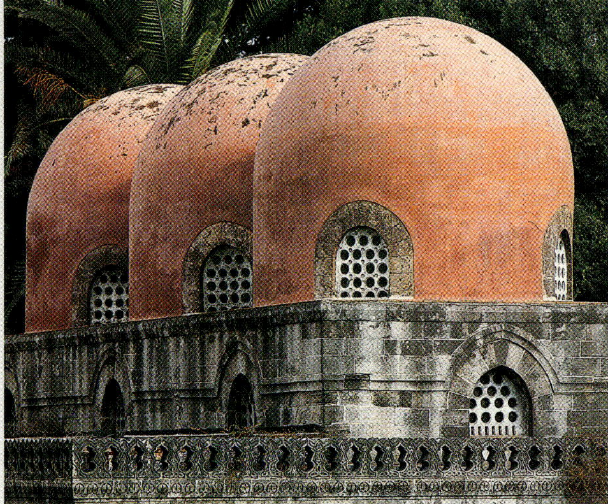

Right:
Domes of San Cataldo, c. 1160. Palermo, Italy.

square plan of the span to the impost of the dome and that facilitate the dispersal of weight onto the surrounding arches. Another common transition element, the tambour, usually has several windows. In some cases, a lantern is placed in the crown of the calotte, allowing more light to enter the interior. In another system for dispersing weight onto the lateral arches, squinches, cone-shaped elements serving the same function as pendentives, are used.

● HISTORY AND TYPES

Like the vault, a symbolic image of the cosmos, the dome is generally considered to be of Minoan origin. (*Tholos* domes are actually pseudo-vaults or pseudo-domes, like the Etruscan.) The Romans frequently employed vaults and domes with vaulting ribs or lacunars (ornamental sunken panels), as in the Pantheon, and domes made of concrete (pp. 232–233). Domes were used as well in Eastern civilizations, especially Persia (from the Parthian dynasty, second century B.C.E.–third century C.E., to the Sassanid dynasty, third–seventh centuries C.E.), where religious buildings dedicated to the cult of fire featured domed halls. At this time also, the concept of the dome as an image of the cosmos at whose center stands the emperor, an incarnation of the Sun god, was perpetuated; the transition of architectural systems based on a square plan to ones with a circular impost (spandrels and squinches) also developed further. Islamic architecture drew inspiration from elements of Sassanid tradition, including the onion-shaped dome, an idealized rotation of the four-centered arch.

Various dome types are also derived from those of the arch. They may be perfectly hemispherical (as in the Pantheon and St. Peter's Basilica), or have a crowning superstructure (as on Brunelleschi's dome for the Florence Cathedral, p. 287). Modern geodesic domes are constructed of prefabricated triangular modules.

Above:
Tyburium on the Certosa viewed from the little cloister, c. 1473. Pavia, Italy.

Left:
Richard Buckminster Fuller, *Geodesic dome on the American Pavilion at the Montreal Expo of 1967.*
Made of steel and plexiglas, the geodesic dome is based on the repetition of a module, so that structures of unlimited size may be built.

Façades

The façade (from the Latin *facies*, "face" or "aspect") is the main front of a building, marking the boundary between its interior and exterior. It may be regarded as the "calling card" of the building, or the image by which it is commonly identified and remembered.

The typical features of a traditional façade are its architectural orders, windows, and doors or portals; it may be decorated with sculpture, bas-reliefs, or marble inlay. A façade often appears as a sort of manifesto of the techniques and styles of a period.

● HISTORICAL NOTES

It was in the ancient Greek temple that the concept of a front adorned with sculptures on the tympanum, to proclaim the building as a holy place, first emerged. Roman architecture creatively emphasized the sculptural

Façade of the Cathedral of Notre-Dame, mid-twelfth century. Paris.

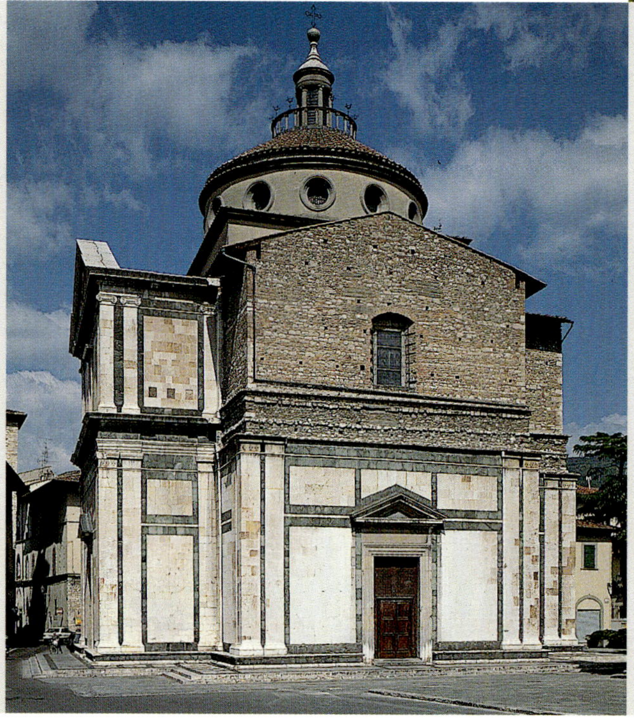

Giuliano da Sangallo, *Lateral façade on one of the transepts of the Church of Santa Maria delle Carceri*, begun in 1475. Prato, Italy.

Francesco Borromini, *Façade of the Oratorio dei Filippini*, 1640. Rome. To achieve symmetry, Borromini "slid" the façade over the body of the building, producing a striking scenographic effect. The main door leads to an entrance hall opening onto the central interior.

aspect. In medieval churches of the basilican plan, the entrance was located on the short side of the building, adorned with a façade; in the Latin cross and Greek cross layouts, the transepts ended in lateral façades. Some buildings had no façades at all, as the feature was "reabsorbed" by the overall structure.

It was in the Renaissance that the architectural value of the façade was fully understood, and its potential was exploited still further in the scenographic style of the Baroque.

Neoclassicism instead codified a static concept of the façade, which in its rhetorical, monumental aspect was to be distinctive of nineteenth-century eclecticism as well. This style was superseded by the modernist currents of the twentieth century, which established a dialogue between interior and exterior space. Fundamental to this trend were the experiments of Mies van der Rohe, the first to adopt the curtain wall, consisting of prefabricated glass panels used to face the structural skeleton of a building. In the postmodern movement, the façade's function as a boundary was to be both revived and refuted.

Ludwig Mies van der Rohe, *Seagram Building*, 1954–1958. New York.

Ferdinando Fuga, *Façade of Santa Maria Maggiore*, 1743–1750. Rome.

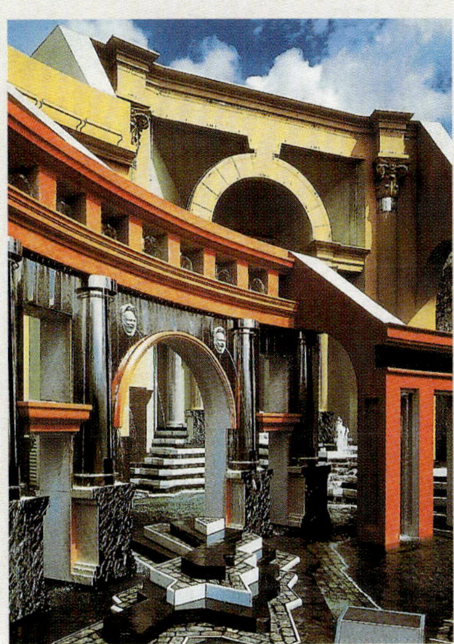

Right:
Charles Willard Moore, *Piazza d'Italia*, 1975–1978. New Orleans, Louisiana. Moore plays with architectural references in combining façades that are not really façades, since they have no buildings behind them and all open onto the same interior space.

Doors, Portals, and Porticoes

Crucially important in the architectural composition of a building is the location of its entrances, involving the arrangement of the main façade, the secondary façades, and any minor structures adjoining the main building. On the urban scale, the location of entrances may declare the outer boundaries of a city (gates) or the location of a public square within the urban fabric.

● DOORS

These are the openings in walls that allow access to, and egress from, the interior space. Since ancient times, the door, usually rectangular in shape, has borne decorative elements on the frame or on the hinged leaves. In the ancient world, fabric (in Latin *velaria*) was often used in place of leaves. City gates, typically monumental in size, sometimes arched at the top, served purposes of defense as well as access.

A distinctive example on the urban scale is that of the *propylaeum*, which in classical Greece and Rome led into the sacred enclosure of a temple. The most famous are those on the Acropolis in Athens, which served as models for neoclassical design in the nineteenth century.

● PORTALS

Portals are used to emphasize the dignity or sacred aspect of a passageway through the outer walls of a building. Early examples of the pseudo-portal have been found in Syria and in the Christian architecture of the fourth and fifth centuries. In these cases, however, the decoration is limited to the cornice and piers. The true portal, decorated with historical or legendary scenes, is distinctive of Romanesque and Gothic architecture. Its monumental size immediately defines it as the most important feature in the composition of the wall. In the sixth and seventh centuries, other elements of portal design began to appear: accentuated lateral embrasures (sometimes decorated with columnar statues); occasionally a lunette; and, above it, in French architecture, a *trumeau*, or central pillar dividing the entrance in half. The portal decorated with historical scenes, a creation

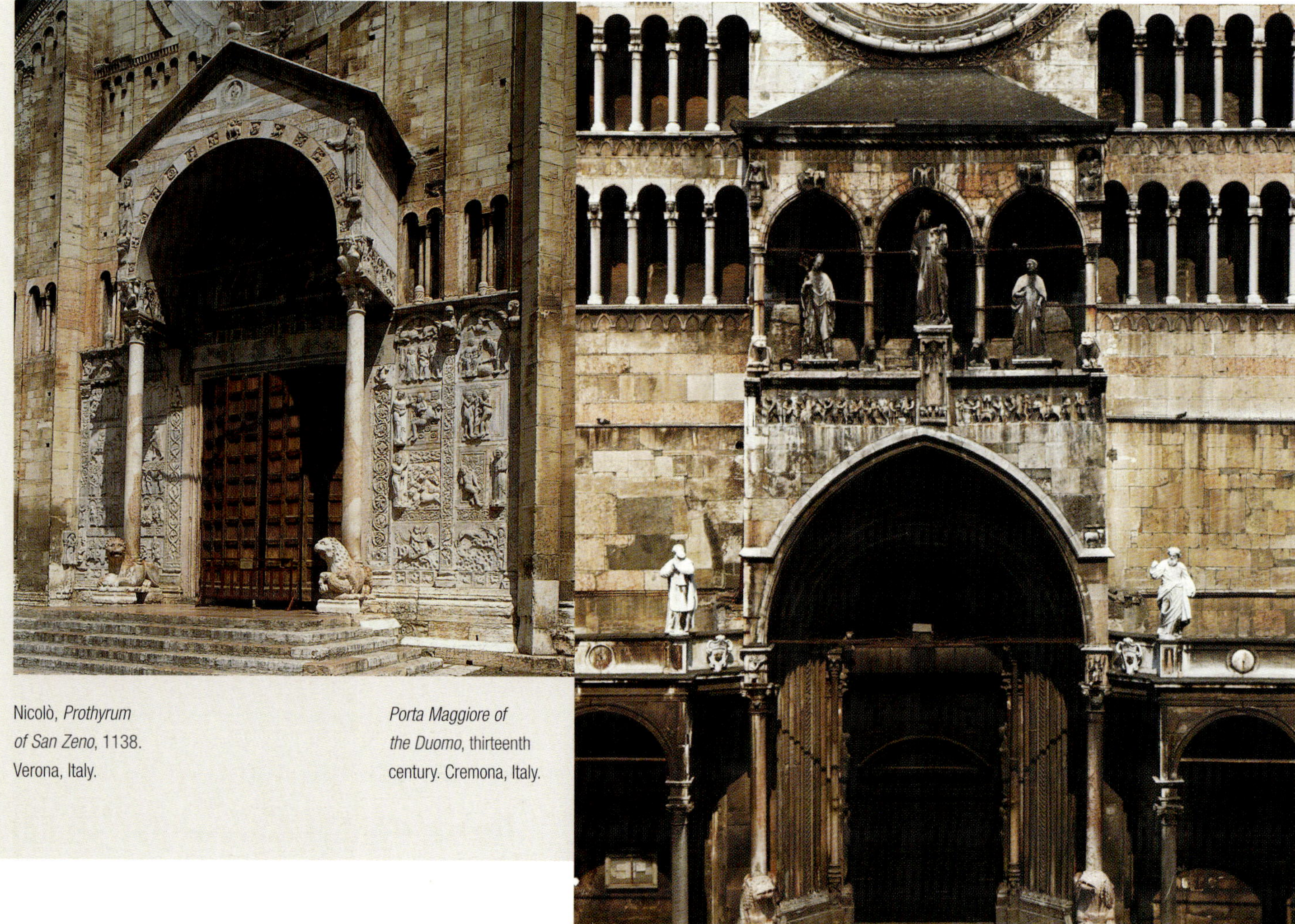

Nicolò, *Prothyrum of San Zeno*, 1138. Verona, Italy.

Porta Maggiore of the Duomo, thirteenth century. Cremona, Italy.

of French and Spanish architecture, was used in complex iconographic programs. Although usually placed on the outside of a building, such a portal sometimes adorned the interior, as in the Romanesque Basilica of the Madeleine at Vézelay in Burgundy. This was unusual in Italy, where a more common type was the portal embellished by a prothyrum (entry porch) projecting from the façade, covered by a roof with two slopes, and occasionally surmounted by a small loggia.

● PORTICOES

An architectural element occupying a position midway between the exterior and interior of a building, the portico is open on at least one side, which is lined with columns or pillars. In monastic complexes and noble civic buildings, it runs around the edge of a cloister or courtyard. On the urban scale, it can also border a street or public square, in which case it is called a loggia.

Leo von Klenze, *Propylaea*, 1846. Munich.

View of Palazzo Vecchio and the Loggia dei Signori in Florence, detail of ancient map, the *Pianta della Catena*, 1472. Florence, Museo di Firenze Com'era.

Portal of the Madeleine, twelfth century. Vézelay, Burgundy, France.

Windows and Stained Glass

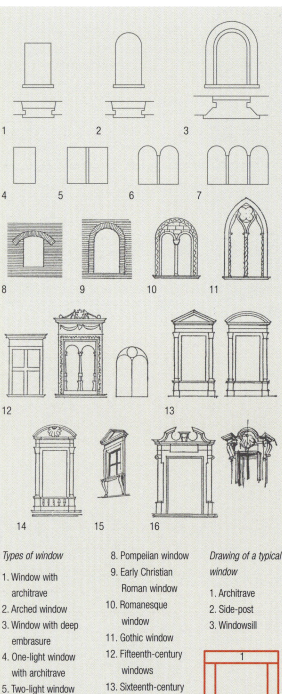

Windows originated in response to the need for light in the interior of buildings and to ventilate them. In the distant past, these openings were shielded by translucent materials such as parchment or alabaster. Glass, the most transparent material, has been used since Roman times. In the Christian world, the large openings in the walls of religious buildings encouraged the development of stained-glass windows, with panes of leaded glass. In Islamic architecture, by contrast, windows are characteristically pierced, lace-like structures made of iron, wood, marble, or other material.

● WINDOWS

A window usually consists of two upright side-posts, a horizontal top element (lintel, flat arch, or platband), and a horizontal bottom element (windowsill). The enormous variety of window styles may vary according to exterior or interior use. Among the rare windows surviving from antiquity, given that so many buildings have fallen into ruin, are those of Trajan's Market in Rome (p. 72) and the Temple of Vesta at Tivoli, an early example of windows used in a temple. In late antiquity and the Middle Ages, a succession of high, narrow windows with a single opening topped by an arch (later pointed) developed into mullioned windows with two lights (openings), then three, and finally several. In early Renaissance architecture, two-light windows, by now more regular and harmonious in form, once again became prominent. Cruciform windows and those topped by a tympanum were also used extensively. Other noteworthy design innovations include the Serlian window, of Roman derivation; the so-called *fenêtre condée,* with outward-curving bars, and the "mascaron" window, tending toward the Baroque. In the seventeenth century, coping (the sloping top course of a wall) over a window became steadily more elaborate, finally developing into a second opening, surrounded by frames of varied shape. Typical of Northern Europe was the bay window, a sort of enclosed balcony, which became widely used in the United States. No substantial changes were made in the various window types until the end of the nineteenth century, when the decorative

Types of window

1. Window with architrave
2. Arched window
3. Window with deep embrasure
4. One-light window with architrave
5. Two-light window with architrave
6. Arched window with two lights
7. Arched window with three lights
8. Pompeiian window
9. Early Christian Roman window
10. Romanesque window
11. Gothic window
12. Fifteenth-century windows
13. Sixteenth-century windows
14. Late-sixteenth-century window
15. *Fenêtre condée*
16. Baroque windows

Drawing of a typical window

1. Architrave
2. Side-post
3. Windowsill

spirit of Art Nouveau introduced an array of imaginative solutions. With the twentieth century, profound innovations in all fields of architecture led to changes in the concept and shape of the window. In the 1920s, Le Corbusier experimented not only with the curtain wall but also with the strip window, an opening that stretched along the entire wall of a building, brightly lighting the interior. Among the types widely used in public and private buildings today are the sash wjndow and windows that open vertically or horizontally.

● STAINED-GLASS WINDOWS

Stained-glass holds a special place in the history of the decorative arts and coincides with major developments in architectural design. Found mainly in Romanesque and Gothic churches, stained-glass windows were used extensively in Western Europe until the sixteenth century and subsequently in Northern Europe. In the nineteenth century, with renewed interest in antique craftsmanship, the technique was revived. Since that time, a number of artists and designers—William Morris, John La Farge, Louis Comfort Tiffany, Henri Matisse, Marc Chagall, and others—have employed stained glass as a vital decorative medium in religious and secular buildings.

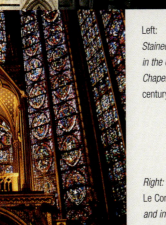

Above:
Bell tower and dome of the Siena Cathedral, thirteenth–fifteenth centuries. Siena, Italy. On the bell-tower, starting from the bottom, are mullioned windows with one light, two lights, three lights, and several lights.

Left:
Donato Bramante, *Palazzo Caprini (then Palace of Raphael),* c. 1510, from an engraving by Antonio Lafréry dated 1549.

Left:
Stained-glass windows in the choir of Sainte-Chapelle, mid-thirteenth century. Paris.

Right:
Le Corbusier, *Exterior and interior of Villa Savoye,* 1928–1931. Poissy, France. A typical example of a building with long horizontal (or strip) windows.

Plans and Planimetry

A building plan is a horizontal section of the structure showing the system by which spaces are organized and the relationship between the exterior and interior. A plan may be "cut" at different levels or floors, with each drawing indicating the thickness of the walls, the dimension of the rooms, and the location and size of doors, windows, courtyards, towers, loggias, and so on. On the basis of the plan, it is possible to identify the architectural style, forms, and elements of a historical building and to determine the era in which it was erected. A plan may therefore be considered a kind of "genetic code" of the building. In a similar manner, the planimetry—a topographical representation of the urban grid—can reveal the history of a city: its origins, phases of expansion, and major additions through a succession of civilizations, cultures, and governing authorities.

Round temple of Baalbek, second–third centuries C.E. Lebanon.

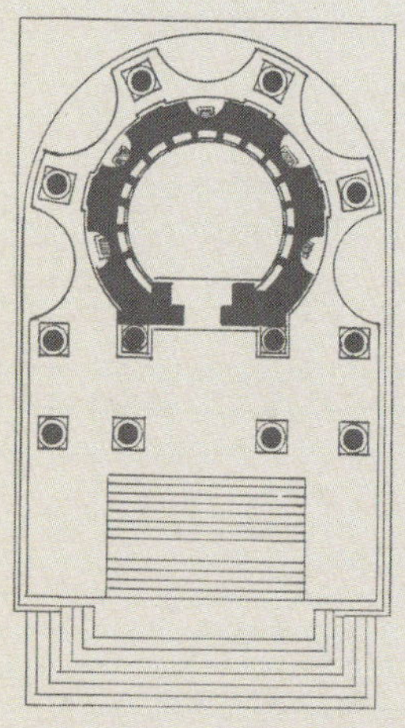

Palace of Diocletian, early fourth century C.E. Split, Croatia.

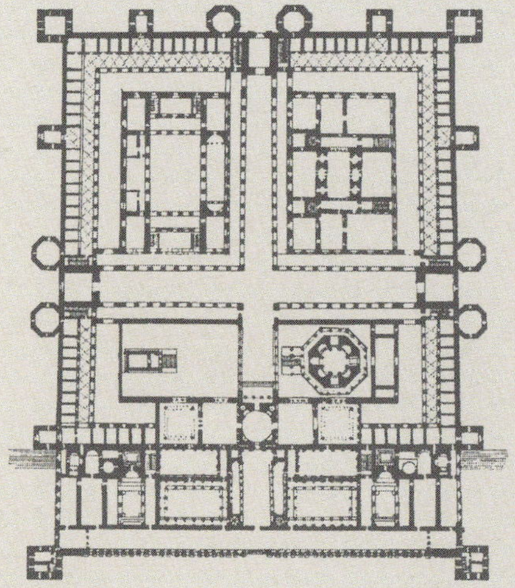

Santa Maria delle Grazie, thirteenth–fifteenth centuries. Milan.

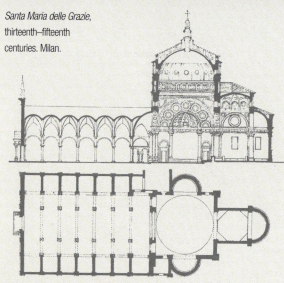

Baptistery, 1153–1356. Pisa.

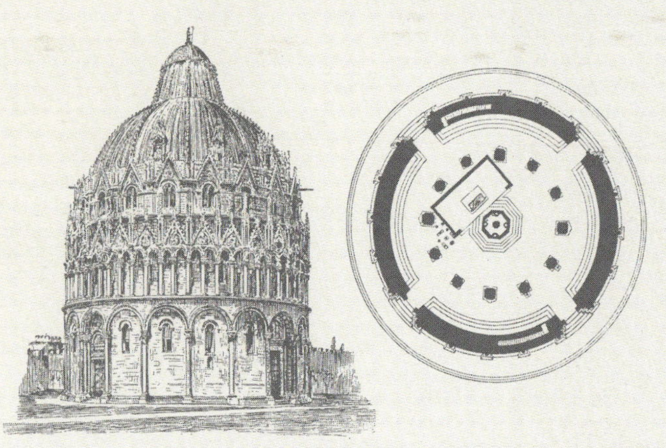

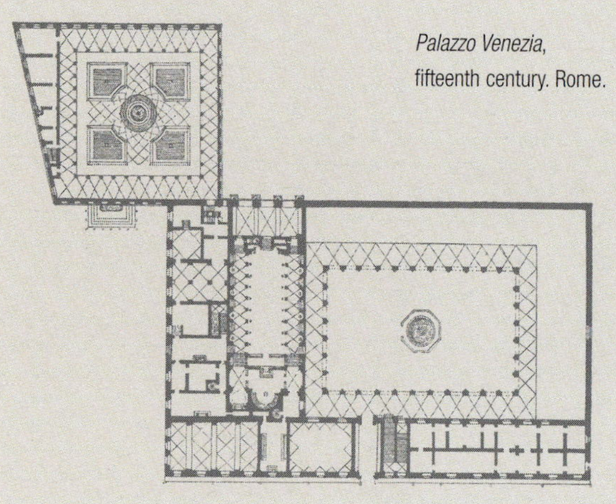

Palazzo Venezia, fifteenth century. Rome.

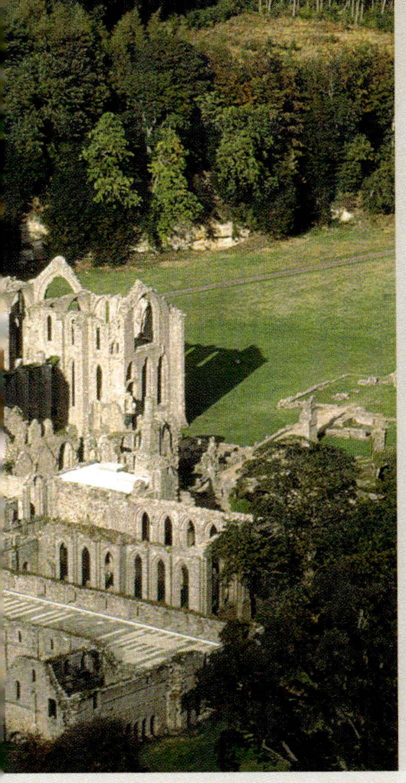

The ruins of Fountains Abbey, twelfth century. Studley, Royal Park, Yorkshire, England. Bernard of Clairvaux, founder of the Cistercian order, sent the architect Geoffroy d'Ainai to England to design the great abbey in accordance with the French model.

● THE BUILDING PLAN

All elements in a building plan are drawn to scale, making it possible to place the structure in a particular cultural context.

For example, the construction system used by Cistercian monks in the Middle Ages was based on a modular repetition of the square, used to configure the entire building.

The rigorous application of this method made it possible to construct very similar buildings even at distances of many miles. As evidence of the relationship between buildings, a plan may therefore reveal changes made in compliance with local tradition or regulation, or may show that the building in question has been inspired by more ancient models. It may, moreover, suggest a derivation from the prototype of a great architect or famous monument.

● URBAN PLANIMETRY

At a broader level, a planimetry (or urban plan) defines the extent and contours of a city at a particular moment in time, a certain point in its history.

By comparing planimetries from different epochs, it is possible to trace the evolution of a particular city or of urban design itself—from the square grid of Greco-Roman culture, to the walled cities of medieval Europe, to the urban sprawl of modern metropolises.

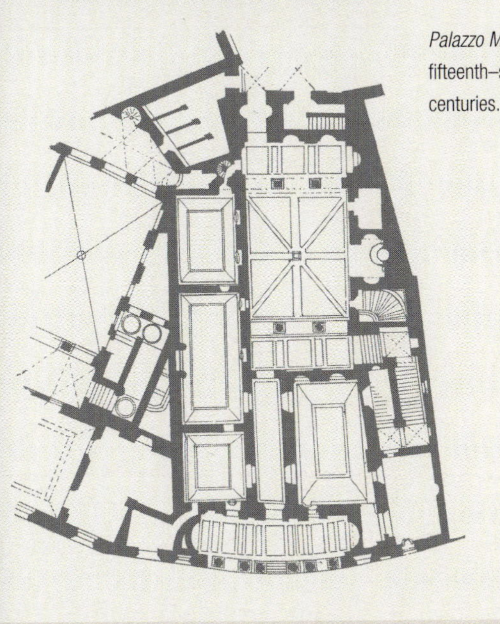

Palazzo Massimo, fifteenth–sixteenth centuries. Rome.

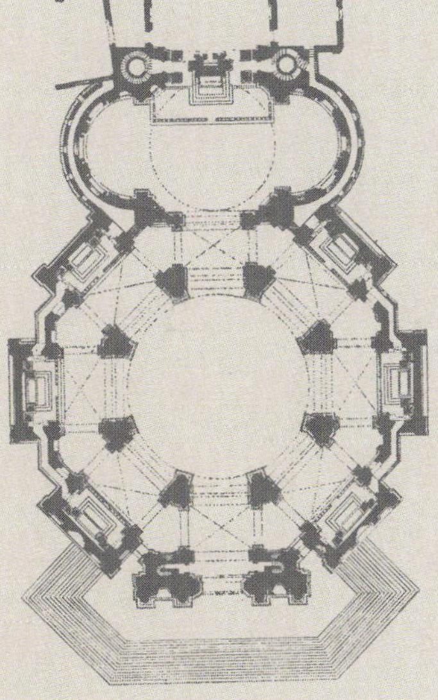

Santa Maria della Salute, sixteenth century. Venice.

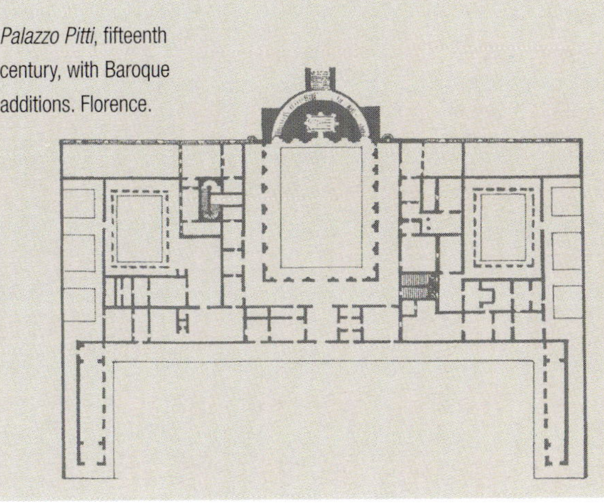

Palazzo Pitti, fifteenth century, with Baroque additions. Florence.

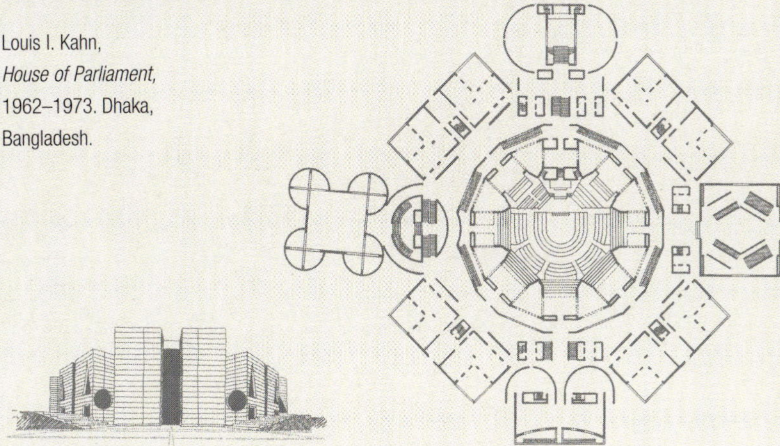

Louis I. Kahn, *House of Parliament*, 1962–1973. Dhaka, Bangladesh.

Styles

Architecture can be interpreted through a kind of linguistic code, based on grammatical and syntactical rules all its own, that is called style. From this point of view, it might be said that Ancient Greece "spoke" Ionic, Doric, and Corinthian, and that the spirit of the Middle Ages was expressed in the Romanesque and Gothic styles—terms, it should be noted, that were coined at a later time. In the Renaissance, architects drew inspiration from the classical world, while in the course of the sixteenth century the style that spread throughout Europe was Mannerism, a prelude to the artifice of the Baroque period, whose influence reached as far as the colonies of the New World. The eighteenth century, especially in France, spoke Rococo, at least until the architectural vocabulary began to express a sense of beauty, harmony, and balance in the language of what is now called Neoclassicism. In the nineteenth century, torn between historicism and modernism, a new concept emerged on both sides of the Atlantic: style as *convention.* Thus was born eclecticism, in which various architectural languages were revived and mingled. It was just this "nonstyle," which, by nullifying the historic dignity of architecture's linguistic code, prepared the way for rationalism and for experiments in the avant-garde. During the twentieth century and in the first years of the new millennium, in fact, the panorama of world architecture has been enriched by a variety of trends and tendencies, most of which defy precise stylistic definition.

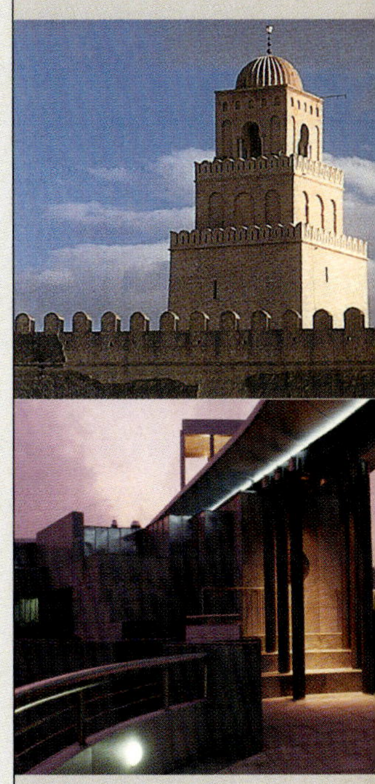

Top:
Minaret of the Great Mosque of Sidi Uqba, ninth century. Kairouan, Tunisia. With its square minaret on tiered levels, this is the most important mosque designed under the Aghlabids, who reigned at Kairouan from 800 to 909.

Above:
Hans Hollein, *Haas House*, 1989. Vienna. The Austrian Hans Hollein, one of the most imaginative post-modern architects, designed a circular patio for the roof of a Viennese shopping center; the patio overlooks the Stephansplatz.

Left:
Lateral nave of a Cistercian abbey, late thirteenth century. Fossanova, Italy.

Antiquity

The term "antiquity," as it is used here, refers to the period extending from the time of the first written records in the Mediterranean basin to the dissolution of the Roman state. If one excludes the hegemony of Greco-Roman architecture, antiquity is distinguished by a number of different systems, which, in the vast area stretching from the Nile Delta to the Persian Gulf, assumed a wide range of expressive forms, as well as contaminations among the various architectural styles. The common denominators in this complex equation were the possibility of rationalizing space, and thus the world, through architecture, and the evolution of human creativity.

● EGYPT

"Precise calculation: the gateway to a knowledge of all things." Thus begins a precious Egyptian document called the "Rhind Papyrus," perhaps the first hymn to numbers and the human capacity for rational thought, the key to understanding universal harmony.

In architecture as well, the stylistic inclinations of Ancient Egypt were not determined by purely aesthetic concerns but by the desire to express certain theological beliefs in concrete images. Accordingly, a certain geometric and spatial organization could serve as inspiration for a working-class village inhabited by artisans, as well as for the layout of a great temple or funerary complex. The Egyptians used the same term to refer to an architectural plan, the foundation of a temple, and a liturgical canon, clearly indicating that the sacred function of a temple was identified with its form.

The Ramesseum (funerary temple) of Ramses II at Luxor (c. 1290–1223 B.C.E., XIX dynasty), for example, was designed to take into account the orientation of the sun's rays, ensuring that they would strike the cult statue at dawn. At Karnak, an ingenious lighting system was devised to illuminate the hypostyle halls, a sort of microcosm with papyrus columns supporting a "sky-ceiling."

The allusion to and emulation of the great edifice of the universe is even more explicit in ceilings decorated like starry skies, as in the pseudo-vault of the Chapel of Hatshepsut (c. 1480 B.C.E.) at Deir el-Bahari, in the vicinity of Thebes.

Courtyard of the temple of Ramses II, c. 1260 B.C.E. Luxor.

DECORATION

An important element in Egyptian architecture is the column, which appears in various types: palmiform (leaves opening upward at the capital), lotus (calyx-shaped leaves closing on themselves), and papyrus (closed capital). In hypostyle halls (whose roofs rested on columns), allusions to the papyrus plant, which grew abundantly along the banks of the Nile, conferred a strong water symbology on the interior, as if it had been inundated by the primordial ocean. Accompanying this quasi-sculptural central element was a whole system of wall decorations inspired by nature, reiterating and interpreting the motif of the papyrus and that of the *uraeus*, or sacred serpent. Not uncommon were carved reliefs and wall paintings depicting scenes of everyday life or episodes from myth and religion.

The image of the lotus flower also appears in heraldic friezes on the piers.

Left and above: *Hypostyle hall in the temple of Amon-Ra*, 1290–1260 B.C.E. Karnak. In the interior of this great temple, featuring 134 columns, light filters from above through typical windows made of perforated stone.

At right, from above: *Funerary complex of Djoser*, detail of decoration in azure ceramics, interior of southern tomb, c. 2680 B.C.E. Saqqara.

Nineteenth-century reconstruction of a hypostyle hall in a temple of the Ptolemaic Age, 150 B.C.E. (from Lepère, "Description de l'Egypte," 1809, I, plate 18). This watercolor shows the splendid, highly varied decoration of Egyptian temples, abounding in symbolic allusions.

MESOPOTAMIA

Mesopotamian civilization influenced the other populations of the Middle East not only through its knowledge of astrology and astronomy, often applied to architecture (the Ancient Egyptians learned how to orient their buildings from them), but also in the development of a decorative style that was later to be reiterated in full by the Persian Achaemenids.

Mesopotamian architecture developed over the course of almost four thousand years, from the Sumerian and Akkadian civilizations (beginning in the fourth millennium B.C.E.) to the Assyrian-Babylonian revival (from the twelfth to the sixth centuries B.C.E.), at the end of which the Macedonian conquest led by Alexander the Great brought an end to the ancient empire. The scarcity of building remains (often no more than foundations, especially from the earliest period) severely limits our knowledge of Sumerian and Akkadian architecure. Our knowledge of the second stage of the region's history, however, is more complete and reliable. Archaeological investigations have unearthed such sites as Khorsabad, a city whose northeastern district was dominated by the imposing mass of the palace of Sargon II (721–705 B.C.E.). Characteristic of Assyrian architecture are the monumental figures of the

Pair of facing human-headed winged lions under the symbol of Ahura Mazda, the supreme divinity, enameled ceramics, from the Palace of Darius I (521–485 B.C.E.) at Susa. Paris, Louvre.

Above:
James Fergusson, *Reconstruction of the Palace of Sennacherib at Kuyunjik,* 1872.

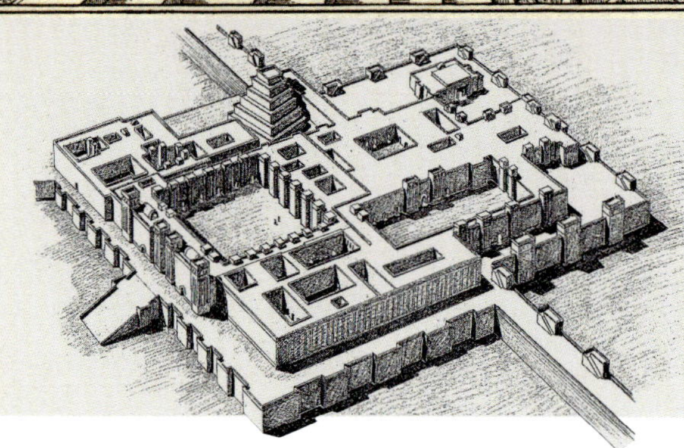

Drawing of reconstruction of Palace of Sargon II at Khorsabad.

lamassu—benevolent spirits with the body of a bull, the head of a human, and the wings of an eagle—which stood guard over the city gates and the entrance to the throne room in an architectural scheme common to other cities as well. The excavations at Khorsabad have yielded column bases assumed to have adorned the front of a portico.

DECORATION

Only a few fragments of the pictorial decoration from the Babylonian palace of Mari (second millennium B.C.E.) still survive. The typical decoration of the later cultures consists of enameled bricks bearing relief figures, such as those from the Ishtar Gate at Babel. The halls of the royal palaces at Nimrod, Nineveh, and Khorsabad were decorated with stone reliefs narrating the feats of the sovereign or depicting religious rites. Commonly used decorative motifs included lotus flowers and rosettes.

THE ACHAEMENIDS

The structural and decorative typologies developed in the Persian Empire under the Achaemenid Dynasty (550–331 B.C.E.) derive mainly from Mesopotamian culture. Yet, while Achaemenid rooms are regular in shape (almost always square, like those of Assyrian-Babylonian architecture), they are not organized around an inner courtyard, but consist instead of immense hypostyle halls. These interiors (*apadana*) take the place of inner courtyards as the vital center of the entire layout. Achaemenid decoration, however, is more similar to that of Ancient Mesopotamia, starting from the use of enameled and relief bricks bearing the same motifs of lions, cattle, and *lamassu*. A splendid example of Achaemenid decoration comes from Persepolis, where the motifs of rosettes and triangular, scaled merlons (crenellations) were used. The basic difference lies in the dual typology of the columns: either with capitals formed of sculpted back-to-back lions, bulls, or griffons, or with a series of scrolls.

View of stairway leading to the apadana, fifth century B.C.E. Persepolis, Takht-i Jamshid, Iran.

● CRETE AND MYCENAE

The Cretan (or Minoan) civilization and the Mycenaean civilization are commonly associated, inasmuch as they were forerunners of what historians have called "the Greek miracle." From the architectural viewpoint, however, it would be hard to find two more different worlds. The fact that Cretan civilization developed in an insular context and Mycenaean culture in a continental

Northern entrance to the Palace of Knossos, seventeenth century B.C.E. Island of Crete.

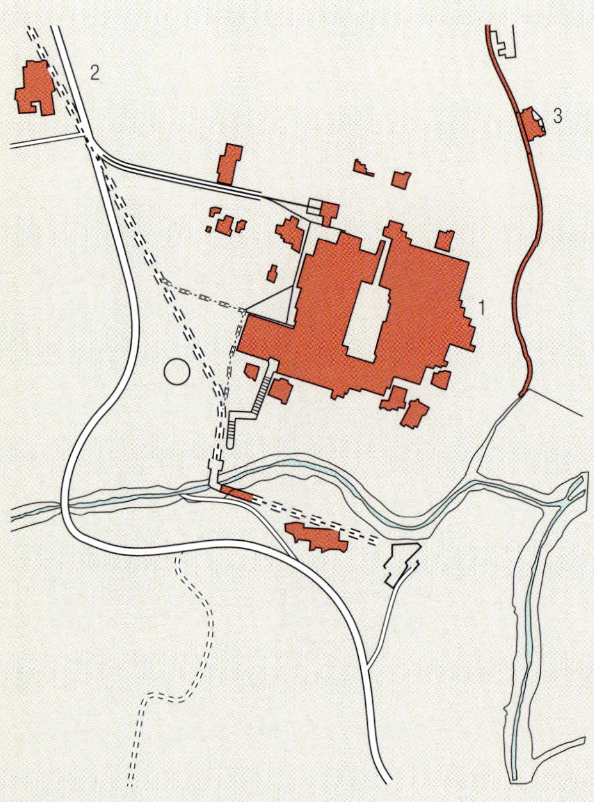

Layout of Palace of Knossos and its surroundings

1. Palace, developed around a central courtyard and surrounded by other less important buildings
2. Small Palace
3. Royal Villa
(from J.D.S. Pendlebury, 1933–1954)

Interior of the Palace of Knossos, seventeenth century B.C.E. Island of Crete.

one (the Greek mainland) determined different approaches to spatial relationships. The Bronze Age citadels of Mycenae and Tiryns were not only encircled by defensive walls but also followed the mountain contours of the terrain, their political center being situated at the highest, most well-protected point. The Cretan palace civilization, by contrast, developed without a sharp division between interior and exterior space. The most recent archaeological campaigns have shown that Minoan palaces were built gradually over an existing urban grid whose road system was organized around a public square, which then became the great inner courtyard of the palace. The first case is an example of a closed system, the second of an open one: Mycenaen urban space was apportioned, with forms and functions that varied according to the location and circumstances; the Minoan palace represented the unitary reduction of a general plan, following the Mesopotamian model. The decorative motifs of Minoan and Mycenaean art show no substantial differences, both being based on natural elements stylized to a greater or lesser degree in geometric forms. The similarities are due to contacts between the two cultures, use of the same architectural types (such as a column whose shaft is tapered at the bottom), and the typical Mediterranean preference for bright colors.

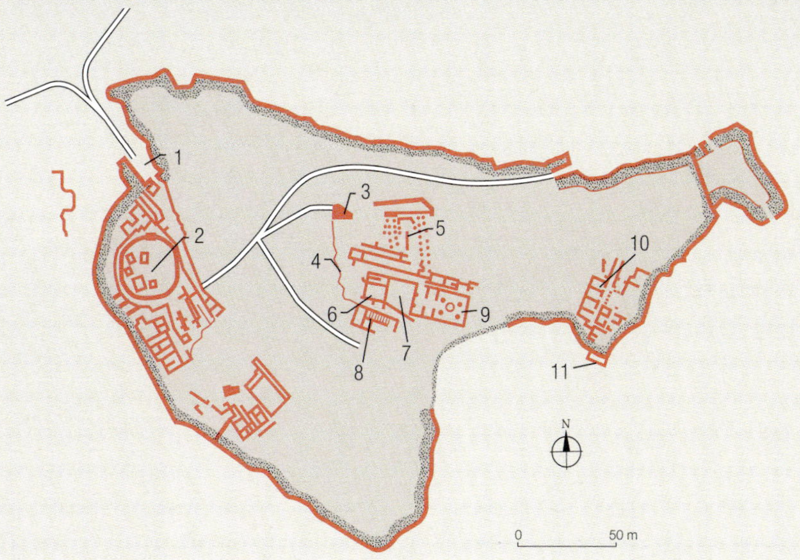

Above:
Ruins of Mycenae.
Peloponnesus, Greece.

Left:
Plan of the Mycenae citadel

1. The Lion Gate
2. Circle of tombs A
3. Palace entrance
4. Retaining wall
5. Temple
6. Throne room
7. Courtyard
8. Stairway
9. Megaron
10. House of columns
11. Tower

The Architectural Orders

In establishing and codifying the architectural orders, the contribution of classical Greece was fundamental. Disseminated throughout the ancient world with the spread of the Roman Empire, the architectural orders originating in Greece survived the collapse of Roman domination, remaining the basic code of architectural style in the West until the late nineteenth century. The main orders are the Doric, Ionic, and Corinthian; not to be overlooked are the Tuscan and the Composite.

● DORIC

Regarded by the Ancient Greeks as the finest, purest order, it was widely diffused by the Dorians, who invaded the Peloponnesus in the twelfth century B.C.E. The Doric order is distinguished by a column-drum (which, in its earliest version, rose directly from the stylobate) and a capital formed of abacus and echinus; it is topped by a trabeation (entablature) decorated with metopes and triglyphs. An acroter (sculpted plinth) is usually present at the eaves of the roof. The sharp-edged flutes on the columns range from sixteen to twenty in number. The top of the column is marked by a collar and rings or annulets. The proportional ratio between the height and diameter of the column is modified by slenderizing, and the height of the trabeation is about one-third that of the column.

● IONIC

This order was created by the Ionians (580–537 B.C.E.), who had settled on the west-central coast of Anatolia (now western Turkey) and on the Aegean

Left:
Diagram of the Doric order.

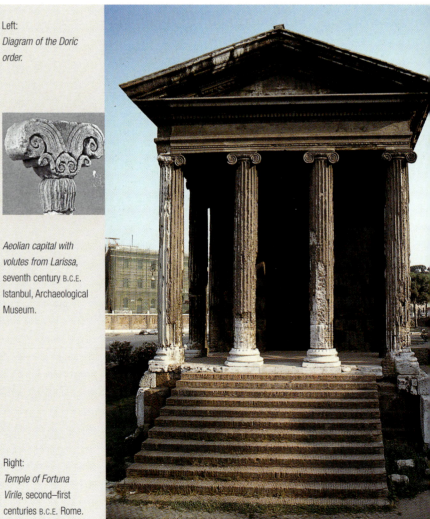

Aeolian capital with volutes from Larissa, seventh century B.C.E. Istanbul, Archaeological Museum.

Right:
Temple of Fortuna Virile, second–first centuries B.C.E. Rome.

islands after their homeland had been invaded by the Dorians. A precursor of the Ionic capital was the Aeolic, distinguished by two spiral scrolls at the sides, inspired by plant forms. The Ionic column is slenderer and less tapered than the Doric, but with more flutes (between twenty and twenty-four) separated by flat ridges. The column rises from an elaborate base resting on a plinth. Above the succession of torus (convex) and scotia (concave) moldings, it may finish in an astragal (beaded molding), either smooth or decorated with egg-and-dart motifs. An astragal can also serve as a collar near the top of the column.

The Ionic capital has a greatly reduced abacus and is distinguished by spiral scrolls united by a frieze bearing an egg-and-dart motif. On the trabeation is a frieze, either smooth or composed of bands surmounted by a cymatium (crown molding) decorated with egg-and-dart motifs on which rests a row of dintels. Above this are the *geison* and the cyma (a projecting double-curve molding). In the Roman version of the Ionic order, the connecting element between the volutes is straight and may be decorated with a plant motif. The fluting in the lower third is replaced by a small torus, and the frieze may be decorated.

● CORINTHIAN

The Corinthian column has a base and shaft similar to those of the Ionic, but its capital is distinctively bell-shaped, with staggered rows of acanthus leaves and small diagonal scrolls under the corners of the abacus. This column was often used in interior colonnades and was conceived as a solution to the "corner problem." The Corinthian order was widely used in Roman architecture, where it was later combined with the Ionic to form the Composite order, in which Ionic volutes are inserted at the top of a Corinthian capital, with an effect of ornamental redundancy.

● TUSCAN

The Tuscan order, so named because it was widely used by the Etruscans, is distinguished by its sobriety of ornamentation. It reiterates the basic features of the Doric order, but with further simplification of the column—now smooth and devoid of decoration on the trabeation.

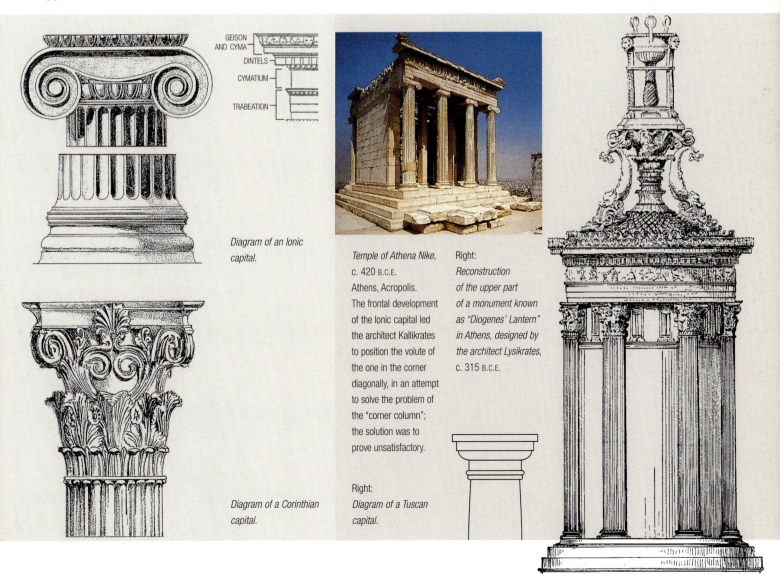

Diagram of an Ionic capital.

Diagram of a Corinthian capital.

Temple of Athena Nike, c. 420 B.C.E. Athens, Acropolis. The frontal development of the Ionic capital led the architect Kallikrates to position the volute of the one in the corner diagonally, in an attempt to solve the problem of the "corner column"; the solution was to prove unsatisfactory.

Right: *Reconstruction of the upper part of a monument known as "Diogenes' Lantern" in Athens, designed by the architect Lysikrates,* c. 315 B.C.E.

Right: *Diagram of a Tuscan capital.*

SYMBOLISM OF THE ORDERS

The symbolic meanings of the architectural orders were explained by the first-century Roman architect and engineer Vitruvius in his treatise *De Architectura.* In that seminal text, Vitruvius establishes relationships between the orders and the pantheon of Greco-Roman gods, implicitly attributing to the former a value that was to remain unchanged in the Renaissance and Baroque traditions.

Accordingly, the Doric order is linked to Minerva, Mars, and Hercules, since these gods—like the temples—arouse little feeling of tenderness or gentleness, but rather a sense of force and solidity. The Corinthian order is compared to Venus, Flora, Proserpine, and especially to water nymphs; its use of floral motifs conveys the corresponding ideas of sweetness, freshness, and pleasure. According to Vitruvius, the Corinthian capital was designed by Callimachus after observing a basket

Gian Lorenzo Bernini, *Colonnade of St. Peter's Basilica*, 1660–1667.

Panthéon (formerly Sainte-Geneviève), 1757–1792. Paris. Designed by Jacques-Germain Soufflot and originally named for the patron saint of Paris, the church was deconsecrated during the French Revolution and renamed the Panthéon in 1791.

"The supreme example of perfect architecture," according to the leading critic of Neoclassicism, Marc-Antoine Laugier, it has a pediment decorated with bas-relief sculptures and fluted Corinthian columns of clearly classical inspiration.

of acanthus leaves arranged with refined taste by a young virgin from Corinth, a fact that further enhanced the implication of delicacy and elegance. Finally, the Ionic order was understood as intermediate to the Doric and Ionic, and thus linked to divinities of a "mild" nature, such as Juno, Diana, and Bacchus.

In keeping with the premises established by Vitruvius, Renaissance theorists and architects such as Leon Battista Alberti, Bramante, Michelangelo, and Sebastiano Serlio, to name only the most famous, identified three basic characteristics of the architectural orders, determined by an obvious correspondence:

Doric order	masculine
Ionic order	feminine
Corinthian order	virginal

These symbolic meanings influenced the typology and structure of monuments, whose orders were selected according to the meaning intended. Since the masculine concept was linked to the heroic feats of martyrs, the Doric order was deemed appropriate to the colonnade of St. Peter's Basilica. The Doric order was also used in military constructions, such as defensive gates and arsenals.

Use of the Tuscan and the Rustic orders was based on the same principle, which was consistently followed until the eighteenth century. The Ionic order was considered well suited to less imposing architectural structures, such as private villas or any buildings of graceful design. The Corinthian order, while providing rich ornamentation in its own right, was frequently used in churches dedicated to the Virgin Mary.

Christian and Byzantine Architecture

Byzantine architecture may be said to have been born from a rib of Greco-Roman art. While starting with the same stylistic code, that of late antiquity, it developed along a path of its own that differed radically from that of its origins.

The rise, peak, and decline of the Byzantine Empire covered a span of more than a thousand years (330–1453 C.E.). Through these centuries and across a vast geographical-cultural area, stretching from Rome to Moscow, a stylistic evolution of enormous scope took place, producing highly original and diversified architectural styles.

The basis of the new stylistic trends was the epochal change wrought by the coming of Christianity and the consequent need to adapt the most ancient architectural typologies to the requisites of the new religion.

● CHRISTIAN ROME

The first city that had to confront this new reality was Rome. The adoption of the civic basilican hall as the new temple signified the transition from a religion delegated to a priestly class to one of communal participation. The structures remained those of Greco-Roman inspiration; the columns were often of the Corinthian order and made of Parian marble, but the decorative elements, such as the mosaics now found in the apse, were decidedly Christian. Circular buildings modeled on the pagan nymphaeum now began to be used for Christian churches. In this case, too, the forms were classical in inspiration, but the sense and meaning were altered by the adoption of

Baptistery of St. John's in the Lateran, first half of the fifth century. Rome. The church was erected by Constantine over a nymphaeum in the Lateran palaces.

Basilica of Santa Sabina, 417–432 C.E. Rome. The Corinthian columns are made of Parian marble, as in the Parthenon.

Christian decorative schemes. Mausoleums, martyries, and baptisteries were reconstructed in the same spirit.

● RAVENNA, ITALY

The chief difference, then, lay in the decoration more than in the architectural form. While such complex, refined works as the altar screens preserved in Ravenna are decorated with floral motifs that might even belong to late Roman culture, the presence of the cross and of peacocks, symbol of the soul, reflect a Christian inspiration. The new decorative schemes continued to rely on the now established Corinthian capital type, whose decoration had become flattened into a kind of lacework, along with the image of the cross. The only other element of significance in this architectural style was the innovative use of the dome or cupola, which usually rose above a circular interior. A fine example of this type is San Vitale in Ravenna, derived from the church of Saints Sergius and Bacchus in Constantinople, the model for all imperial architecture in the ninth and tenth centuries (p. 246).

● GREECE AND RUSSIA

The concept of the dome as the vault of heaven was colored by Christian values, well expressed by placement of the image of Christ Pantocrator ("lord of all things") at the center of the calotte. The presence of a dome not only changed the interior of the Christian church by filling it with light, imbued with spiritual significance, but also modified the appearance and meaning of the building's exterior. In Greece and Russia, domes of oriental shape, rising over buildings of cruciform plan, made each church a kind of miniature city, like a heavenly Jerusalem built of brick.

Interior of Constantinian Basilica, 305–312 C.E. Trier, Germany. Built during the reign of Constantine and consecrated later, it is the oldest example of a basilican hall used as a church.

Left: *Basilica of San Vitale*, 526–547. Ravenna.

View of the domes on the Church of Santa Sophia, 1045–1050. Novgorod, Russia.

Palace of Theodoric, seventh–eighth centuries. Ravenna, Italy.

Barbarian Architecture

Twentieth-century historiography has at last abandoned the negative concept of "barbarian." The term comes from the Greek historian Herodotus, who used the word *bárbaros* ("stuttering") to designate foreigners who spoke Greek badly, even including the Persian Achaemenids (pp. 111, 211). Over the course of time, the word took on a broader negative connotation, applied to any peoples thought to possess only a rudimentary form of civilization. In the nineteenth century, however, German historians began to adopt a different attitude. Germany, the "daughter" of Barbarian civilization, refused to accept the definition of "Barbarian invasions" applied to the moment in history when populations of different cultures first entered the sphere of Roman civilization. They preferred the term *Volkswanderung* ("migration of peoples"), reflecting an awareness of the role played by these cultures and their enormous contribution to the Western world.

● ARCHITECTURE AND CARVED DECORATION

The Barbarians, attracted by the empire's established cultures, soon became Romanized. At first employed as

Slab from balustrade in the Saint-Denis Basilica, Merovingian Age. Saint-Denis, Lapidarium. Judging from surviving fragments, the architecture of Barbarian times employed sculptural elements in which the naturalist forms typical of classicism were stylized.

Left:
Mausoleum of Galla Placidia, c. 425. Ravenna, Italy.

Baptistery of Saint-Jean, seventh century, view of the exterior. Poitiers, France. Compared to the Ravenna model of Galla Placidia's Mausoleum, the French monument is embellished on the exterior by diverse architectural and decorative elements.

unskilled workers in the army, they gradually entered the ranks of state administration and, after the fall of the empire, the so-called Roman-Barbarian reigns. The contribution of Barbarian cultures to medieval civilization is epitomized by their special approach to the question of decoration, which, through their influence, became highly geometric, almost heraldic, and no longer naturalistic. Even the typical elements of Greco-Roman and Late Roman architecture, such as column capitals, were interpreted according to this new sensitivity. Along with the typically Barbarian motif of *tenaille* braiding, other forms of decoration developed that were to be widely used throughout the Middle Ages; among these was the so-called *girale abitato*, a geometric interpretation of vine-tendrils filled with birds, already found in Roman mosaics at Antioch (first century C.E.). The process of Romanizing the Barbarian cultures at some point also began to include conversion to Christianity. Eminently Christian signs such as the cross now began to be interpreted in an entirely new style.

● ARCHITECTURAL TYPOLOGY

The few surviving works of Barbarian architecture are churches and baptisteries. The rare exception of a civic structure may be seen in Theodoric's Palace at Ravenna, Italy; although the origin and function of this building are still debated, it seems to be modeled on Constantinian and Byzantine culture.

Barbarian architects also frequently limited themselves to the reuse of existing buildings. Some basilicas from Merovingian times (fifth–sixth centuries) in France, such as Saint-Martin in Tours, are known to us only through literary descriptions, while the Baptistery of Poitiers is reminiscent of the Mausoleum of Galla Placidia in Ravenna. In Spain, the Palace of Naranco in Oviedo (ninth century) derives from lost seventh-century buildings whose styles were based on a simplification of classical dictates.

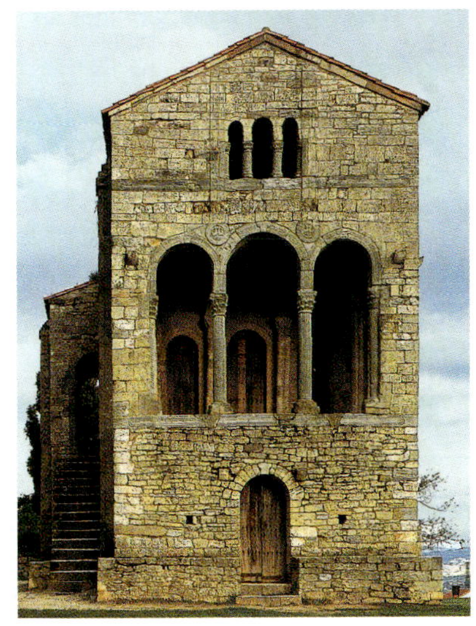

Palace of Santa María de Naranco, ninth century. Oviedo, Spain. The building, constructed for King Ramiro I (842–850), reiterates the style of seventh-century Spanish palaces, a Barbarian interpretation of Late Roman architecture.

Islamic Architecture

Drawings of imperial domes with decoration, from Emile Prisse d'Avennes, *L'Art Arabe d'après les Monuments du Kaire*, A. Morel & Cie., Paris 1877.

Like Byzantine architecture, that of Islam encompasses a domain that extends beyond national boundaries. Faith in Allah, to whose benevolence believers surrender themselves (*islam* means "submission to the will of God"), unites a vast range of different cultures. Slightly more than a century after the Hegira (622), when the Prophet Muhammad departed from Mecca for Medina, Islam had expanded without resistance over an immense territory stretching from the borders of India to southern Spain. (The Frankish ruler Charles Martel halted the Arab Muslim advance northward from Spain at the Battle of Poitiers in 732.)

● BASIC CHARACTERISTICS

The stylistic iterations of Islamic architecture all follow the principle of avoiding anthropomorphic representations. The reasons for this prohibition, which pertains to the figurative arts as well, are to be found in religious tradition.

Although the Koran itself prohibits only the representation of the divinity and any cult that might be associated with such an image (*Sura*, V, 92), traditional commentaries extended the prohibition to images of any living beings except plants. The latter, along with geometric motifs and inscriptions in Kufic (an early Arabic alphabet) thus comprise the most common decorative elements of Islamic architecture. Also characteristic of Islamic architecture are arches of several kinds: horseshoe (or Moorish), four-centered, multifoiled, and intertwined, as well as onion-shaped domes. Typical of ceiling and wall decoration is the *muqarnas* design (a series of honeycomb cells that imparts a sense of movement to the surface). At the same time, Islamic architecture, especially that

Above: *Mausoleum of Tamerlane*, c. 1404. Samarkand, Uzbekistan. Known as Gur-i Mir ("Tomb of the Emir"), this monumental complex includes not only the tomb of the sovereign, topped by a typical imperial dome, but also a mosque and a monastery. Tamerlane (1336–1405) conquered a vast territory: Persia, Iraq, Armenia, Georgia, Anatolia, and portions of Syria and India. At Samarkand, the capital of his empire, he built a number of sophisticated, refined monuments.

Below: *Dome of the Masjid-i Shah*, 1611–1629. Isfahan, Iran.

Below:
Minaret of the Great Mosque, 848–852. Samarra, Iraq. Called *al-Malwiya* ("the spiral"), this minaret of the Great Mosque served as a model for others built in Samarra, and perhaps also for the minaret at the Mosque of Ibn Tulun in Cairo.

Below:
Interior of the Mosque of Ibn Tulun in Cairo (ninth century), from Emile Prisse d'Avennes, *L'Art Arabe*, Paris 1877.

Below:
Drawing of a minaret in Cairo, from Emile Prisse d'Avennes, *L'Art Arabe*, Paris 1877.

of the Umayyad period (661–750), also drew inspiration from Greco-Roman and Byzantine models, as evidenced by the use in mosques of such elements as the column and capital.

● BUILDING TYPOLOGY

In addition to the mosque (p. 48), Islamic architecture has produced such unique building types as the minaret, a typically square or cylindrical tower with a platform serving as a balcony (perhaps derived from the ecclesiastical towers of Byzantine Syria). From the minaret, a *muezzin* (crier) summons the faithful to prayer. Especially striking is the spiral minaret at Samarra (eighth–ninth centuries), inspired by the model of the Mesopotamian *ziggurat*. Beginning in the eleventh century, *madrasas* (derived from an Arab word that means "to study"), institutions of Islamic studies, developed as a common architectural type. A *madrasa* has at least one *iwan* (large vaulted hall) from which the Koran is read, as well as cells for pupils, teachers, and officials around a small courtyard or under a dome.

Contact with other civilizations also led to the construction of buildings used as mausoleums, some of imposing size, such as the Taj Mahal (p. 310).

Arab-Norman, Moorish, and Mozarabic Architecture

The discussion of Islamic architecture (see preceding pages) would not be complete without consideration of the singular mingling of styles that resulted, between the ninth and the fifteenth centuries, from the collision and artistic reconciliation of Islamic and Western civilizations. The term "Arab-Norman" refers to the style of buildings in the southern part of the Italian peninsula during the rule of the Normans (literally, "men from the north"). "Moorish" refers to the style that emerged in Spain and North Africa when Islamic civilization came into contact with Berber culture and the still-thriving Greco-Roman, Visigoth, and Iberian artistic traditions. The term "Mozarabic" (or *mudéjar*, a derivation of the Arab *musta'rib*, or "Arabized") denotes a style that derived from the merger of Christian traditions in southern Spain with Islamic Moorish influences.

● ARAB-NORMAN ARCHITECTURE

In southern Italy, a crossroads of trade and cultural exchange, an enduring Byzantine influence (in Apulia, Lucania, and Calabria) and an Islamic one (in Sicily) had already taken root. The ascendency of the Normans began in 1047 with the conquest of the Campania region by Roberto il Guiscardo, who extended his power in Sicily beginning in 1061. Roberto, who was succeeded by Ruggero II, Guglielmo I, and Guglielmo II, suppressed earlier artistic traditions and encouraged a new, highly original style that interpreted Arab and Byzantine traditions in the context of Christian faith and tradition. In Palermo, Sicily, the Byzantine-style mosaics of the Cappella Palatina formed a harmonious ensemble with its Cosmatesque floors and a *muqarnas* ceiling that rivaled those of Baghdad and Isfahan in splendor. In perhaps the finest monument to this felicitous melding of styles, the Duomo of Monreale

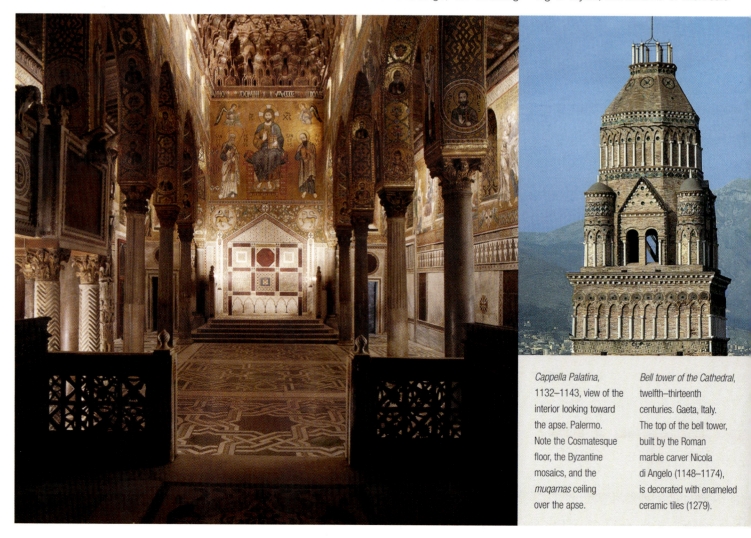

Cappella Palatina, 1132–1143, view of the interior looking toward the apse. Palermo. Note the Cosmatesque floor, the Byzantine mosaics, and the *muqarnas* ceiling over the apse.

Bell tower of the Cathedral, twelfth–thirteenth centuries. Gaeta, Italy. The top of the bell tower, built by the Roman marble carver Nicola di Angelo (1148–1174), is decorated with enameled ceramic tiles (1279).

(p. 263), the intersecting arches in the apse were embellished with enameled ceramics of clearly Islamic tradition. (The interior, similar to that of Cefalù, is Byzantine in style).

On the southern Italy mainland, the Islamic influence was to persist well beyond Norman rule, as exemplified by the Cloister of Paradise in the Amalfi Duomo and by the bell tower of St. Erasmus Cathederal in Gaeta, reminiscent of the minarets in Morocco. Other Italian regions and cities, especially the seafaring republic of Pisa (p. 259), were also to be influenced by Arab culture and style.

● MOORISH AND MOZARABIC ARCHITECTURE

In Spain, a first fusion of stylistic traditions took place under the rule of the Almoravid Dynasty (1056–1147) and another at the time of the Almohads (1130–1269), who controlled Spain and North Africa (Morocco, Tunisia, and Algeria). Dating from this period are, in addition to the world-famous Alhambra near Granada (pp. 282–283), the ribbed dome of the Tlemcen Mosque in Algeria, where elements of Andalusian origin harmonize with others of Persian provenance.

Having survived the Christian *reconquista* of Spain, *mudéjar* architecture was to boast other major achievements in the Cathedral of Toledo and in the Andalusian city of Cordoba, where the Great Mosque, regarded as one of the most imposing structures of any time and place, was transformed into a church, arousing the wrath of the Emperor Charles V, an ardent admirer of Arab art.

Villaviciosa Chapel in the Great Mosque, thirteenth century. Cordoba, Andalusia, Spain.

Left: *Cloister of Paradise,* detail, 1266–1268. Amalfi, Duomo. The play of intersecting pointed arches over slender paired columns recalls similar motifs decorating minarets in Morocco.

Below: *Cloister of San Giovanni degli Eremiti,* 1132. Palermo. Onion-shaped domes, of obvious Islamic derivation, are also distinctive of another Palermo church, San Cataldo.

Romanesque Architecture

The Arch of Constantine in Rome, completed around 315, in an old engraving.

Torhalle, or triumphal gate, after 774. Lorsch, Hesse, Germany. The three arches and composite capitals are reminiscent of the Arch of Constantine in Rome.

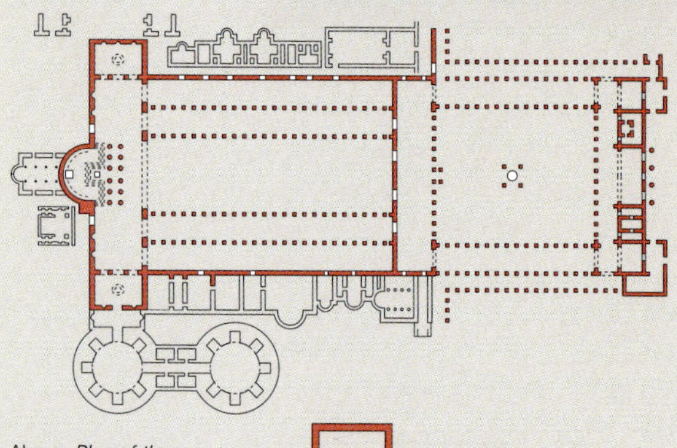

Above: *Plan of the Constantinian Basilica of St. Peter's,* c. 330. Rome.

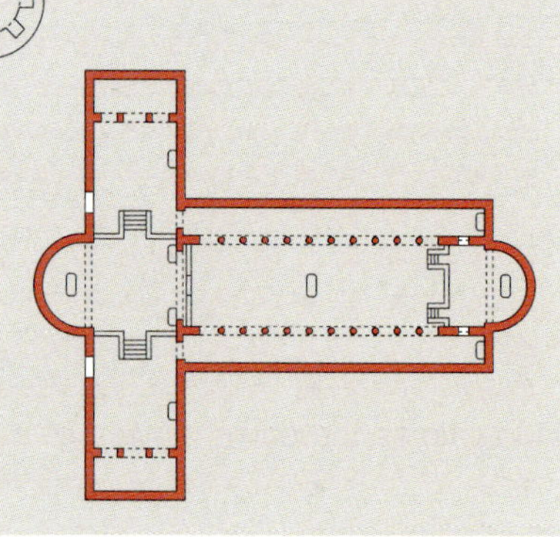

Right: *Plan of the abbey church,* 791–819. Fulda, Hesse, Germany.

The term still conventionally employed to indicate the first great artistic movement of European scope was coined in the nineteenth century to define the architectural style that flourished mainly in the eleventh and twelfth centuries, and to distinguish it from the subsequent Gothic style. The designation—Romanesque—implied an opposition between the presumed Germanic spirit of fourteenth-century architecture and the Roman character of that of the two previous centuries.

● CAROLINGIAN AND OTTONIAN PREMISES

Without oversimplifying, it can be stated with certainty that Romanesque architecture grew like a new shoot from the trunk of the classical tradition. That tradition, however, had been revised at the time of the Carolingian and Ottonian renaissance with the clear intention of symbolically evoking the Roman emperors, Constantine in particular, who had embraced the Christian faith. Not by coincidence, the Arch of Constantine in Rome was the prototype for the triumphal portal (*Torhalle*) of the Carolingian Abbey at Lorsch in Germany, while the Lateran Palace in Rome seems to have inspired that of Aix-la-Chapelle (Aachen). The old St. Peter's Basilica, built during Constantine's reign, with its T-shaped transept, large atrium, and crypt (p. 47) served as the model for many ecclesiastical buildings.

● BASIC CHARACTERISTICS

The essential principle inherited by Romanesque architecture from the Romans, filtered through Carolingian and Ottonian influences, is the organic quality of space, expressed in the clarity of building plans, usually basilican, and in clear-cut structural forms. A primary element of this style is the round arch, which distributes space according to proportional ratios, either double or triple. This system of relationships is part of an "obligatory system" whose starting point is the square module of the span, which is split in half in the lateral naves; this system also governs the proportions of the body of the church and of the transept, narthexes, and atrium. On the basis of the square module, round arches can be used to connect a complex system of alternating columns and piers.

Below:
1. Façade with saddle-roof
2. Façade with composite roof
3. Façade with two towers

Right: *Reconstruction of wall in the central nave of the Cathederal of Modena, Italy, twelfth century.*
1. Clerestory
2. Matroneum or triforium
3. Supporting arches

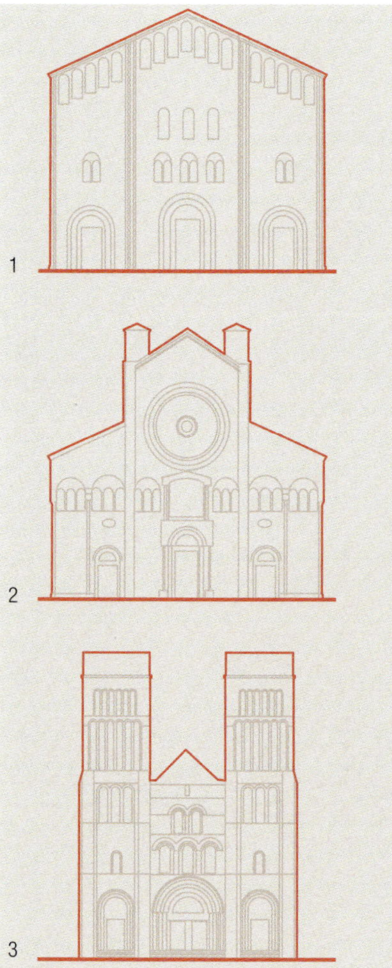

Right:
View of the apse of the cathedral, 1030–1082. Speyer, Rhine Palatinate, Germany.

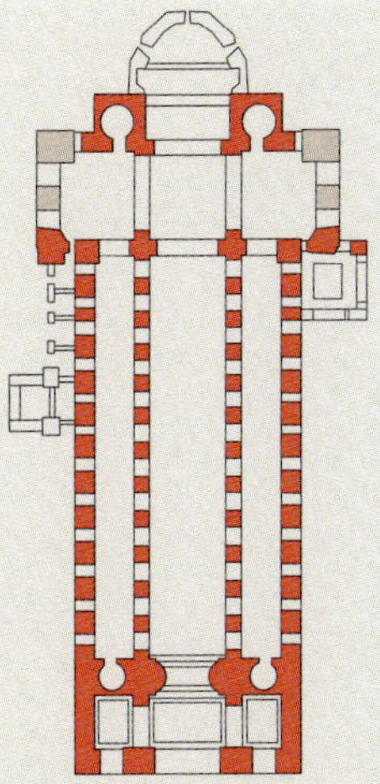

Plan of the Cathedral of Speyer, 1082. Symbol of the political prestige of the Salic dynasty, this church represented, in its complex, grandiose structure, a basic model for the German cathedrals of the twelfth century.

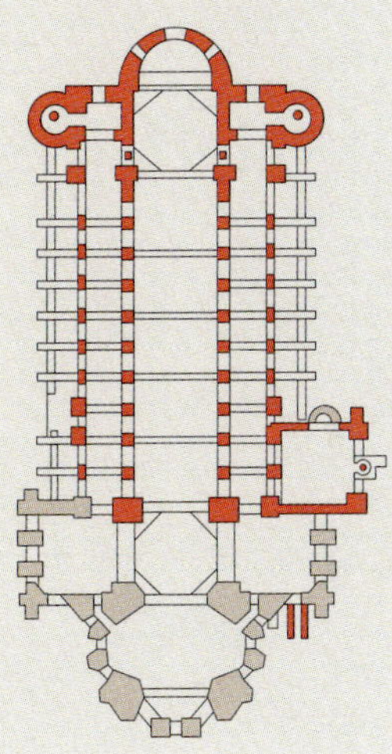

Plan of the Cathedral of Mainz, from 1081. Mainz, Rhine Palatinate, Germany. Each of the two choirs, on the eastern and western side of the building, has a transept and a crypt. The double choir not only enriches the structure but carries a symbolic meaning: the religious requirement of honoring two patron saints.

● CHURCHES

In the different geographical areas of Europe, the Romanesque façade evolved in various forms. In Italian churches and those of southern France, it could be either saddle-roofed (having only two slopes) or monocuspidate (composite roofed, in which the intermediate zone, above the central nave, is higher).

In Spain, Germany, and northern France, façades often had two towers. A rose window often embellished the façade. The apse area was substantially transformed by division into several smaller apses and by the addition of a choir. Ceilings were made of wood or masonry, with a preference for barrel vaults or cross-vaults. Exterior innovations included towers above the intersection between the nave and transept, and domed roofs.

An innovative interior element was the *matroneum*, first designed as a gallery for women along the side of the central nave, later reduced in many churches to an exclusively decorative structure (blind triforium); it was occasionally surmounted by a clerestory (derived from the Middle English *clear story*, or "illuminated level").

Another new solution was the double choir, which included the addition of a western choir opposite the usual one at the eastern side of the church.

Also typical of Romanesque style is a rhythmic series of small, blind arcades articulating the outer walls—on the façades, flanking walls, or apses.

Another fundamental element, which was to be extensively developed in Gothic architecture, is the magnificent sculptural decoration that embellishes portals, capitals, window embrasures, and at times the entire surface of a façade, in a striking variety of forms and motifs.

THE ROMANESQUE STYLE IN EUROPE

Romanesque architecture in Europe may be divided into four principal phases, the first of which, known as "proto-Romanesque" (955–1030), developed in Italy and Catalonia, Spain.

The period of basic stylistic transformation (1030–1080) took place mainly in the Loire, Saone, Normandy, regions of France, and Lombardy in Italy. In the crucial period, that of Romanesque proper (1080–1150), the style spread through Germany, England, and the Scandinavian countries. In the late stage (thirteenth century), the stylistic features were perpetuated, though sometimes contaminated with nascent Gothic style.

FRANCE AND ENGLAND

France, flourishing again after the Norman invasions, was quick to embrace the Romanesque. It was the Norman ruler William the Conqueror who erected the monks' Abbey of Saint-Etienne at Caen in Lower Normandy, while his wife, Matilda, built the nuns' convent of La Trinité there. From Burgundy spread a grand, complex style of architecture that emerged thanks to the Cluniac and Cistercian reform movements, along with dozens of country churches. The mature expression of French Romanesque style is exemplified by Saint-Denis (following pages), a prelude to Gothic architecture.

With the Norman Conquest, the Romanesque style was imported to England, where it found typical expression in churches distinguished by multiple apses or an ambulatory.

ITALY, SPAIN, AND GERMANY

In Italy, too, the style underwent significant evolution, with the development of regional "schools." In the cities rose monumental complexes, elaborated in autonomous styles often showing a

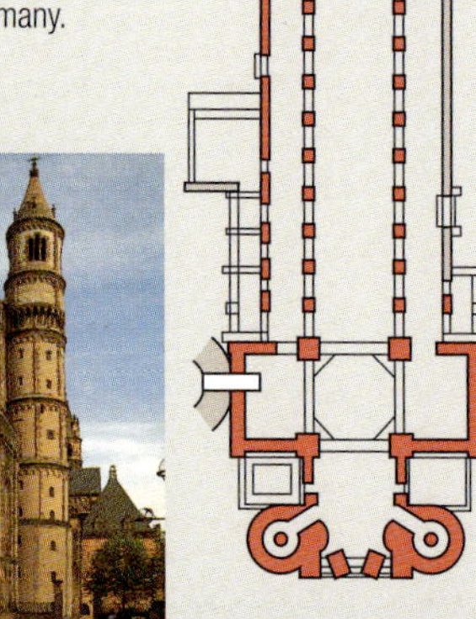

Westwerk *at St. Peter's Cathedral*, late twelfth century. Worms, Rhine Palatinate, Germany.

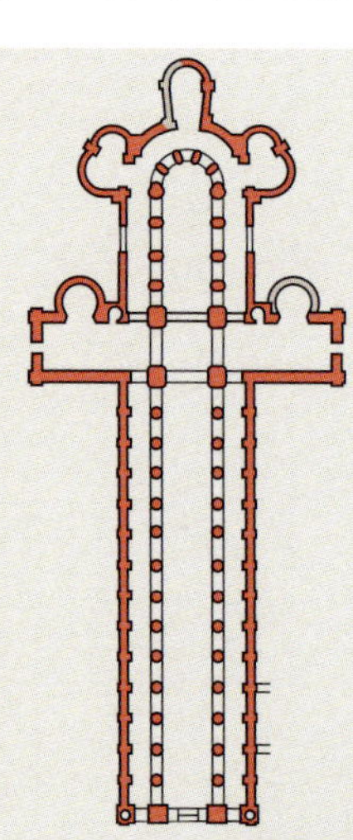

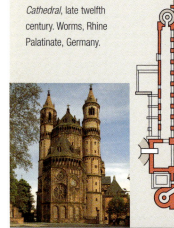

Plan of the Cathedral of the Holy Trinity, begun 1096. Norwich, England. The circular corridor connecting the three apses, of Norman derivation, forms an ambulatory.

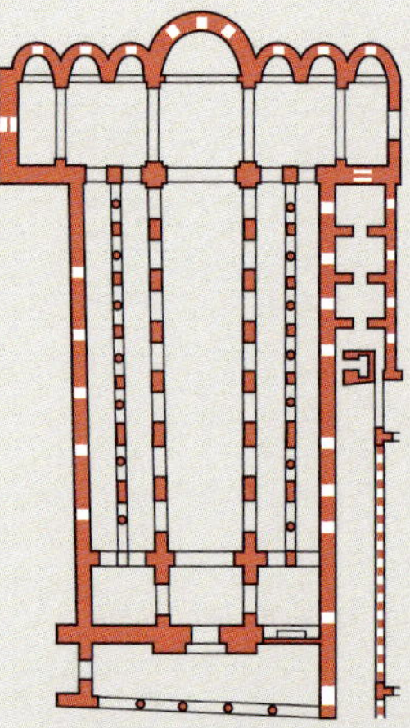

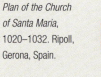

Plan of the Church of Santa Maria, 1020–1032. Ripoll, Gerona, Spain.

Near right: *Notre-Dame-la-Grande*, mid-thirteenth century. Poitiers, Vienne, France.

Far right: *St. John's Chapel*, c. 1078. London, White Tower. Built as both a palace and a defense structure, the White Tower is one of England's most important monuments from Norman times.

wide range of influences, classical and even oriental. Romanesque architecture in Spain is linked mainly to the pilgrimage roads, where Italian architectural modes were soon emulated. Among the most famous monuments are the cathedral of Santiago de Compostela (pp. 264–265) and the serenely balanced Church of Santa Maria at Ripoll.

Germany made an original contribution to Late Romanesque style with the *Westwerk,* a structure at the western end of the church featuring towers with loggias on the first floor and an atrium opening toward the nave, surmounted by a hall usually dedicated to the Archangel Michael.

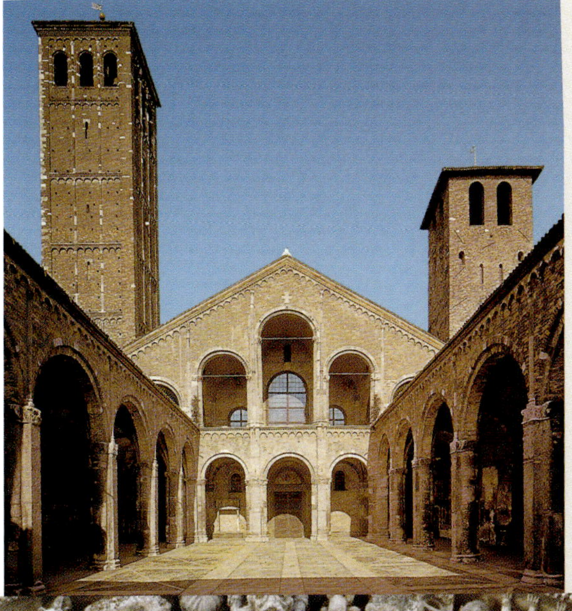

Sant'Ambrogio, ninth–twelfth centuries. Milan. Comacine masters, members of one of the first European guilds of builders and stonemasons, worked in this great complex, where the Constantinian model of the old St. Peter's can still be recognized.

Façade of the cathedral, begun 1093, detail of the rose window. Troia, Foggia, Apulia.

Gothic Architecture

As in the case of many other terms in the history of art, "Gothic" was originally used in a disparaging sense. It was introduced into French by the writer François Rabelais in 1533, and several decades later the Italian Giorgio Vasari referred to the "manner ... formulated by the Goths" as "monstrous and barbarian." On the other hand, the adjective *gothicus* had already been employed in medieval Latin to define codexes written in anything other than *scriptura Romana*. The expression "Gothic" (with the connotation of arbitrary, discordant, and rough) was originally used in reference to the Nordic world as opposed to Latin and Mediterranean culture, which considered itself the exclusive custodian of beauty and harmony. This concept was to persist until the middle of the eighteenth century, when British and French art historians finally began to reconsider the question. In 1797, James Hall proposed the so-called "forest theory," by which Gothic style was said to originate from the primitive wooden structures built in the forest as places of worship by ancient Germanic tribes. More recent studies have refuted all such disparaging hypotheses, and Gothic style has long been acknowledged to possess the same dignity as the Classical and its derivatives. In fact, the nineteenth century was to see a sweeping revival of the Gothic (pp. 160–161).

Interior of the abbey church, view of the windows and clerestory, c. 1140–1238. Saint-Denis, Paris. The Church of Saint-Denis represents the prototype par excellence of Gothic architecture, and not French alone. The first edifice was built at the order of Abbot Suger, an extraordinary figure whose writings have contributed greatly to our knowledge of medieval thought. According to Suger, the light flowing into a cathedral through its stained glass windows is a metaphor of the word of God filling the spirit.

● ORIGINS

Unlike the Romanesque, whose origins have been traced to a variety of locations in Western Europe, the cradle of Gothic architecture is generally acknowledged to be northern France. Only in the nineteenth century, however, was it widely recognized that the first building to "speak" Gothic was the abbey church of Saint-Denis near Paris, built at the initiative of Abbot Suger in 1140. With the luminous structure of the choir surrounded by an ambulatory, the building lent a new maturity to Romanesque features, opening the way for the spread of Gothic style throughout the Ile-de-France.

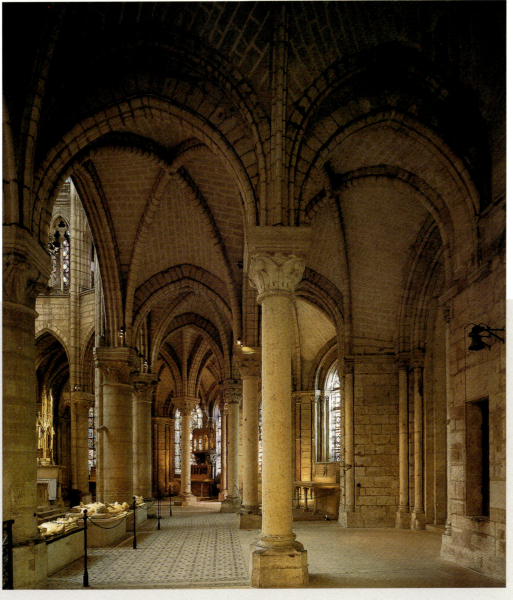

Interior of the abbey church, view of the ambulatory, 1140–1144. Saint-Denis, Paris.

By 1231, most of Abbot Suger's church had become dilapidated and was rebuilt. Only the western narthex, the south tower, and the luminous ambulatory around the choir survive to the present.

Below: *Plan of the abbey church*, c. 1140–1238. Saint-Denis, Paris.

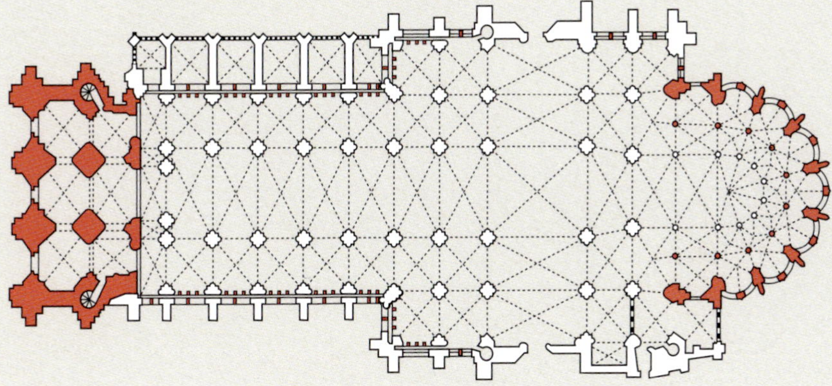

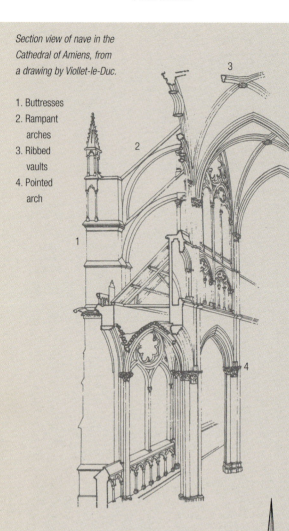

Section view of nave in the Cathedral of Amiens, from a drawing by Viollet-le-Duc.

1. Buttresses
2. Rampant arches
3. Ribbed vaults
4. Pointed arch

Diagram of a "hall church"

BASIC CHARACTERISTICS

Gothic architecture differs most dramatically from Romanesque architecture in the luminosity of its interiors. This derived mainly from the adoption of the pointed arch, which was able to bear heavier loads than the round arch and allowed for the innovative features of much larger windows and less massive piers. Already adopted in the ninth-century in the Islamic architecture of North Africa, the pointed arch was to play a major role in the design of European churches, providing a soaring upward thrust imbued with symbolic and religious import: a striving toward God. Moreover, the greater stability provided by the pointed arch and the ribbed vault made it possible to rely on piers alone for structural support, in place of alternating piers and columns.

While the distribution of elements along the wall of the central nave remained identical to that of Romanesque churches (clerestory, blind triforium or *matroneum*, and bearing arches), the voids were now expanded, and increasingly elaborate decoration was provided by windows and rose windows, often elegantly perforated like filigreed lace.

The presence of such large openings in the wall led to the adoption of new compensation and support systems, specifically flying buttresses and rampant arches, which served the function of dispersing weight (p. 93).

With improved technical methods, the general tendency to soar upward led to the erection of spires atop the towers on the façade and over the intersection of the transept. The manner of decorating also changed, with

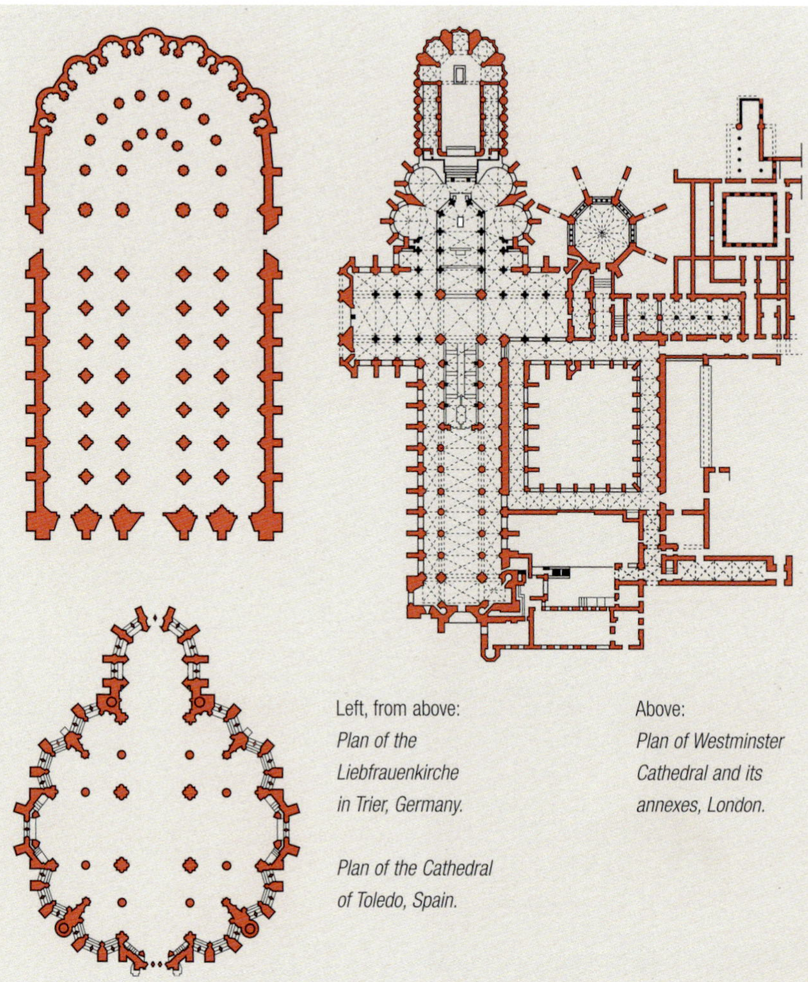

Left, from above:
Plan of the Liebfrauenkirche in Trier, Germany.

Plan of the Cathedral of Toledo, Spain.

Above:
Plan of Westminster Cathedral and its annexes, London.

figured and narrative elements appearing not only on portals and capitals but also on ribbed vaults, bundled piers, and pinnacles. In ornamental friezes, the geometrical patterns typical of the Romanesque tended to disappear in favor of a lively naturalism, expressed in leaves of acanthus, fig, ivy, and thistle. The ornamental element could also consist of stylized foliage motifs (in French, *rinceau*), often adapted to the specific architectural structure.

The layouts, too, became more complex, as the circular plan and the "hall church" (*Hallenkirche*) replaced the Latin cross common in Romanesque architecture. The plan of the hall church—with three or five naves, called "stepped" when the central nave is elevated—conveys the sense of a single great space lit directly by light falling from the windows in the lateral naves.

● CHRONOLOGY AND STYLISTIC DEFINITIONS

The Gothic style continued to evolve, in a variety of forms, over a long period of time, from the fourth decade of the twelfth century to the first decades of the sixteenth, in various regional schools. Its mature stage (lasting roughly from the last decades of the fourteenth to the first four decades of the fifteenth century) is designated by various adjectives describing its manifold aspects.

The term "International Gothic" emphasizes the plurality of stylistic diffusion, while "courtly Gothic" (*Hofkunst* in German) underscores its ties to the courts. "Flamboyant Gothic" (in French *flamboyant* and in German *Weicher Stil*, or "gentle" style) alludes to the sinuous lines of decoration, evocative of twisting, darting flames; it also alludes to the abundant decorative motifs inspired by foliage and flowers. The French term *rayonnant* ("radiant") refers specifically to the rays emanating from rose windows.

The profusion of designations and styles concluded with the Late Gothic (in German *Spätgotik*), which survived until the early sixteenth century, especially in Northern Europe, where the echo of the Italian Renaissance was slow to arrive.

Given its broad geographic scope, the Gothic movement in Europe also produced a variety of typically national styles, as may be seen in the many further variations on this architectural theme.

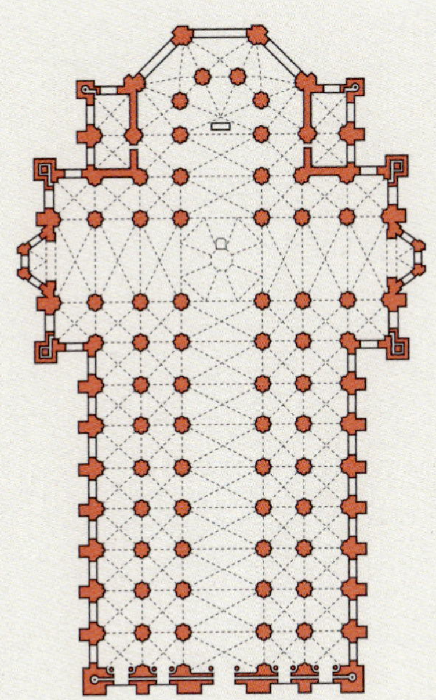

Above:
Plan of the Milan Duomo, Italy.

Right:
The Duomo, begun in 1386 and completed in 1856. Milan.

FRANCE

The spread of the Gothic style in Europe partially coincided with the establishment of more or less definitive national political entities. Not by chance, the most important monuments of this period appeared in cities. It might also be suggested that, in the wake of the Crusades and the expansion of trade routes, Gothic style served as a sort of calling card from the European world to the cultures of the eastern Mediterranean. The leading role in the formulation of diverse stylistic approaches was played by the Ile-de-France during the second half of the twelfth century. By the end of that century, French architects and builders had so thoroughly grasped the technical possibilities of the pointed arch as to create forms of striking impact,

Interior of the cathedral, c. 1235. Strasbourg, France.

Interior of the cathedral, c. 1180–1340. Wells, Somerset, England. This view of the central nave looking toward the apse shows the spectacular solution of the rampant "scissors" arches, which serve the function of supporting the tower over the intersection. The building dates from 1338.

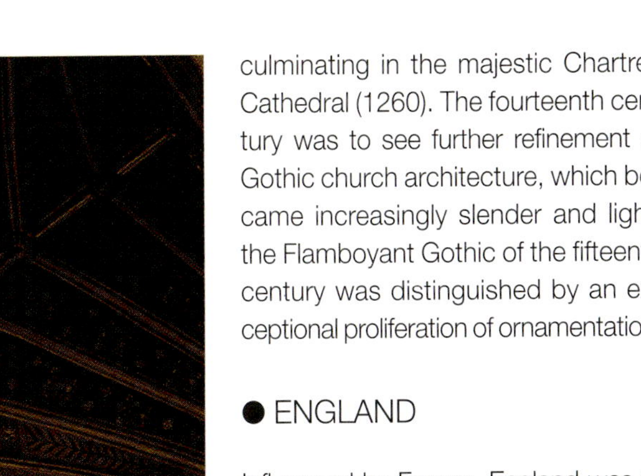

culminating in the majestic Chartres Cathedral (1260). The fourteenth century was to see further refinement of Gothic church architecture, which became increasingly slender and light; the Flamboyant Gothic of the fifteenth century was distinguished by an exceptional proliferation of ornamentation.

● ENGLAND

Influenced by France, England was to formulate a specific national style with its own terminology. "Early English" refers to the period from the end of the twelfth century to the second half of the thirteenth century, including such new formal solutions as the star vaults of Lincoln and Ely. The second half of the thirteenth century to the fourth decade of the fourteenth century saw the evolution of "Decorated Style," featuring ribbing carved with grooves and double curves. And "Perpendicular Style" emerged around the year 1330, lasting until almost the end of the fifteenth century; it is typified by daringly vertical structures, combined with surprising formal inventions.

● SPAIN AND PORTUGAL

Spain and Portugal were relatively slow to embrace the Gothic style, introduced by the Cistercians in the thirteenth century as Islamic domination was gradually diminishing. Another century passed before the first truly Gothic work appeared in Portugal, a prelude to the flourishing of the so-called "Manuelino" style, named after King Manuel I (1495–1521); its Spanish counterpart was the "Reyes Católicos" style.

● GERMANY AND ITALY

In Germany, beginning in the first thirty years of the thirteenth century, architecture showed a French Gothic influence. The Elisabethkirche at Marburg evoked the style of Reims, while the Cologne Duomo was inspired by the cathedrals of Amiens and Beauvais. The original solution of the *Hallenkirche* continued to be used in Germany until the end of the fifteenth century, thanks also to the contribution of master architects such as the Parlers (pp. 280–281).

In Italy, the Gothic style, introduced by the Cistercians, had to confront not only the classical tradition but also the influence of Burgundian architecture, which affected religious and civic buildings to varying degrees.

Above: *Interior of the cathedral,* begun 1248. Cologne, Rhineland, Germany.

Left: *Cross vaults and wooden octagon,* 1322–1340. Ely, Cambridgeshire, England. The church was rebuilt in grand form after the collapse of the tower over the intersection on February 22, 1322.

Left: *Basilica of San Francesco,* 1228–1253. Assisi, Perugia, Italy.

Above: *Castel del Monte,* c. 1240. Andria, Bari, Italy. Burgundian elements appear in this imposing castle with decorations deriving from the Classical age, in keeping with the "proto-humanist" tastes of Frederick II of Swabia.

Chinese Architecture

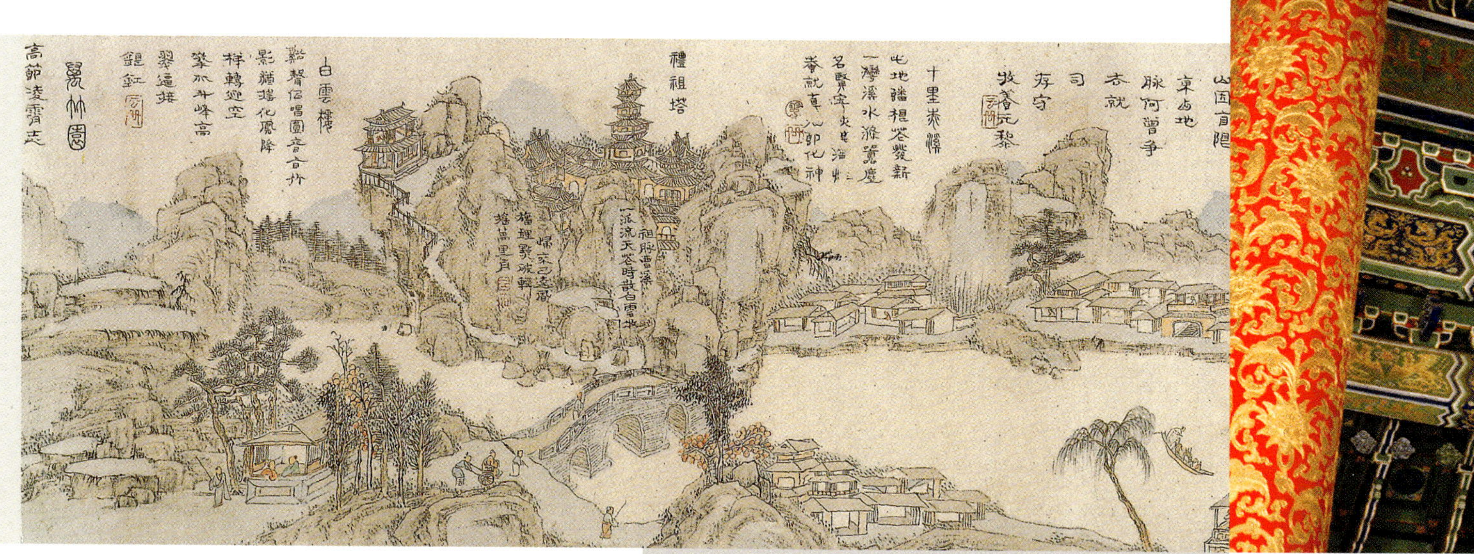

Chinese civilization has a very ancient history and has exerted a powerful influence on the architecture of many Far Eastern countries. Contacts between China and the Western world were extensive in the eleventh and twelfth centuries, when European merchants were embarking on adventurous journeys along the Silk Road and returning to report on the splendid palaces and gardens they had seen at the emperor's court.

● AN ANCIENT TRADITION

While the Great Wall is the most conspicuous sign of China's political unification (third century B.C.E.), the mausoleum of its first emperor, Qin Shi Huangdi at Xi'an, now famous for its spectacular army of terracotta warriors and horses, must have been one of the first great monuments erected during this period. Great mastery is revealed in Chinese mausoleums, the most important architectural complexes surviving from ancient times, as well as in the rock paintings dating from the fourth century C.E. found in the vicinity of Buddhist centers. The tombs of the Han Emperors (202 B.C.E.–220 C.E.) must

Above:
Landscape with temple and bridge over river, detail of scroll depicting the *Temple of the White Clouds*, 1656. Zurich, Rietberg Museum, Drenowatz Collection.

Below:
Model of house, painted terracotta, second century C.E. Kansas City, The Nelson-Atkins Museum of Art.

Pavilion of Good Harvest (Tian Tan, Temple of Heaven), 1420 (restored 1751, rebuilt 1889 after a fire). Beijing, Tian Tan Park. In this circular temple, distinguished by twelve columns standing in a circle around four central ones forming a square, the emperor conducted ceremonies at the solstice of the first lunar month to propitiate the favor of the heavens (in Chinese symbolism the sky is round and the earth square). The different colors of the wooden structural elements show the joining of columns, brackets, and beams. Identical solutions were adopted in stone architecture.

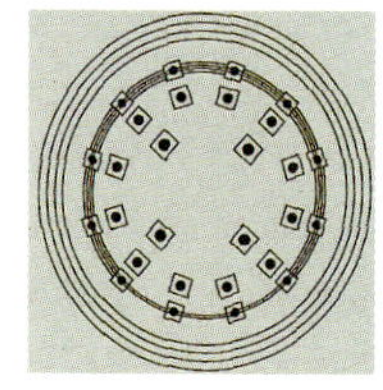

Below:
Brick roof of an ancient building on Mount Qingcheng.

have been made of wood, and their basic plan was later reiterated in stone. The spread of Buddhism from India to China (second century C.E.) determined the development of the Chinese temple par excellence, the pagoda, distinguished by roofs designed in a wide variety of imaginative forms. Outstanding among the monumental urban complexes of ancient China was the imperial Forbidden City in Beijing, one of the few to survive almost intact (pp. 284–285).

● CHARACTERISTICS AND TYPOLOGY

The Chinese term *tumu* (building) indicates the materials used since ancient times for the construction of houses: earth (*tu*) and wood (*mu*). The buildings rested on an embankment of earth, stone, or bricks, depending on the terrain and availability of materials.

The plan was square, with the rooms distributed according to a precise order. The bearing structure was made of timber, with earthen walls serving as partitions between rooms. A characteristic element of these buildings was the roof, which was either curved or flat. Beginning in the Late Han period (25–220 C.E.) roof tiles, often colored, were placed over a layer of insulating clay, which in turn covered wood boards. Typical of this building technique was the system of trusses and brackets, already fully developed by the Warring States Period (475–221 B.C.E.). The curved roof seems instead to have been introduced during the T'ang Dynasty (618–907). Circular buildings were rare, since wood was a material unsuitable to this shape. Cylindrical constructions were intended for public or religious use, as in the spectacular Pavilion of Good Harvest in Beijing. Another distinctive feature of the Chinese building technique is the bridge, in which the voussoirs (stone blocks) either radiated from the span of the arch, as in the West, or were laid vertically and shaped to follow the inner curve of the arch. Designed to enhance the sense of harmony of Chinese buildings was the garden, which was to be extensively developed in Japanese culture. A symbol of the unpredictability of nature, the Oriental garden recreates its manifestations in miniature, evoking the majestic beauty of mountains, rivers, and forests through the harmonious arrangement of plants, rocks, and canals.

Chinese roof types
1. Saddle without overhang
2. Pyramid
3. Saddle with overhang
4. Conical
5. With blunted roof-ridge
6. Intersecting
7. Pavilion
8. Composite on several levels
9. Composite

Renaissance Architecture

The Renaissance was essentially a phenomenon that originated in Italy and spread in different forms to many other countries in Europe. Not by chance, the sense of harmony and balance distinctive of this period was already seen in many medieval buildings in Italy, untouched by the Gothic "vertical soaring" of the North. The term "Renaissance" was used for the first time by the Swiss historian Jacob Burckhardt in his book, *The Civilization of the Renaissance in Italy,* published in 1860. Already in the sixteenth century, however, Giorgio Vasari had used the term "progress of rebirth" in reference to the renewal and flourishing of the arts in the context of a return to the harmony of antiquity; he employed the phrase in opposition to "modern usage," a definition of Gothic style coined a century earlier by Leon Battista Alberti. Even the term "Renaissance" remains too vague to adequately describe all phases of this great movement. Accordingly, the designation "Early Renaissance" is used for the fifteenth century, "High Renaissance" for the period through the end of the third decade of the sixteenth century, and "Late Renaissance" (including Mannerism) beginning in the 1530s.

Façade of Palazzo Strozzi, detail, late fifteenth century. Florence.

Leon Battista Alberti, *Interior of the Church of Sant'Andrea*, c. 1470. Mantua, Italy. Architraves, pilasters, and capitals clearly show a classical inspiration.

Anonymous artist (also attributed to Piero della Francesca and to Giuliano da Sangallo), *View of the Ideal City*, c. 1460–1480. Urbino, Galleria Nazionale delle Marche.

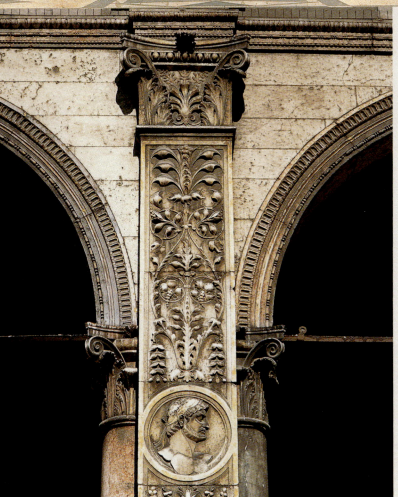

Right:
Andrea Palladio, *Study of proportions of Villa La Rotonda*, from *The Four Books of Architecture*, Venice 1570.

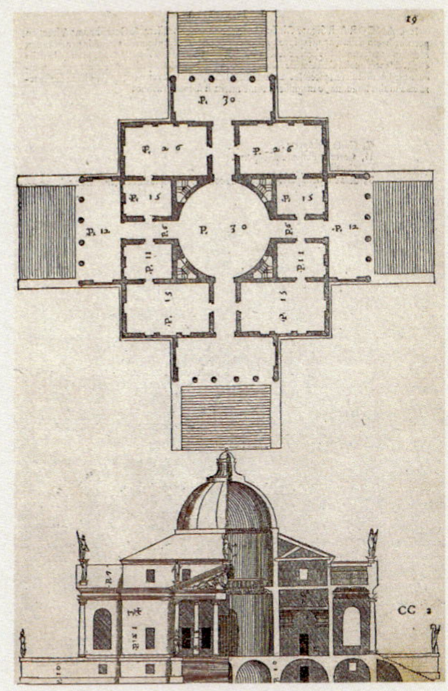

Pilaster with candelabra, late fifteenth century. Verona, Loggia del Consiglio. The candelabra, used as decoration for the pilaster, is an ornamental motif typical of Renaissance architecture.

● BASIC CHARACTERISTICS

The Certosa of Pavia, a former abbey in northern Italy, provides a useful example for the comparison of Gothic and Renaissance styles. The building was originally Gothic and later transformed by Giovanni Antonio Amadeo. What Gothic elements remain in its façade? The exaggerated use of decoration, the lateral buttresses, the statues standing against pilasters, and the pinnacles. What elements can be characterized as Renaissance? The round arches, the classical tympanum over the rose window, the portal without embrasure, the lunette coping over the windows, and the style of the pinnacles. Two other telling examples are the Porta della Carta in Venice and the Arch of Alfonso d'Aragona in Naples. In the Venetian gate, only the rectangular entrance and the statues are Renaissance, while the Neapolitan Arch is a reinterpretation of such ancient models as the arches of Constantine and Septimius Severus in Rome. Among the first to revive the architectural code was Leon Battista Alberti. For the Church of San Francesco in Rimini, known as the Tempio Malatestiano, he drew inspiration from the pagan prototype of the Arch of Augustus in the same city.

The language of Renaissance architecture thus uses the same alphabet as that of the Greco-Roman world. Albeit with variations, the classical orders (Doric, Ionic, Corinthian, and Composite) were revived, along with coffered ceilings and the repertoire of decorative elements (dintels, moldings, egg-and-dart motifs, metopes, triglyphs, archi-

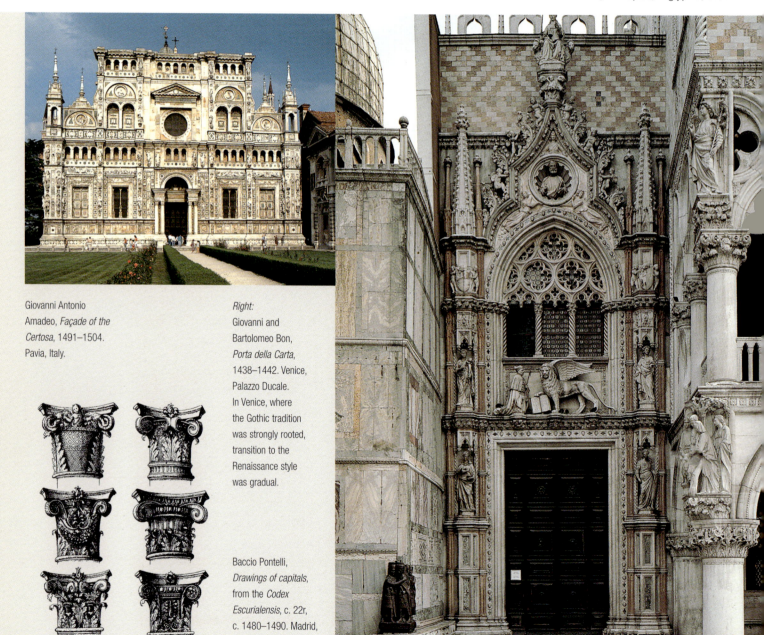

Giovanni Antonio Amadeo, *Façade of the Certosa*, 1491–1504. Pavia, Italy.

Right: Giovanni and Bartolomeo Bon, *Porta della Carta*, 1438–1442. Venice, Palazzo Ducale. In Venice, where the Gothic tradition was strongly rooted, transition to the Renaissance style was gradual.

Baccio Pontelli, *Drawings of capitals*, from the *Codex Escurialensis*, c. 22r, c. 1480–1490. Madrid, Escorial Library.

traves, columns, capitals, and pilasters). Decorative profusion disappears in favor of rhythmic, balanced elements. The pointed arch is replaced by the round arch or the trabeation, and barrel or domical vaults are preferred to cross-vaulting. In churches, however, the Latin cross, the Greek cross, and the central plans are all retained, along with the sloping roof. Renaissance architecture did not, however, restrict itself to slavish imitation of antiquity. Its many innovations were especially apparent in the design of noble palaces and country villas.

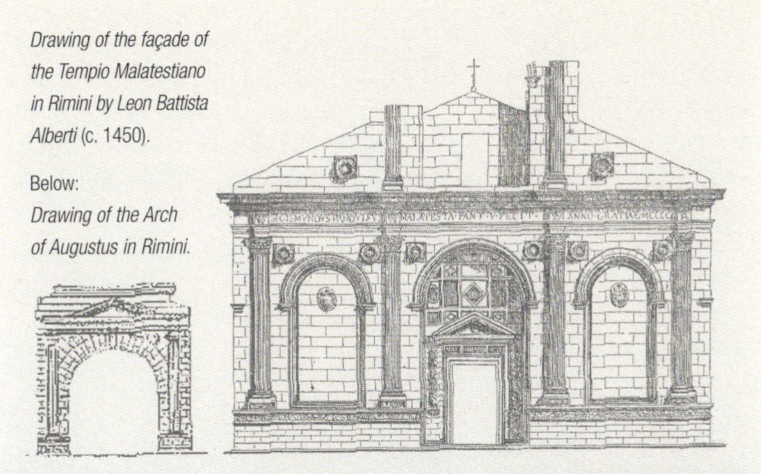

Drawing of the façade of the Tempio Malatestiano in Rimini by Leon Battista Alberti (c. 1450).

Below:
Drawing of the Arch of Augustus in Rimini.

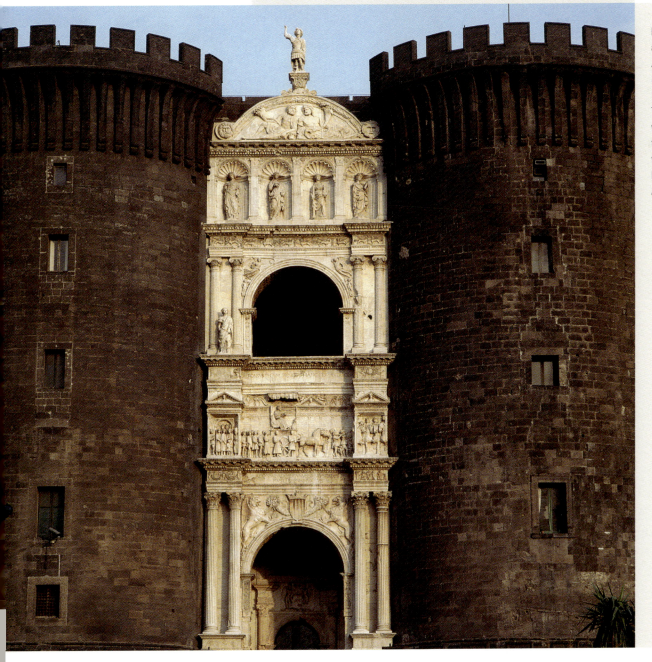

Francesco Laurana and Pietro da Milano, *Arch of Alfonso d'Aragona,* 1455–1466. Naples. This triumphal arch was erected in Naples to commemorate the victory of the Aragonese King Alfonso over the Angevins in 1443.

Below:
Plan and axonometric section of the Pazzi Chapel, 1433–1446. Florence, Santa Croce. The module of the square, repeated three times in the portico and six times in the chapel, is used to create an austere, harmonious space.

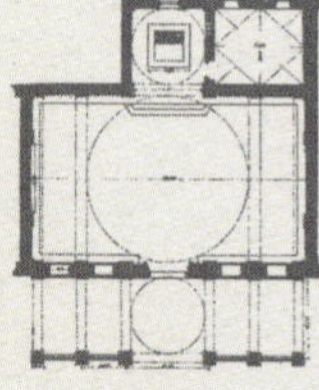

Right:
Filippo Brunelleschi, *Pazzi Chapel*, begun in 1433. Florence, Santa Croce.
The façade is an ingenious combination of vertical elements (columns and pilasters) and horizontal ones (the two trabeations and the roof), topped by a rounded dome. The canopy and the projecting open gallery create a play of fullness and voids.

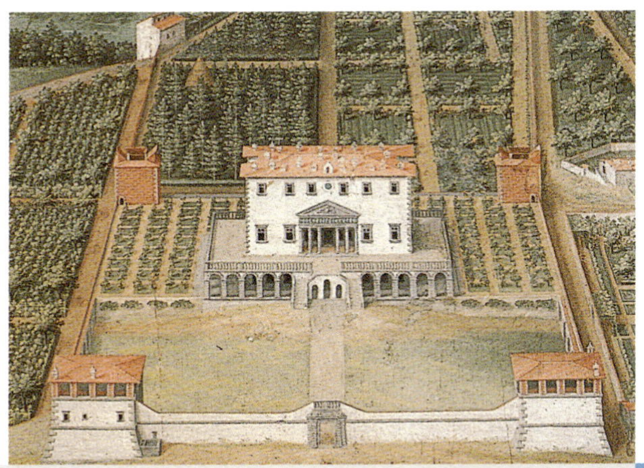

Giusto Utens, *View of the Medici Villa at Poggio a Caiano*, 1599. Florence, Museo di Firenze Com'era.

● THE EARLY RENAISSANCE

The salient features of fifteenth-century architecture are balance and harmony. One of the finest examples of the new style was the Pazzi Chapel in Florence, a synthesis of Brunelleschi's architectural concepts (pp. 286–287). This model was replicated on a monumental scale by Giuliano da Sangallo in the church of Santa Maria delle Carceri in Prato (p. 98). Florence's Palazzo Medici-Riccardi by Michelozzo served as inspiration, decades later, for the Palazzo Strozzi, distinguished by the same simplicity and harmony despite its more imposing form. The Medici Villa at Poggio a Caiano, designed by Giuliano da Sangallo for Lorenzo the Magnificent, is an architectural manifesto of the programmatic references to antiquity typical of the Renaissance, especially evident in the tympanum decorated with mythological scenes.

Pietro Lombardo, *Santa Maria de' Miracoli*, detail of the apse, 1481–1489. Venice. The Early Renaissance style was not a rigid, stereotyped formula, as clearly demonstrated by this Venetian church.

Above and right: *Wooden model and courtyard of Palazzo Strozzi*, 1489–1513. Florence. Enclosed in its austere block of rusticated stone, the palace concludes at the top with an elegant cornice decorated with dintels and modillions that seem to be taken from the trabeation of a Roman temple.

● THE HIGH RENAISSANCE

The course of Renaissance architecture in the sixteenth century was distinguished by a supreme confidence in new means of expression. The equilibrium that characterized designs of the fifteenth century was abandoned, but the result was a greater dynamism and plasticity, as seen in Bramante's new façade for Santa Maria delle Grazie in Milan. On the exterior, the ornamental "rowels" (spiked wheels) and the great concave panels on the lower part of the apse bear witness to a new spatial

Antonio da Sangallo the Elder, *Window on the bell tower of the Madonna di San Biagio*, 1518. Montepulciano, Siena, Italy.

Antonio da Sangallo the Elder, *Madonna di San Biagio*, 1518. Montepulciano, Siena, Italy.

Donato Bramante, *Santa Maria delle Grazie*, view of the apse and tiburium, after 1499. Milan.

Left: Baldassarre Peruzzi, *Villa Chigi (La Farnesina)*, view of the side overlooking the garden, 1508–1511. Rome.

sensitivity, also apparent in the convex façade of Palazzo Massimo alle Colonne in Rome. In La Farnesina, the Roman mansion of Agostino Chigi, Peruzzi reinvented the typology of the villa. Distinguished by two lateral foreparts, it served as the model for suburban villas until the seventeenth-century Villa Borghese and Palazzo Barberini in Rome. During the High Renaissance, however, fifteenth century examples also served as inspiration; the Madonna di San Biagio at Montepulciano appears to be a High Renaissance evolution of Santa Maria delle Carceri in Prato.

FROM LATE RENAISSANCE TO MANNERISM

The sack of Rome in 1527 forced the dispersion of many artists who had been working there, and their diaspora contributed to spread the Renaissance style spread throughout Europe—not only to France, but also to Spain and England.

Architectural projects of the time began to accentuate elements of chiaroscuro, particularly evident in Giorgio Vasari's grand design for Florence's Uffizi Palace, in which a striking contrast is created by the white walls and gray *pietra serena* elements on the exterior. While on the one hand great attention was focused on a philological revival of the ancient orders, on the other hand bold, scenographic effects were increasingly emphasized.

Architects frequently reverted to solutions of striking impact; Giulio Romano adopted a "rustic" order for Palazzo Te in Mantua, Andrea Palladio invented the "giant" order (p. 302), and Michelangelo overturned all canons in his design for Porta Pia in Rome, the emblem of Mannerist architecture.

Above: Giorgio Vasari, *Courtyard of the Uffizi Palace,* from 1560. Florence.

Above: Michelangelo, *Porta Pia*, 1560–1564. Rome.

Left: Jacopo Barozzi da Vignola, *Villa Farnese*, from 1559. Caprarola, Italy.

Below: Giulio Romano, *Palazzo Te*, eastern side, 1524–1535. Mantua, Italy.

From Mannerism to Baroque

While "Mannerism" is a term undoubtedly coined in the mid-sixteenth century, the word "Baroque," in use since at least the late eighteenth century, is of uncertain origin. It may derive from *barroco* (a Portuguese term alluding to the irregular shape of the gibbous pearl) or from *baroco* (a term used in medieval times to signify contrived syllogisms, then extended to indicate pedantic, bizarre reasoning). "Baroque" thus came to be synonymous with affectation, caprice, pretension, and extravagance; in other words, with bad taste and ugliness. One of the first to speak of seventeenth-century architecture in a derogatory manner was the contemporary architect and Neoclassical theorist Francesco Milizia, who in 1781 condemned the work of Borromini as "the ultimate of the bizarre, the ridiculous carried to extremes." Only near the end of the nineteenth century, in the writings of Heinrich Wölfflin, was the style reassessed and recognized as a genuine expression of the human spirit. In his tirade against the Baroque, Milizia had even included the art of Michelangelo, showing that he had grasped at least one important aspect of the new style: its effective evolution from Mannerist modulation and artifice. Typical of Baroque style is a decorative exuberance that finds expression in bold inventions and a progressive accentuation of plastic, dynamic masses. Curved lines and elliptical floor plans predominate, in place of the circular ones typical of the Renaissance. Domes grow increasingly bold, and grand monumental structures offer surprising theatrical effects. To understand the transition between Mannerism and the Baroque, it is enough to compare three types of window: those of Michelangelo on the calotte of the dome over St. Peter's; those of Maderno on the coping over the façade of the same basilica; and those of Borromini in the third lateral order of the façade of Palazzo Barberini. While Maderno's window retains a distinct Michelangelesque imprint, Michelangelo leaves his structure intact (tympanum and window with two sup-

Michelangelo, *Window in the calotte of St. Peter's dome*, 1558–1561. Vatican City.

Right: Carlo Maderno, *Detail of the façade of St. Peter's Basilica*, 1605–1613. Vatican City. Compared to Michelangelo's windows on the dome, those of Maderno on the coping over the façade are more plastic and animated, with the tympanum interrupted by an audacious shell.

porting volutes) and Maderno breaks up the tympanum with a flamboyant shell. While Michelangelo still respects the architectural orders, Maderno draws the eye with surprising plastic effects, already typical of the Baroque spirit. The latter solution is less organic than the former, however, and Borromini was to use an unbroken cornice in place of the fragmented tympanum. The new architectural style had thus reached maturity.

Carlo Maderno, *Façade of the Church of Santa Susanna*, 1597–1603. Rome.
In Baroque architecture, the lateral volutes were progressively reduced in size, while the other elements acquired a sense of greater volume. The Mannerist "rippling" walls of the Church of Gesù were followed by the powerfully sculptural ones of Santa Susanna, the starting point of Roman Baroque.

● SPREAD OF THE BAROQUE STYLE

Radiating from Italy to France and then to Spain, Portugal, and other European countries, Baroque was the first architectural style to leap the boundaries of the Old Continent and take root in the New World, India, and the Philippines. In its mature stage, it was disseminated on a broad international scale.

Guarino Guarini, *Front and profile of the façade of Palazzo Carignano (1678)*, engraving from 1686. Turin, Biblioteca Reale.

Above:
Giacomo della Porta, *Façade of the Church of Gesù*, 1568–1575. Rome.

Francesco Borromini, *Detail of the main façade of Palazzo Barberini*, c. 1630. Rome.
In the third lateral order of the palace, the young Borromini, a nephew of Maderno, designed a more "organic" window than that of his uncle; instead of the fragmented tympanum, an unbroken cornice curves plastically over the shell.

● THE BAROQUE STYLE IN ITALY

Rome, the radiating center of the Baroque style, boasts not only Carlo Maderno, who launched the new fashion in architecture, but also such great innovators as Gian Lorenzo Bernini and Francesco Borromini, as well as Carlo Rainaldi, Pietro da Cortona, Martino Longhi the Younger, Giovanni Antonio de' Rossi, and Carlo Fontana. Working in other Italian cities were the Modenese

Carlo Rainaldi and Gian Lorenzo Bernini, *Piazza del Popolo*, 1662–1679. Rome (photograph from 1930). A trick of perspective makes the two churches of Santa Maria di Montesanto and Santa Maria dei Miracoli appear identical, and the "proscenium" of the three streets (Babuino, Corso, and Ripetta) is symmetrical.

Guarino Guarini, *Dome on the Chapel of the Holy Shroud*, 1667–1690. Turin.

Baldassarre Longhena, *Design of the façade of Santa Maria della Salute in Venice (1631–1687)*. Vienna, Graphische Sammlung Albertina. The church was erected to mark the end of the plague epidemic of 1630.

architect Guarino Guarini (active in Turin and Paris), the Venetian Baldassarre Longhena, the Florentine Gherardo Silvani, and the Neapolitan Cosimo Fanzago. In Apulia and Sicily, the faces of whole cities were changed by the dissemination and appreciation of this new style.

● FROM ITALY TO THE REST OF THE WORLD

Already in 1657, the great French architect Louis Le Vau sought inspiration in Italian Baroque for the distribution of space in the Château of Vaux-le-Vicomte, inspired by suburban villas such as Palazzo Barberini in Rome. The new style began to take on a broad European aspect when Bernini was summoned to renovate the Louvre (1665). During the same period, another Italian architect, Guarino Guarini, was working in France, where such monumental projects as the Place Royale and the Palace of Versailles, celebrating the glories of the French monarchy, were being erected. In England, where Inigo Jones had introduced "Palladianism," the chief representative of Baroque style was Christopher Wren (pp. 312–313). Predominating in Spain, Portugal, and the New World colonies were solutions of splendor and redundancy that culminated in "Churriguerism," a highly decorative sculptural style enriched by elements of Native American that took its name from three architect brothers, José Benito, Joaquin, and Alberto Churriguera, from a family of sculptors in Barcelona.

Left:
Louis Le Vau, *Château of Vaux-le-Vicomte*, 1657–1658.
The château is a typically French architectural category. That of Vaux-le-Vicomte was built for the royal minister of finance, Nicolas Fouquet. The mixtilinear façade is rhythmically marked by pilasters and columns, while the wings are distinguished by the giant order.

Above:
Inigo Jones, *Banqueting House*, 1619–1622. London.
This building, designed in a sober, classical style, shows the influence of Palladio in the bossage (rough stone) on the base and the use of the giant order.

Decorated ceiling of the Cathedral of Santo Domingo, early eighteenth century. Oaxaca, Mexico.

From Late Baroque to Rococco

Johann Bernhard Fischer von Erlach, *Façade of the Karlskirche*, 1715–1716. Vienna. Inspired by Italian Baroque, the church also shows a significant "archaeological" revival in the colossal columns.

Widespread on an international scale (from Portugal to Russia, from Scandinavia to Austria, from the American colonies to those of the Far East), the Late Baroque (or mature Baroque) style is distinguished by the variety and freedom of its forms. In Czechoslovakia, some architects still looked toward Italian Baroque, admitting the same exasperations with local Gothic style, whose development had been interrupted by the Reformation. The revived Italian style, although interpreted in a totally original way, assumed religious and political significance as well. Italy, despite its marginal political position and troubled economy, remained the model for architects from other countries, including the German Johann Balthasar Neumann, the greatest of the Late Baroque architects. In Vienna, Fischer von Erlach, who had studied in Italy, designed the Karlskirche inspired by the work of Borromini and Rainaldi; Johann Lukas von Hildebrandt, a pupil of Carlo Fontana in Rome, designed the Belvedere castle for Prince Eugene. But it was the architects of Central Europe who showed the greatest appreciation for Late Baroque and later for Rococo. Among them were Georg Wenzeslaus von Knobelsdorff (1699–1753), who turned the architectural dreams of Fred-

Right: Christoph Dientzenhofer, *Façade of the church of St. Nicholas*, 1703–1711. Prague. A member of one of the great families of European architects, Dientzenhofer was inspired in part by Borromini's Church of San Carlino (the façade in the form of a giant tabernacle) and in part by Guarini's Palazzo Carignano in Turin (the columns and pilasters). The columns confer robust strength on the first register, and the pilasters confer grace on the other two (in a reversal of Guarini's arrangement).

Below: Luigi and Carlo Vanvitelli, *The Royal Palace of Caserta, seen from the Fountain of Venus and Adonis*, 1752–1774. The relationship between architecture and nature, expressed in pools of water and long straight paths traversing the garden, was inspired by Versailles.

Below: Johann Lukas von Hildebrandt, *Upper Belvedere in Vienna*, 1721–1723.

erick the Great of Prussia into reality, and Georg Bahr (1666–1738), designer of the great German Protestant church, the Frauenkirche in Dresden. In Great Britain, the serene enchantment of Palladianism persisted, serving as inspiration for Colen Campbell (1676–1729) and Richard B. Burlington (1694–1753), and laying the foundation for the Neoclassical style. Italy looked toward the rest of Europe. The Royal Palace of Caserta is an Italian version of Versailles, and the Hunting Lodge of Stupinigi seems a counterpart to the French châteaux. Many Italian architects worked abroad in the centers of European power. In Spain, Filippo Juvarra designed the Royal Palace in Madrid and the Hunting Lodge of Granja near Segovia. In Russia, the grandiose style of St. Petersburg before its Neoclassical renovation was the work of Bartolomeo Francesco Rastrelli and his son, Carlo Bartolomeo.

● ROCOCO

Rococo, frequently identified with Late Baroque, dates from the last fifteen years of the reign of Louis XIV (1661–1715) to the end of the eighteenth century. The term "Rococo" (which contemporaries called *style nouveau*) was employed in a derogatory sense in the third decade of the eighteenth century. The term derives from the French *rocaille* (seashell, an element that had been used to decorate grottoes and pavilions in gardens since the late sixteenth century). The style began with the decoration of interiors, with walls encrusted with branching ornamentation. Trailing branches, leaves, flowers, and vine tendrils, enlivened with birds, cherubs, and Chinese motifs, were generally made of stucco, gilded or painted. Only rarely does the Rococo style assume architectural dignity, however, as decoration of this type was superimposed on Late Baroque forms.

Above: Giovanni Paolo Panini, *Benedict XIV visits the newly completed Fountain of Trevi*, c. 1744. Moscow, Pushkin Museum.

This enormous fountain stood at the front of the newly built Duke of Poli's palace, whose façade was expropriated.

Left: Bartolomeo Rastrelli, *Monumental staircase in the Winter Palace*, 1752–1763. St. Petersburg.

Rococo decoration was superimposed on Late Baroque structures.

Early Indian Architecture

Left:
Thomas Colman Dibdin, *View of the interior of a* vihara *in the Ajanta caves*, lithograph from the second half of the nineteenth century.

Below:
Interior of a caitya *in Grotto XIX*, sixth century C.E. Ajanta, Maharashtra.
The *caitya*, with a ceiling formed of raised arches, has richly decorated walls. At the back of the apse, the relief sculpture of a standing Buddha adorns the front of the *stupa*.

Below:
Bodhika capital, from the Column of Ashoka, third century B.C.E. Sarnath, Archaeological Museum.

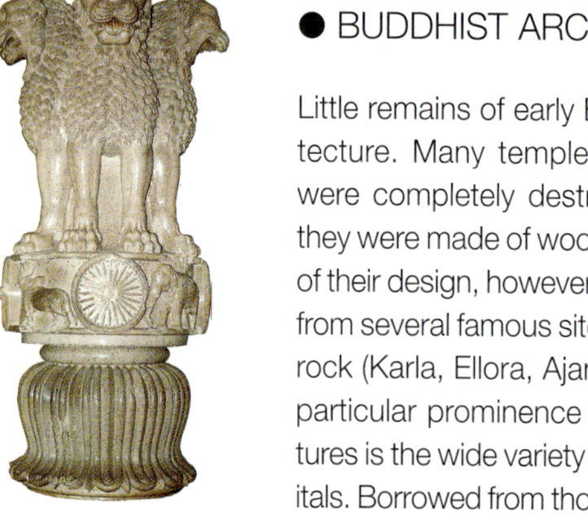

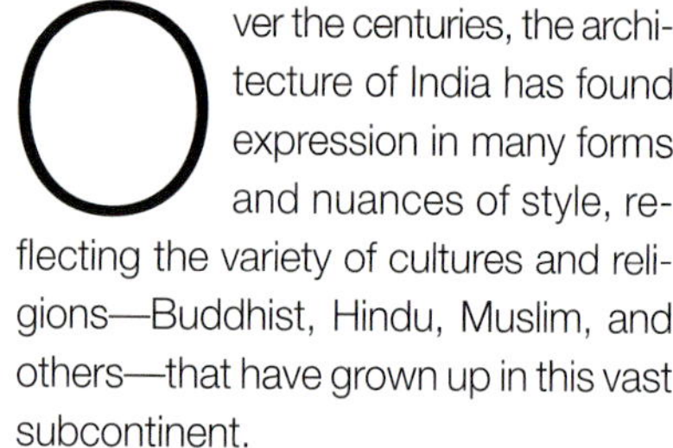

Over the centuries, the architecture of India has found expression in many forms and nuances of style, reflecting the variety of cultures and religions—Buddhist, Hindu, Muslim, and others—that have grown up in this vast subcontinent.

● BUDDHIST ARCHITECTURE

Little remains of early Buddhist architecture. Many temples and palaces were completely destroyed because they were made of wood. Some sense of their design, however, can be gained from several famous sites excavated in rock (Karla, Ellora, Ajanta, p. 245). Of particular prominence in these structures is the wide variety of column capitals. Borrowed from those of Persia, Indian column capitals recapitulate a number of types: forked with animal figures leaning against them, back-to-back, bulbous, goblet-shaped, and spherical (often topped with an abacus). Especially elaborate are *bodhika* capitals, on which appear, from bottom to top, an upside-down lotus flower, animal figures, and a pulvin (convex base). The simple *sira* capital, instead, is a corbel (supporting projection). Another important feature is the raised arch, often repeated in series to form the structure of a ceiling.

Buddhist building types are those still found in cliff monasteries today: the *vihara*, consisting of a central cloister surrounded by monks' cells; the *caitya*, a prayer hall of basilican plan with one or three naves, also common to Chinese architecture; and the *stupa* (p. 49), the

Ratha entrance, seventh–eighth centuries C.E. Mahabalipuram, Madras.
This is one of the rare surviving monolithic temples (*ratha*) hewn out of the rock, constructed in the ancient port of the Pallava Dynasty (400–750 C.E.) on the Gulf of Bengali.

building par excellence of Buddhist tradition, distinguished by a proliferation of sculptural door decorations (*torana*), reminiscent of Hindu temples.

● HINDU ARCHITECTURE

Hindu temples may be classified as belonging to one of three basic styles. Of these, the *nagara* is typical of the temples of Khajuraho (p. 253), Konarak, and Bubaneswar in northern India. Erected on a base, they rise like mountain peaks topped with distinctive pinnacles (*sikhara*), symbolizing a bowl of water placed above the *amalak* ("pure essence") or, according to an anthropomorphic interpretation, a crowned head. The Dravidic style originated in southern India during the sixth and seventh centuries in the "city of the seven temples," near Madras. Here each building (*ratha*) is carved out of a single mass of granite. From this style was to develop, in southern India, the typical stepped tower, often enlivened by a swarm of brightly colored human figures. Distinctive of the *vesara* style, which developed in the sixth and seventh centuries under the reign of the Chalukya Empire, is the star-shaped temple.

● ISLAMIC ARCHITECTURE

Beginning in the eleventh century, peoples of Muslim faith began to settle in India, where Islamic architecture was distinguished in particular by four-centered multifoil arches, along with bulb-shaped or ovoid domes. The most splendid Islamic structures, such as the famous Taj Mahal (pp. 310–311) were built under the Mogul Dynasty.

Temple of Sri Meenakshi, seventeenth century. Madurai, Tamil Nadu.

Pre-Columbian Architecture

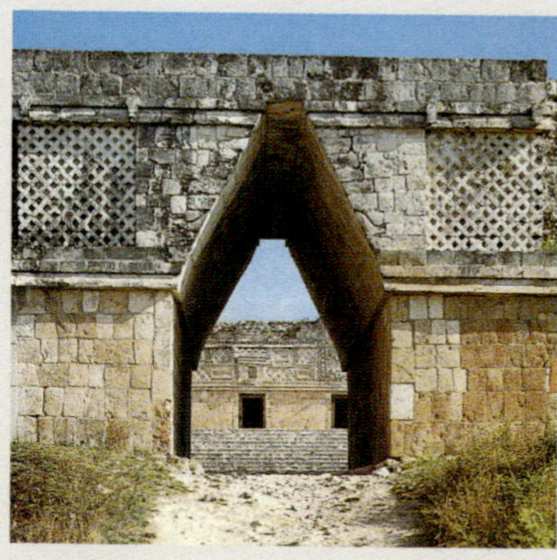

Maya culture, *Nun's Courtyard*, entrance to the south building. Uxmál, Yucatan, Mexico. The passageway leading to the Nun's Courtyard, so called by the Spanish for its resemblance to a cloister, consists of a typical pseudo-arch with overhanging voussoirs.

Above: Toltec art, *Temple of the Morning Star with "Atlas" warrior columns*, tenth–twelfth centuries C.E. Tula, Hidalgo, Mexico.

Below: Maya-Toltec culture, *El Caracol (Observatory) and, in the background, the Pyramid of Kukulkan*, c. 1050. Chichén Itzá, Yucatan, Mexico.

From this cylindrical tower, Maya astronomers studied the stars to produce a remarkably accurate calendar.

In the vast territory of Central and South America, a number of different civilizations, each with its own artistic characteristics, flourished between 2000 B.C.E. and the end of the sixteenth century C.E. In their use of architectural forms and decorations, however, a certain continuity and homogeneity is evident, due mainly to a religious identity based on shared cult forms.

● BASIC CHARACTERISTICS

The architecture that developed before the Spanish conquest in the geographical area of Mexico, Central America, and the Andes was characterized by the column-architrave system. The arch was unknown to the Toltecs, Mayas, Aztecs, and Incas, who instead used pseudo-arches produced by carving openings in monolith stones or by arranging the voussoirs of a wall to form a triangle. Rare but imposing are buildings of circular shape, such as the spectacular astronomical tower at Chichén Itzá.

Pre-Columbian columns generally resemble square-section pillars without a base or capital, although in Maya constructions a rudimentary pulvin (convex base) was sometimes used. At times carved in relief with images of warriors, this type of pillar may also be decorated with geometric motifs. Doors narrowing at the top are another typical feature of this style.

Circular chulpa built of stone, twelfth century C.E. Sillustani Peninsula, Peru.

Left and above: Maya culture, *Temple (or Pyramid) of the Inscriptions*, exterior and funerary crypt, seventh century C.E. Palenque, Chiapas, Mexico. The central stairway of the pyramid leads to the top of the structure, which gives access to the funerary crypt where a monolithic sarcophagus containing the body of the Maya King Pacal (615–683), closed with a massive stone slab decorated with relief incisions, was found in 1952.

Below: *Huaca Esmeralda*, detail of decoration with rhomboid motifs. Chan-Chan, Trujillo, Peru.

● ARCHITECTURAL TYPOLOGIES

Pre-Columbian civilizations are famous for their step-pyramids dedicated to cults of the sun and moon (pp. 300–301). Used as sacrificial altars, they were also astronomical observatories and sometimes served a funerary function. Maya architecture is also typified by lordly mansions consisting of rectangular buildings erected on tiered bases.

Typical of the Andes culture are *kulpi* house-tombs in the vicinity of Lima, Peru, generally built of stone and usually with a round floor plan (or, more rarely, polygonal or quadrangular with rounded corners). With ceilings formed of pseudo-vaults, they contained living quarters in the upper room and tombs in the lower room dug out of the soil. The *kulpi* are similar in structure to the funerary *chulpas* of Peru, found around Lake Titicaca, which are also made of stone and are cylindrical in shape.

● DECORATIVE ELEMENTS

Much of the architectural decoration is geometric, based on motifs that seem derived from textile patterns: rhombus, grille, serrated triangle, meander, and serrated meander.

In addition to these decorations are others of religious inspiration, such as the plumed serpent and the mask of the jaguar-god.

Neoclassical Architecture

Joseph Michael Gandy, *Architectural Visions*, 1820. London, Sir John Soane's Museum.

According to the German archaeologist and art historian Johann Joachim Winckelmann (1717–1768), the first great theorist of Neoclassicism, "the only way to achieve greatness and, if possible, to be inimitable, is to emulate the ancients" (1764). What, then, is the innovative factor in a movement inspired by the classical world, which had already been the model for many of the styles that developed in the West? It has already been seen how European architecture had, over the centuries, elaborated variations on the theme of antiquity, rather than merely imitating the Greco-Roman stylistic codes. In the Middle Ages, the classical tradition was revived for the purpose of demonstrating continuity between the Roman Empire and the one that marched under the banner of Christianity, while the architects of the Early Renaissance rediscovered classical building techniques by studying ancient monuments and identifying their basic elements (such as the column-trabeation-arch). After the codification of rules in the fifteenth century, however, European architecture departed from classical standards with the advent of Mannerism, culminating in the bizarre, striking effects of the Baroque. Lastly, the Late Baroque and Rococo styles had intensified these trends in both their structural and decorative aspects, largely abandoning the sober equilibrium of the Early Renaissance. Thus the Neoclassical reaction (1750–1840), although this was hardly a return to the Quattrocento. The differences were considerable, beginning with a stricter philological approach, determined largely by direct knowledge of ancient monuments unearthed in

Right:
Antonio Joli, *The Temple of Neptune at Paestum*, 1759. Caserta, Palazzo Reale.

major archaeological expeditions. The great archaeological finds on the Palatine Hill in Rome (1729), at Hadrian's Villa in Tivoli (1734), and above all in the ancient cities of Herculaneum (1711) and Pompeii (1748), buried for centuries by the eruption of Mount Vesuvius, were the starting point for a series of excavations that attracted theorists, travelers, and artists from all over Europe and gave rise to famous collections of engravings that were critically important to the development of the new style.

● A NEW THEORY OF STYLE

Albeit with uncertainty and errors, a distinction was made for the first time between Roman and Greek art, and the generic concept of antiquity was abandoned. The relative merits of Greek and Roman creations were widely debated. The apostle of this new trend was Winckelmann, who had formulated his theories while engaged, beginning in 1755, as the librarian of a splendid collection of books owned by Cardinal Albani in Rome. In his *History of Ancient Art,* he distinguishes four periods of ancient art: the "archaic" of pre-Phidian Greece, the "sublime" of the fifth century B.C.E., the "beautiful" of the fourth century B.C.E., and the "decadent" of the Roman era before the birth of Christ. Bold new theories, fundamental to the development of Neoclassicism, were advanced in Italy by Francesco Milizia; by the German Anton Raphael Mengs; and by two Venetians, Carlo Lodoli (1690–1761), a Franciscan priest, mathematician, and opponent of the Baroque, and Francesco Algarotti (1712–1764), the author of an important essay on architecture published in 1753.

Jacques-Germain Soufflot, *Dome of the Panthéon (formerly Sainte-Geneviève),* 1757–1792. Paris.

William Thornton, Stephen Hallet, Benjamin Henry Latrobe, Thomas Ustick Walter, and others, *The U.S. Capitol Building,* 1793–1814. Washington, D.C. Thornton's project won a competition held in 1793; although it was later modified, the building was to retain a consistent Neoclassical style.

● BASIC CHARACTERISTICS

Neoclassicism in architecture may be summarized in two words: simplicity and rationality. In aspiring to emulate the harmony and balance of Ancient Greece, it rejects the superfluous ornamentation of Baroque and Rococo; banned are the unexpected and irrational in form, which is now dictated primarily by function. The Neoclassical palace indulges in no scenographic effects, and its elements clearly reveal their structural function. The difference is exemplified by two palaces, the Stroganov (1750–1754) by Rastrelli and the Small Hermitage (1764–1775) by Jean-Baptiste Vallin de la Mothe, both in St. Petersburg, which was swept by a wave of Neoclassicism under Catherine the Great (r. 1762–1796). Although the two buildings have many elements in common, their differences are significant. The Stroganov palace has a molded cornice that culminates in a tympanum above the central body, emphasized by projecting pilasters. The windows on the *piano nobile* (main floor) and lower floor are rounded at the top (those at the center being even with the tympanum), while those at the mezzanine level are framed by a wide molded cornice. The façade concludes with pilasters at the corners. The resulting effect is one of dynamism and plasticity. The Small Hermitage, by contrast, has a dentiled cor-

Below:
Bartolomeo Rastrelli, *Façade of the Stroganov Palace*, 1750–1754. St. Petersburg.

Above:
Jean-Baptiste Vallin de la Mothe, *Façade of the Small Hermitage overlooking the Neva*, 1764–1775. St. Petersburg. While retaining certain elements in common with the older Stroganov Palace (giant order, bossage on the base, rectangular front), the Small Hermitage shows important differences. For example, instead of the molded cornice culminating in a central tympanum, the building designed by de la Mothe has a dentiled cornice that serves as architrave. Simple windows are used instead of rounded ones or those framed by a molded cornice. In the ten years between the construction of the two palaces, dynamism and plasticity had yielded to linearity and equilibrium.

nice of the architrave type that projects above the columns. The windows are simple; those on the first floor and *piano nobile* are arched. The projecting columns are connected to the façade by two pilasters. The resulting effect is one of linearity and equilibrium. Although the stylistic code is the same as that of Late Baroque, the results are quite different. The search for rationality led architects such as Ledoux and Boullée (pp. 318–319) to design ideal buildings that carried to an extreme the theories of Lodoli and Algarotti, constituting a prelude to rationalism.

● NEOCLASSICISM IN THE WORLD

The Neoclassical style met with international success. Although first theorized in Italy, it was adopted in that country only later. In tune with the spirit of the Enlightenment, it found ample space in Russia, where Neoclassicism marginalized such Late Baroque architects as Rastrelli. In France, Neoclassical architecture crossed the historic divide between monarchy and revolution to enter the Napoleonic Era and the Bourbon Restoration. Neoclassicism seemed appropriate to the ideal of liberty in the United States, and to the president-architect Thomas Jefferson. American architecture was influenced by the neo-Palladian style originating in England.

Alexandre Pierre Vignon, *La Madeleine*, 1806–1842. Paris. The Neoclassical elements adopted in the Napoleonic Era were still being used during the Bourbon Restoration.

Karl Gotthard Langhans, *Brandenburg Gate*, 1799–1791. Berlin (photograph from 1907). In the Prussia of Frederick the Great, Neoclassical architecture was well suited to the ostentation of military power.

John Nash, *Cumberland Terrace*, 1826. London, Regent's Park.

Neo-Gothic, or Gothic Revival Architecture

The revival of the style most typical of the Middle Ages emerged in England during the mid-eighteenth century, at the time of the amateur architect and writer of "Gothic novels," Horace Walpole (1717–1797). Strawberry Hill, his eccentric country house overlooking the Thames, launched a "Gothic Revival" fashion that was to last throughout the nineteenth century. This phenomenon, in contrast to the prevailing Neoclassicism, had the value of re-evoking the national style. The new version had an exotic flair, however, reflecting the taste for *chinoiserie* (things Chinese) that had pervaded European architecture and decorative arts as early as the 1720s. The renewed interest in Gothic architecture originated from the need to complete buildings that had remained unfinished for centuries. The rediscovered style soon prompted a debate on the need for forms and solutions suited to a "modern" architecture, able to satisfy the needs of a society now fast becoming industrialized, with the utilization of such new materials as iron and glass and the introduction of such new building types as railway stations and mechanized bridges. Studies aimed at a philological revival of the old "language" proliferated. Among the most widely diffused texts were *The True Principles of Pointed or Christian Architecture* (1841), by Augustus Welby Northmore Pugin (pp. 330–331), and the *Essay on the Origin of Gothic Architecture* (1797), by James Hall. Eugène Emmanuel Viollet-le-Duc (pp. 328–329) played the dual role of theorist and architect. The return to Gothic was strongly opposed by advocates of Neoclassicism, which they deemed the only legitimate style derived from tradition.

View of Strawberry Hill, the country house of Horace Walpole, 1750–1770. Twickenham, Middlesex, England. Horace Walpole was a successful writer who contributed to the dissemination of the Neo-Gothic style with his novel *The Castle of Otranto* (1764).

Horace Jones and John Wolfe Barry, *Tower Bridge*, 1886–1894. London. The drawbridge was lifted by a steam-driven mechanism, replaced by an electrical device only in 1976.

Walter Stuler, *Accounting Room in the Castle of the Hohenzollern*, 1850–1867. Württemberg, Germany.

Nicola Matas, *Façade of Santa Croce*, 1853–1863. Florence.

● THE NEO-GOTHIC STYLE IN THE WORLD

The Neo-Gothic style spread far. Prominent examples in the United States included the Brooklyn Bridge (pp. 68–69), whose trestles are evoke Gothic ogival arches, and the spires of Trinity Church soaring upward among the skyscrapers of New York. But the vast echo of Gothic Revival was determined chiefly by the preference of the great power of the time, which legitimized the style as an alternative to the Neoclassical in a grandiose architectural undertaking. In 1835, the British government decided to renovate the House of Parliament in Neo-Gothic style (pp. 330–331). Several Gothic buildings in Great Britain had already been restored and enlarged in the style now adopted for the seat of government. In Austria and Germany, too, the Neo-Gothic style was a concrete expression of the recovery of a national identity, through a style of different tradition, though no less authoritative, from the Greco-Roman one. The grandiose castles of Ludwig II of Bavaria (1864–1886), obviously evoking a fantastic dimension of Nordic tradition that could never be expressed by Neoclassicism, were to become the model, in the twentieth century, for the homes of Walt Disney's princes and fairies. The Neo-Gothic style found success in Italy as well—from the "castles" and villas of antiquarians, to the façades of Santa Croce and Santa Maria del Fiore in Florence.

Giuseppe Fancelli, *Gothic Revival castle of John Temple Leader*, c. 1860. Vincigliata, Fiesole, Florence.

Eduard Riedel and Georg Dollmann, *Castle of Ludwig II of Bavaria*, from 1869. Neuschwanstein, Germany.

A Neo-Gothic portal on a bridge over the Po, 1865. Piacenza, Italy (old photograph). The bridge, built using technologies that were highly modern for the times, was constructed of iron, a material synonymous with progress. Running beside the tracks were broad sidewalks for pedestrians. The railway bridge was dismantled only in 1931, as it could no longer withstand the weight of the new locomotives, unimaginable at the time it was built.

Eclecticism

Left:
Ludwig Persius, *Heilandskirche*, 1841–1844. Potsdam-Sacrow, Germany. For monuments such as this one, of Romanesque inspiration with Late Antiquity and Byzantine roots, Heinrich Hubsch coined the term *Rundbogenstil* ("round arch style") in 1878.

Right:
John Nash, *Royal Pavilion*, 1818. Brighton, England.

Giuseppe Jappelli, *Caffè Pedrocchi and Pedrocchino*, 1816–1831 and 1837. Padua, Italy. Jappelli remained faithful to the Neoclassical tradition for his elegant design of the Caffè Pedrocchi, but he did not hesitate to annex to it the Neo-Gothic structure of the "Pedrocchino" a few years later.

The emergence of Gothic Revival as a dominant force in late-nineteenth-century architecture had raised the question of conventionality of style. While centuries-old ties to the classical tradition could no longer prevail over other approaches, none of the various alternatives could fully satisfy the requirements of a swiftly changing society. Not even the preference of engineers for the use of iron, a sturdy and reliable material with distinct ornamental potential, was sufficient to solve the problem. Once the concept of Classicism as the only legitimate style had been abandoned, the possibility of resorting to a broad diversity of approaches, to be used in accordance with specific circumstances and individual taste, came to be recognized. The historical styles thus became a sort of interchangeable "architectural dress," in keeping with a taste that in the decorative arts as well was turning to eclectic solutions.

● ECLECTICISM IN THE WORLD

The Classical style had now become only one of several architectural solutions. It was still used in some major architectural projects, such as the Roman monument to Vittorio Emanuele II in 1884 (pp. 326–327), for which Giuseppe Sacconi drew inspiration from the architecture of Imperial Rome. In the same public square, a decade later, Sacconi designed a headquarters for the Assicurazioni Generali insurance

Right:
Charles Garnier, *Opéra*, 1862–1875. Paris. After having traveled extensively between Rome and Athens, Garnier in 1861 won the competition for the Paris Opera House, a building finished fourteen years later in a redundant Neo-Baroque style.

Henry Hobson Richardson, *Monumental stairway in the New York State Capitol Building* (late nineteenth-century photograph). Albany, New York.

Henri Labrouste, *Reading room*, begun 1868. Paris, original site of the National Library. After long periods in Italy, where he studied Roman aqueducts and planned the restoration of the temples at Paestum (judged too avant-garde in his own country), the Parisian engineer and architect was one of the first to recognize the importance of iron. The reading room he designed for the National Library has sixteen cast-iron columns supporting nine small eggshell domes.

company, inspired by the fifteenth-century Palazzo Venezia (p. 19). In Great Britain, John Nash (pp. 324–325) adopted an impeccable Neoclassical style for the mansions in Regent's Park, London (p. 159); later he created an imaginative pavilion at Brighton inspired by Arab architecture. In the United States, Henry Hobson Richardson (1838–1886) showed a preference for the Romanesque; after having studied examples throughout Europe and worked in Paris with Labrouste and Hittorf, he drew inspiration from that style for the design of mansions, libraries, and department stores of massive, imposing form. Romanesque architecture saw a kind of revival in England as well, where, in its so-called "Norman" version, it evoked national tradition. In Germany, the tendency was toward a style somewhere between that of Late Antiquity and the Byzantine, while France opted for the Baroque, displaying an image of grandeur that evoked the splendor of the Sun King.

Modernism and Art Nouveau

Josef Hoffmann, *Palais Stoclet*, 1905–1911. Brussels.

Otto Wagner, *Karlsplatz subway station*, detail, 1898. Vienna.

The reevaluation of style itself had led architects, with the contribution of theorists such as Jean-Nicolas-Louis Durand (1760–1834), to shift the terms of debate from the consistency of utilizing classical orders to the function and role of a building. "The orders are not in fact the essence of architecture," wrote Durand in his *Précis of the Lectures on Architecture* (1802–1805). "Decoration itself," he concluded, "is a chimera and the expense to which it leads a folly." The Neo-Gothic experience and the widely read texts of Eugène Emmanuel Viollet-le-Duc had strongly contributed to the reexamination of architectural history and, given the intrinsic nature of the Gothic, to a focus on structural aspects. The premises of a new response to the problem of style thus were established.

● MANY NAMES FOR THE SAME STYLE

Between 1890 and 1910, Art Nouveau spread all over the world, the Americas included. The name derives from a shop opened in Paris in 1895 that specialized in distinctly modern objects. The German name *Jugendstil* came from the magazine *Jugend,* published in Munich in 1896. In Italy it was known as Liberty, after the London department stores owned by Arthur Lasenby Liberty, which sold floral-patterned fabrics and other items. *Sezessionstil*, the term adopted in Vienna, alludes to the Viennese Secession (1897), a group that declared war on official art. Modern Style was the designation preferred by the British.

● BASIC CHARACTERISTICS

The salient feature of this style is a sinuous line inspired by the world of plants. Curvilinear design became the distinguishing characteristic of Art Nouveau jewelry, furnishings, balustrades, glass panels, and even building exteriors. Another distinctive feature was the use of industrial materials such as iron, cast iron, and majolica. Any reference to the architectural orders was banned, and the structure of a building became identified with its decoration.

● ORIGINS AND DEVELOPMENT

Art Nouveau was inspired by the Arts and Crafts Movement, which had developed in England, in a new relationship between art and industry (p. 31). While Art Nouveau assimilated the aesthetic ideals of the British movement, it rejected the social component. In close contact with the Viennese Secession (led by the architect Otto Wagner), it was also enriched by the work of such outstanding figures as the Scottish architect and designer Charles R. Mackintosh (pp. 334– 335) and the Spanish architect Antoni Gaudí (pp. 336–337). The main centers of Art Nouveau were Vienna, where Joseph Maria Olbrich (1867–1908) designed the Secession House, and Brussels, where Victor Horta (1861–1947) designed buildings melding decoration and structure, while Henry van de Velde (1836–1957) explored the possibilities of the new style in graphics and the applied arts.

Giovanni Michelazzi, *Villino Liberty*, 1911. Florence.

Joseph Maria Olbrich, *Secession House*, 1897–1898. Vienna. The Secession House, built as an exhibition hall for the works of a group of avant-garde artists (including Gustav Klimt, Josef Hoffmann, and Olbrich himself) was immediately judged a radical break with Viennese artistic tradition. Over the entrance appears the inscription, *Der Zeit ihre Kunst der Kunst ihre Freiheit* (To each age its art, to each art its freedom).

Left: Otto Wagner, *Majolikahaus*, detail, 1898–1899. Vienna.

Victor Horta, *Maison du Peuple in Brussels* (1897), in an old photograph. The commission to design a great center of social life was conferred on Victor Horta, a member of the Social Democratic Workers' Party. The building, now destroyed, housed offices, shops, a performance hall, and a café. The entire structure was based on an exposed iron framework.

Japanese Architecture

An ancient tea house on the lake. Naha, Okinawa.

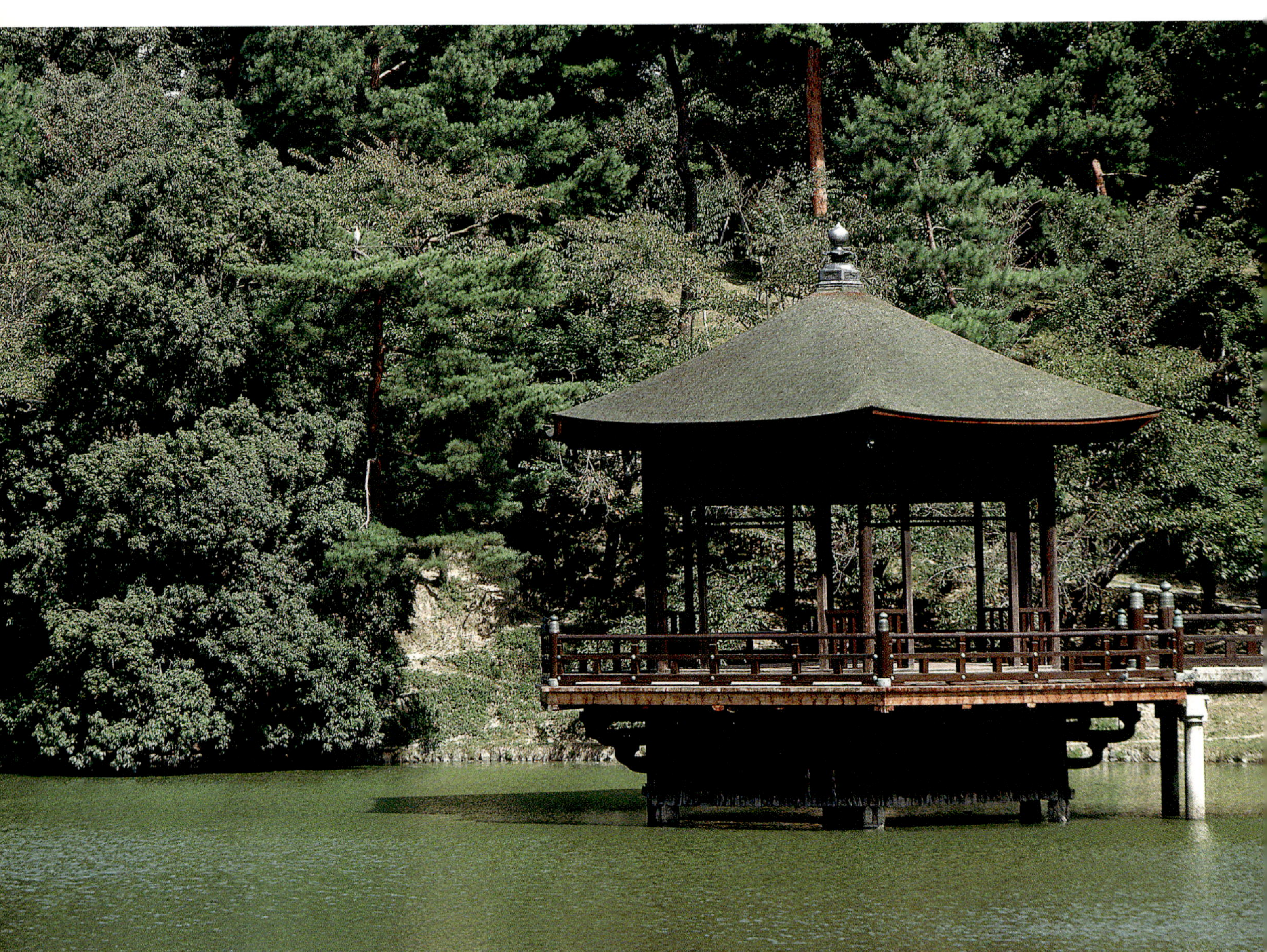

In its formal aspects, Japanese architecture has been strongly influenced by the building methods of the Chinese (pp. 136–137). These techniques came to the Land of the Rising Sun with the spread of Buddhism around the middle of the sixth century C.E., during the reign of the Emperor Kimmei. (Chinese writing had already been in use for some time.) Until the arrival of Buddhism, Japan had been dominated by the national cult of Shinto ("the way of the gods"), an animistic religion that attributes spirituality to various aspects of nature and to any emotion capable of evoking a higher dimension. While in the sixteenth century Japanese contacts with Europe were intensified with the arrival of Protestant and Catholic missionaries, starting in the mid-seventeenth century Japan was to remain in total isolation for two hundred years, with all foreigners prohibited from approaching its shores.

With the resumption of Western contact following the accession of Emperor Meiji (r. 1867–1912), the unique fascination of Japanese culture began to exert a strong attraction in the Western world, which continues to look to Japan as a source of inspiration and mutual exchange, especially in the field of architecture.

Right:
The temple complex of Itsukushima-jinja, seen from the "Great Torii," 1241–1571. Miyajima Island.

Overlooking the bay of Hiroshima on the Inland Sea, this temple was once regarded as one of the three most beautiful places in Japan.

Below:
System of beams in the Phoenix Hall, 1053. Temple of Byodo-in, Kyoto Prefecture.

● ORIGINS AND BASIC CHARACTERISTICS

The most ancient traditional houses (*haniwa*) are recalled only in a few terracotta models, which show similarities with the houses of other East Asian countries. The typical rural house, made of wood, paper, and straw, had a raised floor, a veranda, and a wide-sloping roof sometimes covered with reeds. Typically Japanese buildings include temples, palaces, fortified castles, and storehouses for rice built on piles. Traditional Japanese building systems have survived especially in rural houses and Shinto temples. The latter are surrounded by an enclosure with a trapezoidal gate (*torii*), surmounted by an architrave that overhangs supporting pillars. Temples of the time typically followed a hall plan, of extreme simplicity, with a pillar on the outside supporting a tympanum. One variation was the cruciform floor plan, with an entrance on the long side. A salient feature of these buildings was the close relationship between structure and decoration. With the introduction and rapid expansion of Buddhism, pagoda temples, typical of Chinese culture, became widespread and exerted a distinct influence on Shinto buildings as well.

● EAST AND WEST

When, after almost two centuries of isolation, the Land of the Shoguns complied with the demands of the United States that it reopen its ports and resume contact with the rest of the world (1853), Japanese art was revealed to the amazed eyes of Western artists. Claude Monet went so far as to design his garden at Giverny in the style of the polychrome woodcuts from the Far East that were becoming so popular in Europe. The time was ripe for Eastern culture to pique the interest of architects as well, who welcomed the stimulus and inspiration of a tradition so radically different from the Greco-Roman. In 1874 an Englishman, Josiah Conder, founded the Institute of Architecture, a vital center of cultural exchange at the University of Tokyo. Leading European and American architects then began to work in Japan. Among these was Frank Lloyd Wright (pp. 342–343), who in 1916 designed the Imperial Hotel in Tokyo (now destroyed), with the assistance of the Czech architect Antonin Raymond, who was to remain in Japan for the rest of his life and design a number of buildings. In the 1950s especially, Japanese architects began to emerge on the international level with avant-garde projects, thanks also to the worldwide fame of their leading figure Kenzo Tange (pp. 360–361). But traditional Japanese architecture continued to be a source of inspiration for the West, especially in the austere, essential, geometric character of its interiors, where sunlight entered from great sliding verandas often overlooking splendid gardens. House and garden were in fact joined in a virtually indissoluble whole, so much so that the ideograms *ka* ("house") and *tei* ("garden"), when linked together, denote the concept of home.

Above:
Teahouse in the Ritsurin garden. Ritsurin Koen, Takamatsu.

Interior of a modern Japanese house.

Claude Monet, *The Water Lily Pond at Giverny*, 1917. Paris, Musée d'Orsay. The painting shows the garden of Monet's house at Giverny, in Normandy, where he went to live in 1883. The typically Japanese-style bridge appears in many other contemporary illustrations.

Right:
Kano Akinobu, *Il Ryogoku Bridge on the Sumida River*, from the series *Views of Edo*, early nineteenth century. Tokyo, National Museum.

Modern Classicism

Plans for factories never built, designed by Peter Behrens and collaborators around 1909.

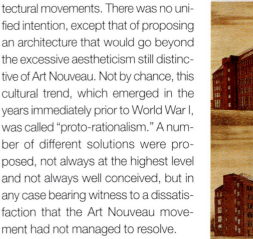

Even such a movement as Art Nouveau, which developed as an original response to the needs of late nineteenth-century Western society, soon encountered opposition and severe criticism. The term "Modern Classicism" refers, as a matter of convention only, to the architects who, in the first decade of the twentieth century, took a position against the still predominant Art Nouveau. This was not a true movement, consisting instead of isolated figures inspired by an intuition of new architectural movements. There was no unified intention, except that of proposing an architecture that would go beyond the excessive aestheticism still distinctive of Art Nouveau. Not by chance, this cultural trend, which emerged in the years immediately prior to World War I, was called "proto-rationalism." A number of different solutions were proposed, not always at the highest level and not always well conceived, but in any case bearing witness to a dissatisfaction that the Art Nouveau movement had not managed to resolve.

Above:
Adolf Loos, *Looshaus on the Michaelerplatz*, 1910. Vienna.

Right:
Peter Behrens, *Detail of the AEG turbine factory*, 1909. Berlin.

Adolf Loos, *Steiner House*, 1910. Vienna.

● ADOLF LOOS

While starting from a position close to that of Otto Wagner, Adolf Loos (1870–1933) soon abandoned the principles of the Secession, seeing in them a new despotism no less dangerous than those of the Greco-Roman or Neo-Gothic traditions. His concept of architecture rejected originality at all costs, favoring simplicity and the banning of any type of ornamentation. One dimension of the Arts and Crafts Movement that Loos did revive was the artisanal and "human" aspect of building, which caused him to refute the priority of the project itself in favor of the architect's constant presence on the worksite, allowing him to verify every detail in person. Loos's teachings were to be crucially important to subsequent generations of architects.

Top:
Auguste Perret, *Interior of the Esders industrial tailoring firm*, 1919. Paris.

Right:
Auguste Perret, *Interior of the Church of Notre-Dame*, 1923. Le Raincy, Seine-Saint Denis, France.

● PETER BEHRENS

A figure of major importance in early-twentieth-century industrial architecture, Behrens (1868–1940), a German, was inspired by the ideas of William Morris. In 1907, as head of the General Electricity Company AEG in Berlin, he applied his fertile imagination to the design of turbine factories, management buildings (p. 64), workshops, and products of various kinds. During the course of his career, Behrens developed a dry, powerful style, almost entirely free of historic influences, in which the utilization of new materials was a key factor.

● TONY GARNIER

A French architect and city planner instilled with the ideals of nineteenth-century socialism, Garnier (1869–1948) was chiefly concerned with the urban problems of the industrial world. He promoted the concept of the "garden city" in his plans for a *Cité Industrielle* (1901, published 1917), partially realized in his native Lyon, where in 1915 he designed the Edouard Herriot Hospital, composed of airy, pleasant pavilions separated by broad lawns.

● AUGUSTE PERRET

The son of a builder, the Frenchman Perret (1874–1954) was one of the first architects to use exposed reinforced concrete without concealing its structural function (as in the Esders industrial tailoring firm in Paris) and to give it a decorative function (as in the Church of Notre-Dame at Le Raincy).

Avant-garde Architecture

Rudolf Steiner, *Second Goetheanum*, 1924–1928. Dornach, Switzerland. Founder of the Free University of Science of the Spirit and theorist of anthroposophy, a mystical social philosophy that asserts that humans have a faculty of spiritual cognition, the Austrian Rudolf Steiner (1861–1925) dedicated the headquarters of his study center to Goethe, creating one of the most singular examples of Expressionist architecture. For his first building (1913–1920), of curvilinear plan, he used seven different types of wood, reflecting the seven principles of his mystic doctrine. Destroyed by fire in 1922, the Goetheanum was redesigned and rebuilt in reinforced concrete by Steiner himself. In the interior, some of the rooms are conceived as esoteric caverns.

Rudolf Steiner in his studio, with the model of the first Goetheanum (photograph from 1914).

Since architecture had wiped the slate clean of previous traditions, it now came into close contact with the pictorial experiments being conducted by the historic avant-garde art movements. The first decades of the twentieth century were thus to see various architectural styles that assimilated and made use of the new trends in art.

● EXPRESSIONISM

In the strict sense, "Expressionism" refers to the works of a group of artists who, in 1905 in Dresden, Germany, established the current known as *Die Brücke* ("The Bridge"). The movement promoted new, subjective forms of expression without foundation in academic training. The paintings of Kirchner, Heckel, Schmidt-Rottluff, and others emphasized the troubled human condition, suspended between pain and death, emitting the "primal scream" that lies deep in every individual. The architects who shared these inclinations, opposed to ideas such as those of Adolf Loos ("architecture is not an art ... anything that serves a purpose should be excluded from the sphere of art"), closed ranks against functionality in favor of creativity and an imagination bordering on the visionary. In their approach, architecture was intended to arouse emotion through soft, organic, enveloping forms that appear to come from the glistening realm of crystals or the mysterious world of grottoes. Architectural Expressionism evolved in part from Art Nouveau, by way of inspiration from the plant and mineral world close to the forms of Gaudí, and with a glance at Behrens (the first to design industrial architecture of striking visual impact). Its leading figures were a number of German architects, the designers of projects almost all of which are now destroyed or were never built, in part due to their idealistic nature. Among these was Hans Poelzig (1869–1936), the designer in 1918 of the Grosses Schauspielhaus in Berlin, a massive theater demolished in the 1970s (p. 59); Erich Mendelsohn (1887–1953), who in 1920

Erich Mendelsohn, *View of the Einsteinturm (Einstein Tower) and section drawing*, 1920. Potsdam. This astronomical observatory, commissioned from the German architect by Einstein-Stiftung, was designed for spectrum analysis research in relation to the theory of relativity. With their aggressive, massive forms, some of the project sketches (p. 337) resemble the finest Expressionist works.

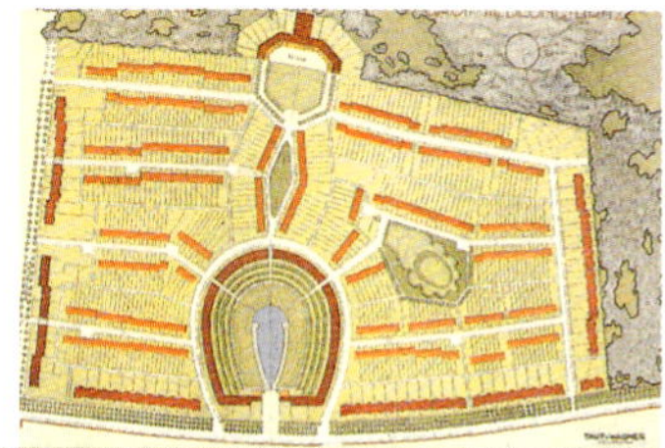

Bruno Taut and Martin Wagner, *Urban plan (1925–1927) of the Britz District in Berlin.*

Bruno Taut and Martin Wagner, *Britz District on the Liningstrasse*, 1925–1927. Berlin. One of the first to take an interest in theories on *Glasarchitektur* ("glass architecture"), Taut joined the Expressionists in 1918. He worked later in Berlin, Cologne, Stuttgart, Dresden, and Frankfurt, and in the early 1920s he was the municipal architect of Magdeburg. He was to leave Germany with the rise of the Nazis; after traveling in Japan and Russia, he settled in Ankara, Turkey, for the rest of his life.

designed the tower of the Observatory and Astrophysical Institute of Potsdam, still in service today; Bruno Taut (1880–1938), attentive to the problems of urban planning and famous for his Glashaus built in 1914 for the Deutscher Werkbund of Cologne (a glass pavilion in which the reflection of water in a basin interacts with light filtering through a dome); and Fritz Hoger (1877–1949), who restored dignity to brick (and clinker in particular). Predominantly European in inspiration, Expressionism made a significant contribution to other twentieth-century avant-garde movements and exerted its influence on such architects as Gropius (pp. 350–351) and Mies van der Rohe (pp. 352–353).

Fritz Hoger, *Chilehaus*, 1922–1924. Hamburg. The sharp corners confer a particularly dramatic aspect on this imposing building, while the bricks take on a decorative value.

Josef Gočár, *Entrance to the twin houses at Hradcany*, 1912. Prague, Tychonova Street (old photograph). An architect, urban planner, and teacher, Gočár (1880–1945) was one of the leaders of the Czech Cubist movement, backed by the critics Václav Steč and Vincenč Kramar.

Giacomo Balla, *Patriotic Song in Piazza di Siena*, 1915.

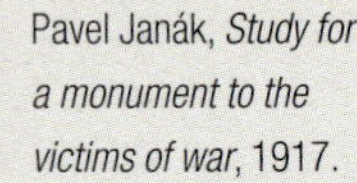

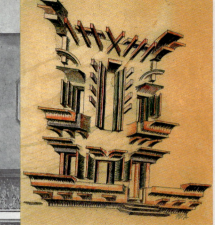

Pavel Janák, *Study for a monument to the victims of war*, 1917.

Antonín Prochazka, *Design for a desk*, 1916. Brno, Moravian Gallery.

● FUTURISM

As stated in Marinetti's *Manifesto* (February 20, 1909), Futurism scoffed at bourgeois respectability and hailed modern industrial civilization. Speed, machines, electricity, and war were regarded as the defining myths of progress. The movement dissolved with the first signs of social crisis following World War I, but a second stage, which was to spread throughout the world, developed around Balla, Depero, and Marinetti, who in 1915 had called for the Futurist Reconstruction of the universe. Futurist architecture anticipated the approaches of Le Corbusier (pp. 348–349) and Gropius, as evidenced in Marinetti's and Sant'Elia's *Manifesto* of 1914, but nothing was to remain of it except the drawings of Sant'Elia (pp. 338–339) and buildings and designs by Mario Chiattone (1891–1957).

● CUBISM

Although this was the most famous style in the history of twentieth-century avant-garde painting, thanks mainly to the work of Picasso and Braque, its direct contribution to architecture was meager. The only truly Cubist buildings were those designed in Czechoslovakia between 1912 and 1915 by a few

Jacobus Johannes Pieter Oud, *Café de Unie*, 1924–1925. Rotterdam.
The signs and their wording are an integral part of the project.

Gerrit Rietveld, *House of the interior decorator Truus Shroeder*, 1924. Utrecht.
The walls and uprights in this three-dimensional space show the same rhythmic lines as those in the paintings of Mondrian.

Piet Mondrian, *Composition*, 1929. Belgrade, National Museum.

Bohemian artists. Nevertheless, the Cubist approach to positioning objects in space and its revolutionary view of the world exerted a strong influence on the likes of Le Corbusier (who was also a Cubist painter at one stage in his career) and van Doesburg in the Netherlands.

● "DE STIJL" OR NEOPLASTICISM

Founded in 1915 at Leyden, Holland, by Theo van Doesburg (1883–1931), a painter and later an architect, the magazine *de Stijl* was for fifteen years the dialectic tool of a group of commercial artists, architects, and painters (including Piet Mondrian) who embraced the ideals of rhythm, economy of expressive means, and rigorous construction. Known also as "Neoplasticism," the movement aimed at a radical transformation of art in contrast to the "visionary and dynamic" confusion (as it was termed by Mendelsohn) of the Expressionism embraced by the Amsterdam School. As in Mondrian's paintings, the buildings are distinguished by vertical and horizontal lines, primary colors (red, yellow, and blue), and smooth planes. After the death of van Doesburg, the group broke up into individuals pursuing other trends in art, who were to exert an influence on Rationalism.

● CONSTRUCTIVISM

Coined by the Russian art critic Nikolai Punin in 1913 to define the slender, machine-like metal structures created by Vladimir Tatlin, the term "Constructivism" was to enter the language as a label for the aesthetic ideology of Bolshevik Russia in the 1920s. Close to the concepts of Futurism, whose revolutionary impetus and formal premises it shared, this new form of expression, which encompassed painting, sculpture, architecture, and drama, challenged bourgeois aesthetics with the intent of reestablishing an art for the masses. Unlike Italian Futurism, from which it distanced itself upon the rise of Fascism, Constructivism could count on a state structure that implemented, in its early stages, the concepts of Marx and Lenin. In 1932, under Stalin's dictatorship, art circles were suppressed and the process of transformation first promulgated by Trotsky as a project of "permanent revolution" was suspended.

Paradoxically, the chief symbol of Constructivism remained the scale model for a "sculptural architecture" that was never built. Designed by Tatlin, the Monument to the Third International was to have been a towering double-spiral with revolving overhead rooms, suspended like a bridge over the Neva River. Indeed only a few Constructivist building plans were ever realized. Among these were the Labor Building in Moscow and the Pravda headquarters in Leningrad (St. Petersburg), designed by the Vesnin brothers, who specialized in social clubs for the working class and theaters.

Important for his contacts with Western Europe, where he worked on several

El Lissitzky, *Drawing for the Wolkenbügel ("Cloud Hanger")*, 1924–1925. It was El Lissitzky himself who gave the name of "Cloud Hanger" to this bizarre office building, conceived as a sort of skyscraper formed by a vast number of blocks extending horizontally. It was never constructed.

Above:
El Lissitzky, *Photomontage of the design for the Wolkenbügel ("Cloud Hanger")*, 1924–1925.

occasions, was the painter, architect, and designer El Lissitzky, whose style in the 1920s resembled that of De Stijl. His enthusiastic comment about the Pravda building in Leningrad offered an apt and succinct definition of Constructivism: "All of the accessories ... signs, advertising, clocks, loudspeakers, elevators, are an integral part of the project and are integrated into a unitary whole. This is the aesthetics of constructivism" (1929).

Konstantin S. Mel'nikov (1890–1974) is known for the Rusakov Workers' Club in Moscow, whose sharp, geometric masses spread out like a fan.

Konstantin Stepanovič Mel'nikov, *Rusakov Workers' Club*, 1927–1929. Moscow. The building has a large auditorium on the ground floor and three more in the projecting bodies—a sort of multiplex cinema before its time.

El Lissitzky, *Axonometric projection of the International Red Stadium on the Lenin Hills in Moscow*, 1925.

The Soviet Pavilion at the Press Exposition of Cologne, 1928.

The Modern Movement

Walter Gropius, *Plan of the Bauhaus building*, 1925–1926. Dessau, Germany. The building is composed of two bodies, a rectangular one containing classrooms and workshops and an L-shaped one that houses the auditorium, stage, kitchen, and canteen. The five-story building contains twenty-eight apartments for students, bathrooms and a gymnasium; the administrative offices are located on the bridge that crosses the street.

Walter Gropius, *Main entrance to the Bauhaus with the two-story bridge*, 1925–1926. Dessau.

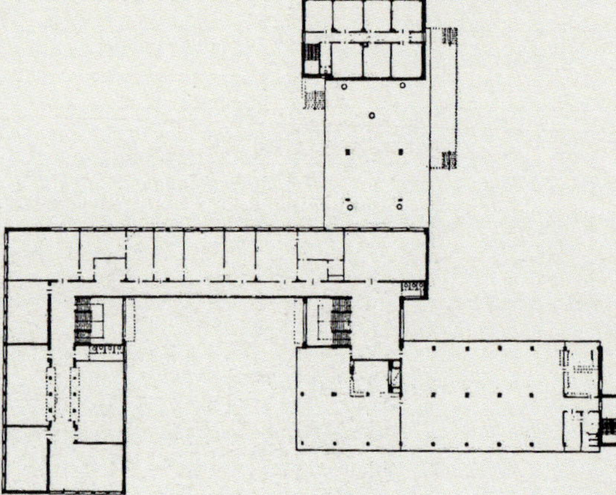

In the years following World War I, industry emerged as the most powerful economic force in the West, giving rise to new urban problems and the need for mass residential buildings.

The theoretical bases of the early avant-garde movements, linked to idealistic programs for "changing the world," now acquired a universal dimension. In architecture, some trends, such as that of Cubism, were abandoned; others, such as Futurist concepts of the industrial city, were absorbed and re-elaborated according to principles of unqualified rationality.

● AN ARRAY OF NAMES

The term "Modern Movement" entered architectural history in 1936, introduced by Nikolaus Pevsner's book *Pioneers of the Modern Movement from William Morris to Walter Gropius*. The text was published four years after an exhibition held at the Museum of Modern Art in New York entitled "Modern Architecture," an homage to architecture as practiced by such masters as Wright, Le Corbusier, and Gropius, to name only the most famous. Since the roots of this architecture are to be found in reasoned analysis, the movement is also known as Rationalism. The guiding principle of the Modern Movement is the axiom formulated by Louis Sullivan, "form follows function," according to which the appearance of a building or object does not depend on purely aesthetic considerations, but on the purposes it must serve.

The term "Functionalism," reflecting an essential quality of a Modernist work, is therefore also used.

Walter Gropius, *The Bauhaus seen from the southeast*, 1925–1926. Dessau. At right, the five-story building with studio-apartments for students. In the wing connecting the two structures at the bottom, distinguished by large windows, are the canteen, auditorium, and stage. To the left is the section containing the workshops.

Above: Walter Gropius, *Axonometric drawing of building plan for the Residential District in the Dessau-Törten suburb*, 1926–1928.

Below: Walter Gropius, *View of the Dessau-Törten suburb*, 1926–1928.

● THE BAUHAUS

The Bauhaus (p. 31), the first and most famous school of architecture and industrial design in the twentieth century, was founded in 1919 at Weimar, Germany, by Walter Gropius. The Bauhaus headquarters, which moved to Dessau in 1925 because of the hostility encountered in the academic and bourgeois circles of Weimar, was designed by Gropius in reinforced concrete and glass, according to strict principles of functionality; it is a sort of manifesto of the Modern Movement.

Extending over several floors, with separate wings for the various activities (classrooms, student dormitories, and an auditorium), the building includes a bridge on two levels that crosses the street and leads to a great curtain wall behind which lay the workshops. The building, according to Gropius, "reflects the spirit of the times and is far removed from the representative form of the symmetrical façade. One must walk around this building to fully grasp its three-dimensional aspect and understand the function of its elements." Its simple, geometric forms fully satisfied the desire for clarity and order that had already emerged with De Stijl and that now was moving in the direction of a "new objectivity" (another component of Rationalism), in which nothing should be emotional or subjective.

● EUROPEAN RATIONALISM

With the Bauhaus (which was to be shut down by the Nazi government in 1933), Germany assumed a guiding role in establishing the ideals of the Modern Movement, summarized as follows: the architect has a social function; he must provide the greatest benefit to society at the least expense; useless, expensive ornamentation is banned in favor of rational forms that best serve the function for which they are designed; all design issues are related, and the architect must assume responsibility for the whole, designing everything from "a spoon to a city." Maintaining a positive relationship with industry was considered vital, in order to fully exploit its potential. It was equally important to provide mass low-cost housing, as it is the moral imperative of governments to guarantee the minimum necessities of life (*Existenzminimum*) for every individual. The problem must be confronted methodically, by studying the optimal design, facilities, and physical orientation of housing complexes. Theory was put into practice with the achievements of Ernst May (1886–1970), the municipal housing councilor in Frankfurt, Germany, and those of Hans Scharoun (1893–1972), commissioner for the reconstruction of Eastern Prussia from 1919 to 1925. Gropius, too, designed apartment buildings, basing his projects extensively on technical, economic, and social concerns. In Russia, projects for shared housing and urban complexes carried the concept of collectivism to extremes, but the basic premise was not far from that of Le Corbusier's "Housing Unit" (1946–1952) in Marseilles (p. 45); the Swiss architect, a leading figure of the Modern Movement, arrived at that solution from his model-house design displayed at the 1925 International Exposition of Decorative Arts in Paris.

● OTHER CURRENTS

The architects did not restrict themselves to designing. The universal character of the Modern Movement and its attempt to improve the quality of life through standardization were demonstrated, beginning in 1928, at Interna-

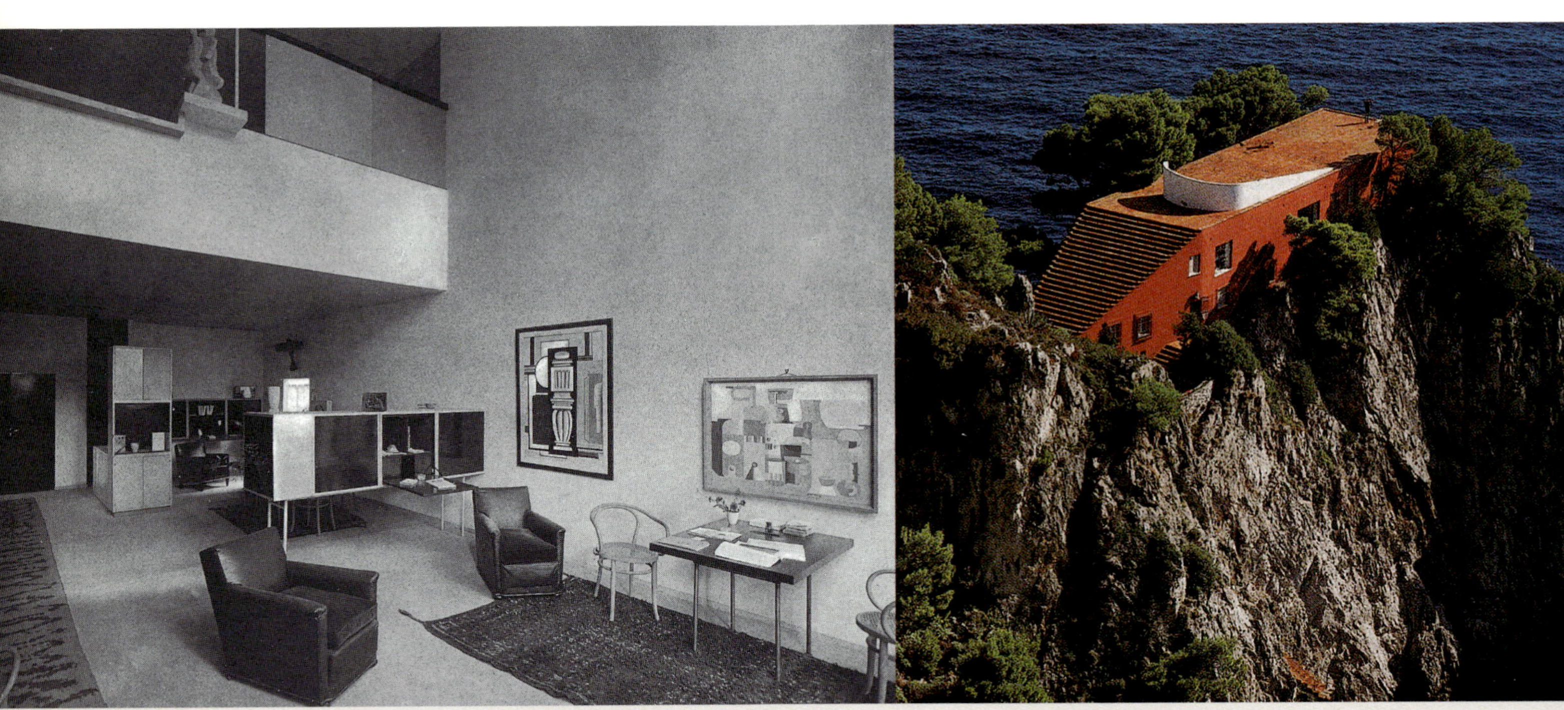

Above:
Le Corbusier and Pierre Jeanneret, *Interior of the model-house,* International Exposition of Decorative Arts, Esprit Nouveau Pavilion (Paris, 1925).
At the inauguration of the exposition, the Esprit Nouveau Pavilion created such a scandal that it had to be concealed behind a fence. This contemporary photograph shows the prototype of a housing cell for apartment buildings constructed of reinforced concrete and entirely prefabricated, thus substantially lowering the cost of building.

Right:
Hugo Häring, *Plan of Gut Garkau model farm,* 1924–1925.
Lübeck, Germany.
The interior areas, especially the great U-shaped trough, dictate the plan. It was designed for a vast agricultural enterprise, only partially built.

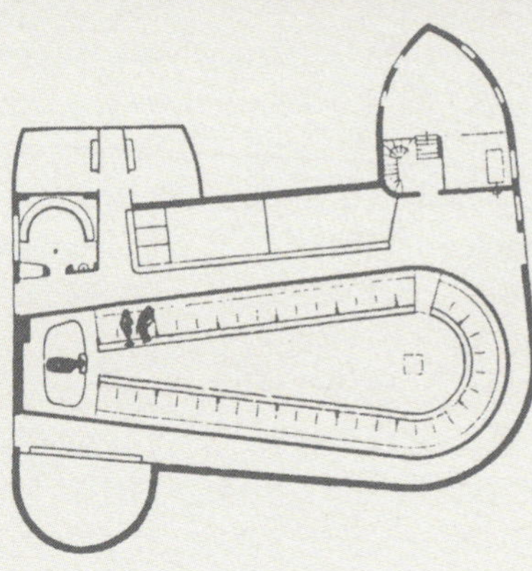

Above:
Adalberto Libera, *Malaparte House,* 1938–1943.
Capri, Italy.
Owned by the writer Curzio Malaparte, the villa designed by Libera (p. 186), a member of the Gruppo 7 and the Italian Movement for Rational Architecture, skillfully resolves the relationship between tradition and modernity.
Perched on the tip of Cape Masullo, the building extends over three floors; at the top is a terrace, reached by a stairway that is also part of the building's roof.

tional Congresses of Modern Architecture (CIAM), where architectural concepts and methodologies were discussed with unflagging attention to social and economic realities. This gave rise to formal decisions from which sprang other currents, such as Italian Rationalism (exemplified by Adalberto Libera), at first supported by the Fascist Party. The German Hugo Häring (1882–1958) was essential to the development of organic architecture and, to some extent, ecological architecture. His concepts of *Organwerk* ("organic work," tending toward functionality) and *Gestaltwerk* ("formal work," dependent on the former and the basis of formal change) were to influence Alvar Aalto (pp. 354–355) and Hans Scharoun.

● THE AMERICAN EXPERIENCE

The concept of organic architecture, originating from diverse currents in Europe, was the guiding spirit of American Rationalism, which flourished within the sphere of the Chicago School. Its point of departure was the theory advanced by the sculptor Horatio Greenough (1805–1852) who, in opposition to the eclectic style of the nineteenth century, hailed nature as the model to be followed in the creation of new forms. This concept, albeit without Greenough's theological implications, was taken up by Sullivan (p. 340), who declared that in nature "form follows function." In this view, Functionalism should be consistent with the laws of nature rather than mechanistic, as had been theorized in Europe. It was no coincidence that Frank Lloyd Wright drew inspiration from traditional American houses dating from Colonial times (p. 342). For this great architect, interior living space must be linked continuously with the outdoors and, although each element forms part of the whole, each must have its own identity. The American movement was enriched by many outstanding European architects who emigrated to the United States during the Nazi years.

Thanks largely to U.S. economic power, it became possible to build architectural complexes that had been unthinkable in Europe. Architects were now forced to take measure of unique urban realities.

Above:
Frank Lloyd Wright, *View of the Coonley House from the garden,* 1908. Riverside, Illinois. Designed by Wright for Avery Coonley, the house, surrounded by gardens, is decorated on the outside with majolica tiles enameled in geometric patterns.

Above:
Aerial view of New York in the 1930s.

Right:
Frank Lloyd Wright, *Plan of the Coonley House at Riverside.*
The plan demonstrates Wright's attention to the interaction between unified structure and individual architectural features.

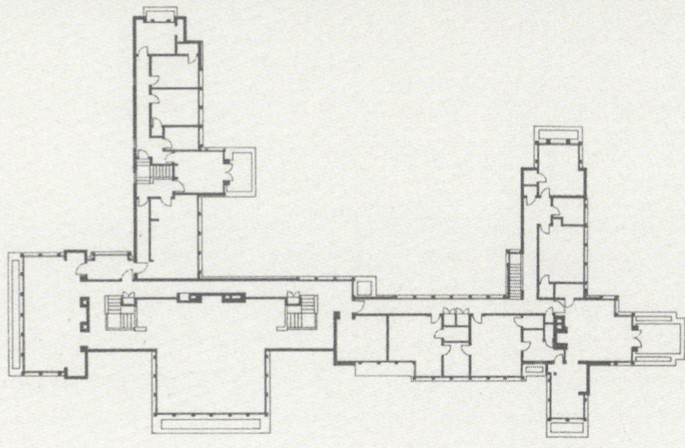

The International Style

Le Corbusier, *Chapel of Notre-Dame-du-Haut*, 1950–1954. Ronchamp, France.

Although international architecture was dominated by the Modern Movement for years after World War II, a process of revision began to emerge that eventually developed into open criticism and gave rise to a number of new solutions beginning in the 1970s.

● THE HISTORY OF A NAME

The term "International Style" was coined by the historian Henry-Russel Hickcock and the architect Philip Johnson for the "modern" designs produced in Europe during the period 1922–1932. The term first appeared in their book, *The International Style: Architecture Since 1922*, published on the occasion of the New York Exhibition of Modern Architecture, organized in 1932 by Johnson himself, then the director of the Museum of Modern Art. The book specified the stylistic principles deemed fundamental to the projects designed during that period: architecture as volume; projects distinguished by order and clarity; the elimination of all forms of decoration in favor of attention to details, each to be realized with meticulous care. This aesthetic canon immediately assumed an international dimension, and the term "International Style," which had been deemed suitable for expressing the global dimensions of Rationalism, was extended to the architectural experimentation of the postwar period. Until the late 1970s this was to remain, albeit with many variations, the official language of modern architecture from Japan to the United States, from Sweden to Australia.

● HERITAGE OF THE MASTERS

The epochal change that took place after World War II did not spring from a new generation of architects. The same figures that had made Rationalist architecture great after World War I were those now at the forefront of postwar developments. Aside from Le Corbusier who, having obtained French citizenship, had collaborated with the militarist regime of General Pétain, other leading lights—including the Germans Gropius and Mies van der Rohe, the Hungarian Marcel Breuer, and the Austrian Richard Neutra—had emigrated to the United States with the rise of Nazism. It was they who were to lay the foundation for the architectural style of the future. The CIAM also resumed activity during this period. Virtually all the great masters of that gen-

Kisho Kurokawa, *Karuizawa Capsule House*, 1972. Tokyo.

James Stirling (with Michael Wilford and Malcolm Higgs), *Faculty of Historical Sciences*, 1964–1967. Cambridge, England. The two spectacular wings, rising to a height of seven floors, house offices and seminar halls opening at right angles off the great glass-domed reading room in the library, with book stacks on the floor below it.

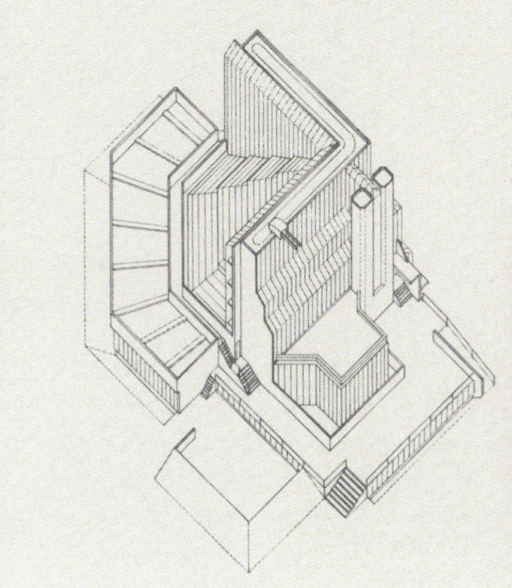

eration continued to work until at least the mid-1960s, and the International Style became, in the end, a cultural dictatorship against which some of these same architects were later to rebel.

● VARIATIONS ON A THEME: BRUTALISM

The works of Le Corbusier, such as the sanctuary of Ronchamp, the Chandigarh projects in India (p. 29) and the Maisons Jaoul at Neuilly (outside Paris), are considered the cornerstones of a style that came to be called Brutalism, in which the aesthetic quality of concrete was first appreciated. The term was coined in Great Britain in 1954 to define the stylistic current that flowed from Le Corbusier's projects and were characterized by the use of exposed reinforced concrete (in French, *béton brut*). Although precedents may be found in the "modern classicism" of Auguste Perret (p. 171), Le Corbusier renewed the tradition, reviving the very expressiveness that had been condemned by Rationalism. The trend was soon followed everywhere, from Italy to England, from the United States to Latin America (where the leading proponent was the Brazilian Oscar Niemeyer, who was also to work in Italy, France, and Algeria).

● METABOLISM

The current labeled "Metabolism" developed in Japan. In the wake of Kenzo Tange (pp. 360–361), who had worked in the studio of Kunio Maekawa (1905–1986), a collaborator of Le Corbusier, the ideas of the Swiss master had spread as far as the Land of the Rising Sun. The decision to leave concrete in open sight was accompanied by a reconsideration of the relationship between public and private space; the latter was reduced to a high-tech "capsule" that could be replaced in case of wear or deterioration, as in a kind of structural "metabolism." With this concept of apportioning space came a revival of the hypothesis of articulated mega-structures in which the architectural design was adapted to meet changing requirements, in an almost "protein" or "biological" form. The Metabolism Movement, having failed to attain its objectives, dissolved after the International Exposition of Osaka in 1970, and different currents were then pursued by each of the architects involved.

Below:
Ludwig Mies van der Rohe, *Design model for a glass skyscraper in Berlin.* 1922.

Right:
Ludwig Mies van der Rohe, *860–880 Lake Shore Drive*, Chicago, 1948–1951. Chicago, Illinois. Two soaring apartment towers, designed without terraces or balconies, display unqualified geometric rigor.

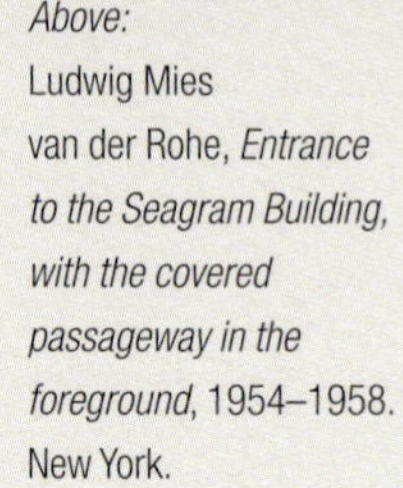

Above:
Ludwig Mies van der Rohe, *Entrance to the Seagram Building, with the covered passageway in the foreground*, 1954–1958. New York.

Eliel and Eero Saarinen, *The buildings of the General Motors Company in Detroit in a contemporary illustration*, 1951.

● EUROPEANS IN THE UNITED STATES

Throughout his career, Ludwig Mies van der Rohe (pp. 352–353) remained faithful to the premises of the Modern Movement. In 1938, having tried in vain to establish a working relationship with the Nazis, the German architect immigrated to the United States. He soon recognized the immense possibilities in his adoptive country, where the needs and prerogatives of American society were in keeping with his own artistic proclivities. More than twenty years after his first sky-

Right:
Walter Gropius (TAC Studio), *Pan American Building*, 1958–1963. New York. This landmark structure, with a helicopter pad on the roof, is like an immense octagonal tower, supported by a steel structure and enclosed in a grid of prestressed concrete.

scraper sketches, Mies van der Rohe was to design glass-and-steel towers that took root in the American architectural landscape. Among them was the famous Seagram Building in New York, completed in 1958 with the collaboration of Philip Johnson; one of the first skyscrapers of the "new generation," it had a continuous façade of bronze-colored metal and burnished thermal glass. An uncompromising spirit, Mies van der Rohe is the polestar of Rationalist architecture. Drawing inspiration from him were such figures as Eero Saarinen (1910–1961), a native of Finland who followed his father Eliel (1873–1950) to the United States. The Saarinens collaborated on the design of buildings for the General Motors Company, in part inspired by Mies van der Rohe's ITT (Illinois Institute of Technology) complex in Chicago, 1946.

● GROPIUS AND THE TAC

Walter Gropius (pp. 350–351) left Nazi Germany in 1934 with the hope of being able to return. After three years in London, however, he settled in the United States, where he taught at Harvard University. In 1945, with six younger colleagues, he founded The Architects Collaborative, TAC. This studio, with its high-profile projects, was in large part responsible for undermining the supremacy of the International Style. The lessons taught by Gropius became the legacy of his pupils, though each of them followed a separate path. Two of his most brilliant pupils were Ieoh Ming Pei (p. 365) and Marcel Breuer (1902–1981), the latter oriented toward the revival of a regionalist language, a vital feature of which was the use of local materials such as wood and split stone.

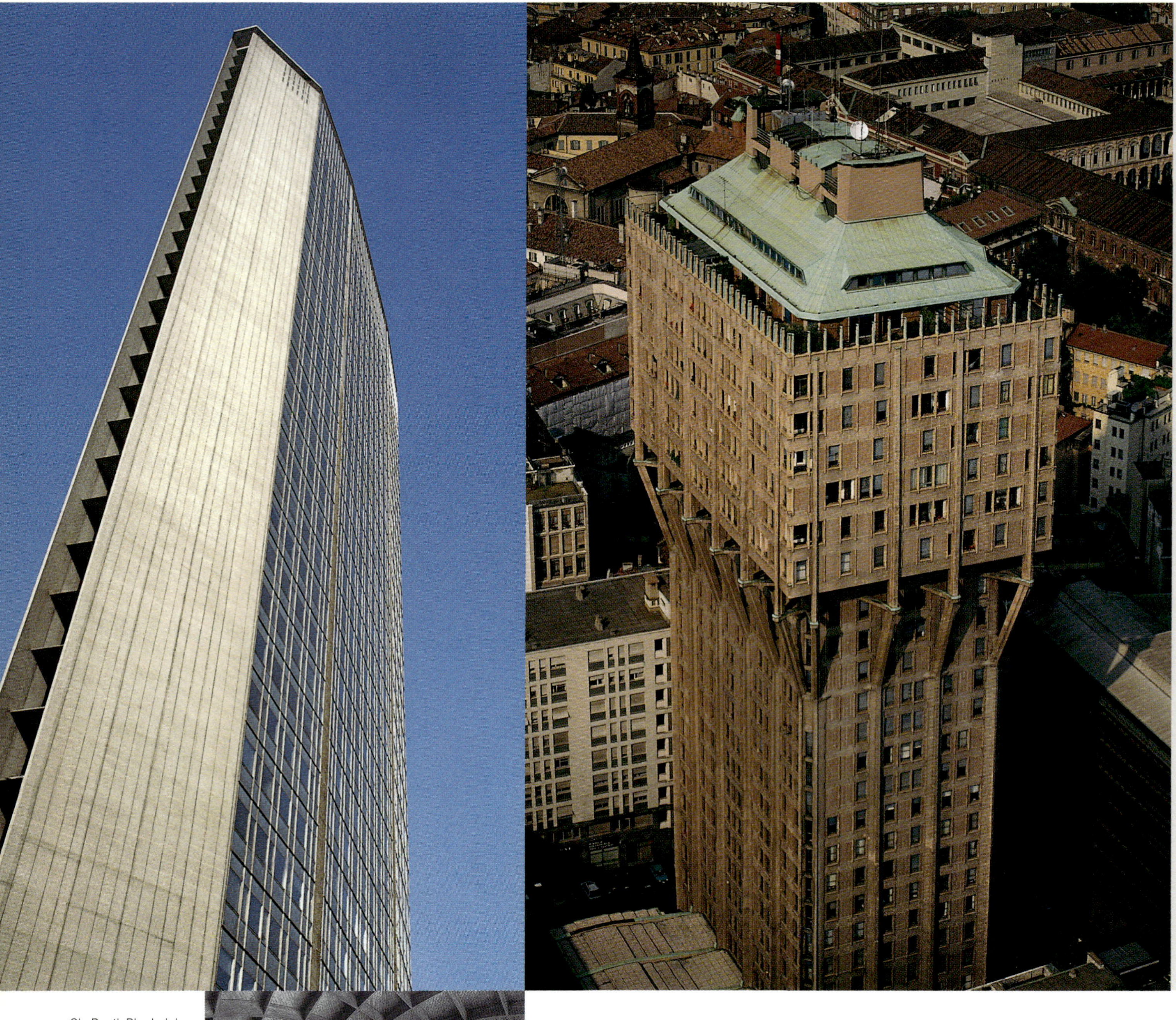

Gio Ponti, Pier Luigi Nervi, and others, *Pirelli skyscraper*, 1953–1961. Milan.

Pier Luigi Nervi, *Hangar*, 1939–1942. Orbetello, Grosseto, Italy. Destroyed at the end of World War II, the hangar had geodetic roofing that covered an area of 43,000 square feet and was supported by only six lateral pylons.

● NERVI, PONTI, AND THE ITALIAN ARCHITECTS

Italian architects also drew inspiration from Mies van der Rohe, and their projects became fully consonant with the International Style. In Italy, moreover, the Rationalist tradition was rooted in the work of Giuseppe Terragni, Luigi Figini, Adalberto Libera, and other members of the Gruppo 7. (The group was founded in 1926, dissolved in 1931, and transformed into the MIAR, Movimento Italiano per l'Architettura Razionale, later absorbed into Fascist organizations). In the hangar for the Orbetello airport (now destroyed), the engineer Pier Luigi Nervi (1891–1979) developed a system of roofing with angular beams. His experiment, conducted in parallel to that of Italian Rationalism, was to bear its finest fruits in the 1950s: the UNESCO Building in Paris; the Palazzetto dello Sport in Rome, designed in collaboration with Annibale Vitellozzi; and Milan's Pirelli skyscraper, by Nervi and Gio Ponti in collaboration with Fornaroli, Rosselli, Valtolina, Dell'Orto, and Danusso.

Left:
BBPR Studio,
Torre Velasca,
1950–1958. Milan.
Ernesto Nathan Rogers, a partner in the studio that designed the building, promoted a theory of "environmental preexistence," i.e., that the architectural value deriving from the history of a place should suggest modern but familiar solutions. The details of the 325-foot tower are reminiscent of Castello Sforzesco and the Duomo in Milan.

Above:
Ignazio Gardella,
Casa alle Zattere,
Condominio Cicogna,
1953–1958. Venice.
Gardella, one of the masters of Italian Rationalism, was inspired by the unique character of the site. The building is at once modern and imbued with historical and artistic memory.

Below:
Pier Luigi Nervi and Annibale Vitellozzi,
Palazzetto dello Sport,
1958. Rome.
Circular in plan, the building has a roof supported by fork-shaped structures that extend inside the ribbed ceiling. The design reflects a perfect integration of the ideas of the architect Vitellozzi with the engineering solutions of Nervi.

Louis I. Kahn,
Medical Research Building (Richards Laboratories),
1957–1964.
Philadelphia, University of Pennsylvania.
After having painted a series of watercolors depicting the medieval towers of San Gimignano in Italy, Kahn designed the Richards Medical Research Laboratories as a series of blocks with tower annexes that rise 30 feet above the pavilion roofs. The obvious allusion to medieval Tuscan architecture is combined with the highest technology of the day. Stairwells containing the air-conditioning system project from the profile of each block. The projecting blocks, fundamental to the style of the building, are made of concrete faced with brick.

● CRISIS IN THE INTERNATIONAL STYLE

Already by the 1930s, Alvar Aalto (pp. 354–355) and Frank Lloyd Wright (pp. 342–343) had expressed concern that architecture was being impoverished by the Modern Movement, whose limitations they had noted. The process of revision may be said to have concluded by the late 1960s, by which time many architects had already taken new directions. In the mid-1950s, for instance, a neo-Liberty current emerged in Italy. The work of Guido Canella, Gae Aulenti, and others during this period made clear historical references not only to the turn-of-the-century Liberty style but also to the architectural memories of specific places. This was to give rise to the "Regionalism" of Ignazio Gardella and of the BBPR Studio (from the initials of the architects Banfi, Barbiano di Belgioioso, Peressutti, and Rogers), whose express intent was to recover the visual memory of historical architecture within a Rationalist context. The American Louis Kahn (1901–1974), who had emigrated from Estonia in 1905, advocated "reference to the values of history" revisited in the light of modern technology. In his radical revision of the International Style, Kahn started from Rationalist positions, with a renewed and embellished Brutalism, and ended by expressing his style in a sort of reversal of the "form follows function" dictate, declaring that function evokes form. In other words, by observing a building and understanding its function and practical objective, one finally comes to recognize its innermost nature.

Contemporary Architecture

The 1970s witnessed profound changes in Western society, as expressed by student protests that swept from the campuses of American universities to the European continent. The crisis may be said to mark the end of the first stage of industrialization, a phenomenon that developed in the United States and the major European nations during the twentieth century and exerted a profound influence on the evolution of architectural styles. The attempt at regularizing building production, the search for solutions that could solve any problem through the imposition of so-called standards, now began to show its limitations, calling into question the very principle of Rationalism as well as the basic premises of the International Style. The quality that now began to be valued above all was creative ingenuity, which can never be reduced to formulas, no matter how complex. In the 1970s, as the social and cultural role of the architect became a subject of heated debate all over the world, the West became increasingly aware that the technological premises underlying Rationalism were fragile indeed. The need for a radical structural revision and the launching of new initiatives and design methods, in keeping with a civilization now commonly referred to as "post-industrial," began to be felt. From the 1970s through the 1990s and into the new century, a new generation of architects developed a multitude of innovative stylistic approaches.

Above:
Philip Johnson, *Roofless Church,* 1960. New Harmony, Indiana.

Right:
Mario Ridolfi, Ludovico Quaroni, Carlo Aymonino, and others, *INA-Casa buildings,* 1949–1950. Rome, Tiburtino District. The artfully irregular arrangement of these apartment buildings, the utilization of local materials, and the sophisticated asymmetrical effect evoke the traditions of Roman popular housing.

Above:
Wallace Kirkman Harrison, *View of the New Metropolitan Opera House by night,* 1959–1966. New York, Lincoln Center. The monumental arches bear witness to a reinterpretation of new architectural styles in a historical key.

Below:
Philip Johnson, *AT&T Building,* 1978–1982. New York. This skyscraper, more than 650 feet tall, is faced in pink granite which softens and ennobles the steel structure, terminating in a kind of molded tympanum clearly inspired by Art Nouveau forms.

Above and below:
Michael Graves, *Humana Building,* 1982. Louisville, Kentucky. The skyscraper has twenty-seven floors of offices. Its most distinctive feature is the base on the street front, a sort of portico.

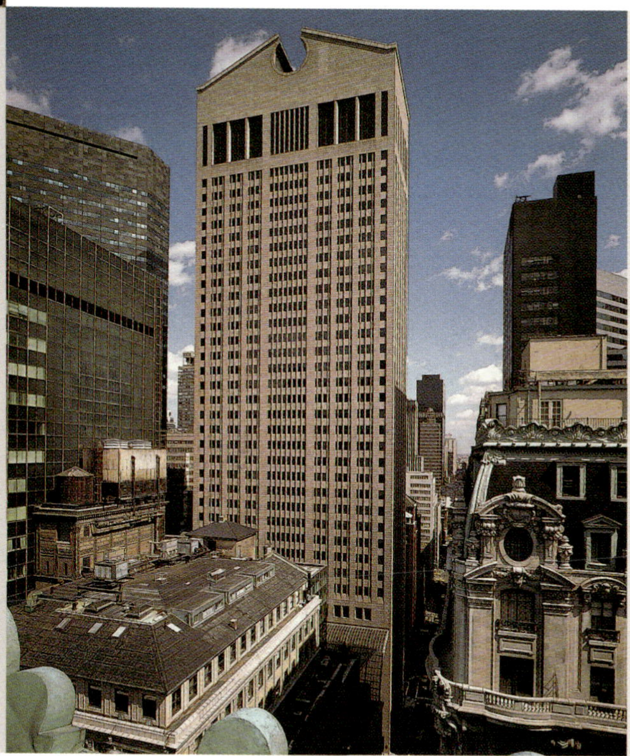

● THE POSTMODERN MOVEMENT

The first such movement, which emerged around 1975 and continued to develop until the late 1980s, Postmodernism departed from the rigid schemes of Rationalism and returned to a historical relationship with forms, at times ironic, in the awareness that a building may have a humorous component.

ORIGINS

The term "Postmodern," applied to architecture for the first time in 1975 by the architects Charles Jencks and Robert A. Stern, had previously been employed by literary critics to indicate a return to the genre of the narrative, structured in an organic approach that restores the original meaning to words.

A forerunner of Postmodern architecture has been found in the "traditionalism" of the 1920s, but, as noted previously, the revival of local styles and those linked to a specific historical context, combined with modern techniques and building systems—closer to a description of Postmodern—was a trend that emerged in Italy in the 1950s and in the United States soon thereafter.

LEADING FIGURES

An early theorist of the Postmodern movement was the American architect Robert Venturi, who wrote an essay in 1962, titled *Complexity and Contradictions in Architecture* (published four years later), that would prove highly influential.

The Postmodern reaction to the International Style can be seen in the stylistic evolution of Philip Johnson. An architect of broad outlook who collaborated in the realization of the Seagram Building, a pure example of the International Style, Johnson began to turn in the direction of Postmodernism as early as the 1960s. The tendency can already be seen in such projects of his as the New Harmony Roofless Church (p. 188), whose reference to the Native American tent placed it clearly in the realm of historicism. Toward the end of the 1970s, with the AT&T Building in New York (p. 189) Johnson created one of the signature structures of the Postmodern style. The real innovation of the building consists of the dialectical relationship between modernity and history, rendering the image of the skyscraper in elegantly *rétro* terms. The skyscraper is thus transformed from an emblem of modernity to a historical reference—even if the history is that of America, the country that, more than any other, seems projected into the future. The first to introduce the historical styles (Classical, Baroque, and Neoclassical) into contemporary architecture, albeit with an ironic twist, was Charles Willard Moore (1925–1995). In his celebrated "Piazza d'Italia" (p. 99), designed for the Italian community of New Orleans in honor of their native land, Moore recreated a place of nostalgic kitsch—a quality that made it even more "true." In the words of Jencks, "A Postmodern building is, to put it briefly, a building that communicates on at least two levels at the same time: to the other architects and a minority who under-

Right:
James Stirling,
Hall of statues in the New Staatsgalerie,
1977–1996.
Stuttgart, Baden-Württemberg, Germany.

Above:
James Stirling,
View of the New Staatsgalerie and Music School,
1977–1996.
Stuttgart, Baden-Württemberg, Germany.

stand the real meaning of architecture, and to a broader public or the inhabitants of the place who are concerned with other issues such as comfort, traditional construction and lifestyle."

It is precisely this ambiguity in which are played out the aesthetics of Postmodernism, officially celebrated in Hans Hollein's "Strada Novissima" exhibit at the Venice Biennale of 1980, directed by the Italian architect Paolo Portoghesi. The latter, an expert on Italian seventeenth-century architecture, had recognized the value of history and tradition in the conception of new architectural creations. By taking this approach, he was able to satisfy the new requirements of the Islamic community in Rome by designing the grandiose, now famous mosque annexed to the Islamic Cultural Center.

Along the same lines, but in a more homogeneous context, is the multiform architecture of the Scotsman James Stirling (1926–1992), who assembles consolidated historic forms, such as that of the tower, in the New Staatsgalerie and Music School of Stuttgart. The two structures are imagined as elements of the same architectural complex, the great reservoir of memory being, in this case the city itself.

In the Berlin Schützenstraße, by contrast, the Italian Aldo Rossi (1931–1997) includes references to the past as if it were the architecture itself that is telling the story, with the building façades evoking the severe austerity of seventeenth-century Florentine palaces.

The Postmodern style is so elastic as to allow—even encourage—entirely unexpected results, such as the Humana Building in Louisville, Kentucky, by Michael Graves (1934–), whose architectural pursuit focuses on the dual aspects of citation and reinvention. His intention was to abandon the cold aspect of a "box-like" skyscraper in favor of another form that would be both surprising and emotionally engaging.

Hans Hollein, *Façade for the Strada Novissima at the "The Presence of the Past" exhibition,* 1980. Venice Biennale.

Left: Paolo Portoghesi, *Interior of the mosque,* 1975–1993. Rome. Portoghesi plays on a revival of the sinuous lines of Moorish and Mudéjar tradition.

Above: Aldo Rossi, *Project for the Theater of the New World,* 1980. Venice Biennale.

Right: Aldo Rossi, *Project for apartment building on the Schützenstraße,* 1992–1998. Berlin.

● DECONSTRUCTIVISM

The term "Deconstructivism" derives from a method of analyzing texts devised by the French philosopher Jacques Derrida, with whom such architects as the Swiss Bernard Tschumi (1944–) and the American Peter Eisenman (1932–) collaborated at various times. In a 1984 essay, for example, Derrida reverses Martin Heidegger's term *destruktion* ("destruction") by attributing a positive significance to "deconstruction": a procedure that lays bare, in the analysis of a text, the artificial "constructions" that are often unconscious but always implicit.

The concept of deconstructivism—neither a true movement nor a style, since it has philosophical rather than theoretical bases—made its official entry into the history of architecture in 1988. In the summer of that year, Philip Johnson and Marc Wigley organized an exhibition at the Museum of Modern Art in New York called "Deconstructivist Architecture." A few months earlier, the Tate Gallery in London had held the first "International Symposium on Deconstruction," which was open to artists as well as architects.

PRECEDENTS

Although the origins and development of Deconstructivism can be said to date from the 1980s with the New York exhibition, various antecedents can be identified. Among these are the works of SITE Incorporated (Sculpture in the Environment), a company founded in 1969 by the Chicago-born architect James Wines (1932–). Wines defined the aesthetic of "de-architecture" as an expressive art, based on irony, that does not disdain extreme graphic languages such as that of the comic strip, and calls into question the overpowering rule of consumerism in America.

For the Best Products chain of supermarkets, SITE invented buildings that seem to be in ruins. At its store in Houston, the high outer wall appears to be chipped away and crumbling; while at the Sacramento store, a seemingly permanent fracture appears in a corner of the building each day at opening time but then moves back to become an entrance.

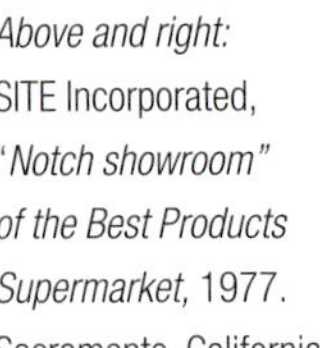

Above and right:
SITE Incorporated,
"Notch showroom" of the Best Products Supermarket, 1977.
Sacramento, California.

Above:
James Wines and SITE Incorporated,
"Indeterminated façade showroom" of the Best Products Supermarket,
1975. Houston, Texas.

LEADING FIGURES

Deconstructivism—whose representation in the New York exhibition included Eisenman, Tschumi, and Frank O. Gehry, as well as the group of Viennese architects called Himmelblau Bau-Coop and the Iraqi Zaha Hadid—did not restrict itself to undermining the concept of solidity, but went so far as to revolutionize the very meaning of architecture. Little now remained of the conventional sense of structural harmony and completeness; every building project became autonomous,

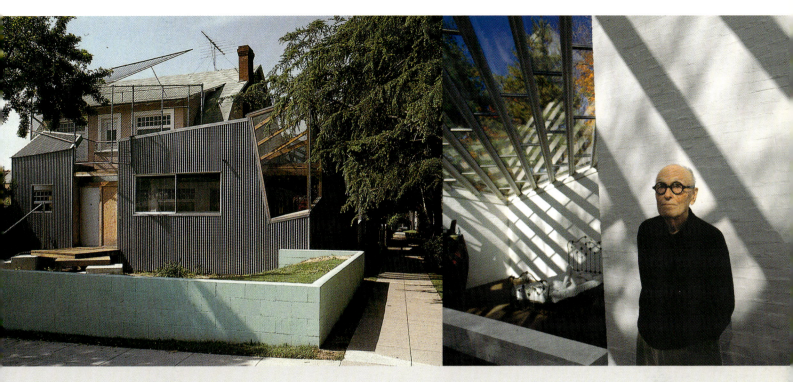

Frank O. Gehry, *Gehry House*, 1978. Santa Monica, California. In 1977, Gehry renovated an "old house, uniform but attractive" for his family in an anonymous neighborhood of Santa Monica, California. The new house became a sort of manifesto of Deconstructivism and made the Canadian architect world-famous. Utilizing scrap materials, corrugated sheeting, and wire mesh, Gehry added a kitchen, dining room, and terrace, which partially surround the existing building.

Above: *The architect Philip Johnson on the glassed-in roof of his house in Cincinnati.*

Below: Peter Eisenman, *Aronoff Center for Design and Art,* University of Cincinnati, 1988–1996. Cincinnati, Ohio. The structural deformation of the center is based on calculations by sophisticated computer programs.

left to the unbridled fantasy of its designer. Sometimes it seemed that the hand of a giant had crumpled an ordinary house into a shapeless ball, or that an entire apartment building had been violently shaken by an earthquake. But every irregularity is real: if a wall seems to lean, it really does so; if a ceiling is suddenly lowered because the "box" of the building seems to split open, it has really happened. Deconstructivist buildings thus appear as a metaphor for the contemporary world and implicitly criticize the view of the International Style that humans are exclusively rational beings. To the contrary, as noted by Eisenman (who came from the Modernist experience of the group of architects called the New York Five), Deconstructivism fluctuates between "reason and madness" and is linked in some way to Postmodernism, if only in that it views Philip Johnson as a primary source of inspiration.

An important role is also played by computer-based design. The architect's models are then analyzed and reconfigured as necessary—making possible, among other things, unusual shapes and deformations.

● HIGH TECH

An abbreviation of "High Technology," this phrase designates the architectural direction, explored from the late 1970s to the last years of the twentieth century and still a leading current today, that makes use of the most advanced engineering techniques.

The term was popularized with the success of a book by Joan Kron and Suzanne Slesin titled *High Tech* (1978), published on the occasion of an exhibition held by the Museum of Modern Art in New York. Antecedents of the High Tech style may be recognized in the "engineering" architecture of the late nineteenth century (exemplified by the Eiffel Tower), in part taken up again by the Russian Constructivists in the 1920s.

LEADING FIGURES

The first stylistic manifestations of this new trend, such as the Georges Pompidou Center in Paris (p. 370) and the main office of the Lloyd's of London insurance company, tend to emphasize the aesthetics of the machine and its innate aggressiveness. Although the theoretical premise is that of clarity (a building whose structural logic is immediately clear), the effect is much more complex.

And this is precisely the provocative, groundbreaking aspect of High Tech design; as the French architect Jean Nouvel (1945–) writes: "A building must communicate the anxiety of an epoch." Thus, a museum is made to resemble a factory, and the southern side of the spectacular Institut du Monde Arabe in Paris is an immense glass wall lit by 240 photoelectric cells.

Richard Rogers & Partners, *Staircase towers faced with steel panels in the Lloyd's building*, 1978–1986. London. The architect pays homage to the architecture of engineers, an important current in nineteenth-century Britain, while at the same time inserting a "mechanical monster" into the heart of the City.

Jean Nouvel, Gilbert Lezénés, Pierre Soria, and Architecture Studio, *Southern side of the Institut du Monde Arabe building*, 1981–1987. Paris.

Below:
Herzog & de Meuron, *View of the new Tate Gallery*, 1994–2000. London. The expansion of exhibition space for the Tate Gallery of Modern Art, inaugurated in May 2000, involved the renovation of the Bankside power station, distinguished by a 325-foot smokestack. With nearly 100,000 square feet of floor space, the Tate has become Europe's largest gallery of modern art.

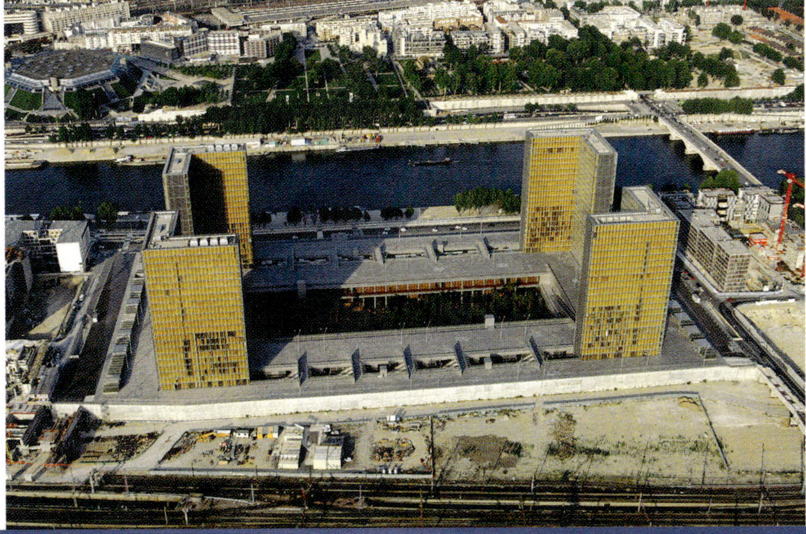

Left:
Dominique Perrault, *View of the new Bibliothèque Nationale de France*, 1988–1997. Paris, XIIIe Arrondissement. The four L-shaped towers of France's new National Library, overlooking a great garden-plaza, contain some 650 miles of bookshelves.

Alvaro Siza, *Church of Santa Maria and Parish House*, 1990–1996. Marco de Canavezes, Portugal. In this religious building, the sense of spirituality is intensified by the pure white of the outer walls.

● MINIMALISM

Coined in the mid-1960s, this term was first used in reference to literature, motion pictures, and painting. As in the figurative arts, Minimalist architecture—whose leading figures have included the Swiss Jacques Herzog and Pierre de Meuron, the Portuguese Alvaro Siza, and the Frenchman Dominique Perrault—reduces the expressive means to a minimum, avoiding any emotional involvement on the part of the spectator. The lesson of the Modern Movement and the International Style have not been entirely discarded by this current, which has also been influenced by Poor Art, Land Art, and Conceptual Art. Purity of form and geometric lines have been quietly reconsidered as possible solutions for the new architecture.

Fumihiko Maki, *Sports complex*, 1980–1984. Fujisawa, Japan.

OTHER TRENDS

The complexity of artistic and cultural currents in the last three decades of the twentieth century defies easy labels, not attempted even by architects themselves, who often embrace a number of different styles in the course of a career. The sections below summarize some of the most important trends in the global panorama of contemporary architecture.

RATIONALISM AND ARCHITECTURAL ARCHETYPES

The galaxy of Rationalism "revisited" ranges from world-famous projects by the Chicago studios of Murphy/Jahn and SOM—the latter founded in 1936 by Louis Skidmore (1897–1962) and Nathaniel Owings (1903–1984), joined in 1939 by John Merrill (1896–1975)—to the futuristic concepts of the Japanese Fumihiko Maki (1928–) and the pure, white architecture of Richard Meier (1934–), whose salient feature is harmonious integration with the landscape.

Above: Joan Otto van Sprechelsen and Paul Andreu, *Grande Arche de la Défense*, 1989. Paris. The enormous cube-shaped arch contains a conference and exhibition center.

Left: Mario Botta, *Museum of Modern Art*, 1989–1995. San Francisco.

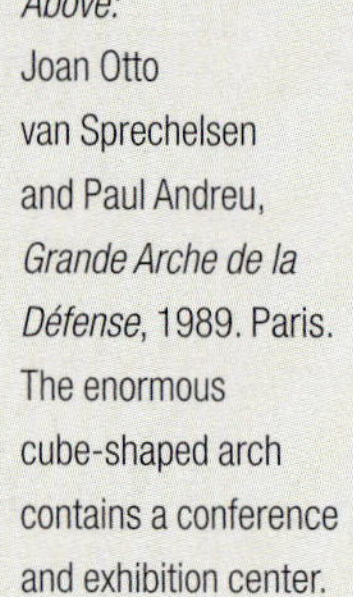

Left: Richard Meier, *Douglas House*, 1971–1973. Harbor Springs, Michigan. The structure emerges dramatically from a forest of fir trees on the shores of Lake Michigan.

Right: Charles Willard Moore, *Sea Ranch Condominium*, 1965. Sonoma County, San Francisco, California. The architect brings an ecological approach to his choice of a traditionalist design with the use of simple but evocative building methods.

For others, the objective is simplification and a return to archetypes. These are sometimes used in combination, as in the single-family house by the Swiss architect Mario Botta (1943–), a sort of dress rehearsal for his San Francisco Museum of Modern Art, in which the playful component emerges even more strongly. A similar aspect is evident in the designs of Oswald Mathias Ungers (1926–), who likewise searches for archetypes. Archetypical forms are also applied to megastructures, such as the Grande Arche de la Défense in Paris and the Spencer Theatre in Alto, New Mexico.

Himmelblau Coop, *Law office in Falkenstraße*, 1983–1988. Vienna. In 1995, Coop Himmelblau ("Blue-Sky Cooperative"), founded seventeen years earlier in Vienna by W.D. Prix, H. Swiczinsky, R.M. Holzer, and F. Stepper, put the "l" in parentheses and became Coop Himmelb(l)au ("Blue-Sky Construction Cooperative"). This roof office with an overhanging framework combines and reinterprets the Postmodern and High Tech approaches.

ORGANIC ARCHITECTURE

As seen previously, the architectural trend of "metabolism" (p. 183) represented an attempt to apply processes of living organisms to building design, and the concept of organic architecture began to emerge in the projects of Alvar Aalto and Hans Scharoun. More recently, such other architects as Frei Otto (1925–) and Zvi Hecker (1931–) have drawn inspiration from the processes of biological growth.

ECOLOGICAL ARCHITECTURE

More than a stylistic trend, this represents an approach to design that the Finnish architect Juhani Pallasmaa has labeled "ecological functionalism."

The solutions, based on the principle of respect for the environment regardless of the stylistic code being employed, may be based on tradition or the way a building is set within the natural context.

HETEROTOPIA

Literally, this word means architecture "of another place." In observing, for example, the renovated law office of the Himmelblau Coop in Vienna, one has the impression of standing before an alien presence that has sprung from some twilight zone of the imagination. Such projects, based on very high technology, have burst onto the urban scene like fragments of a bizarre, unreal world.

Above:
Glenn Murcutt, *Simpson-Lee House*, 1989–1994. Mount Wilson, New South Wales, Australia. Built of iron, steel, and scrap material, this residential design exploits the natural ventilation of the site, natural sunlight, and local rainfall to create an ecological building in perfect harmony with the environment.

Index of names

The numbers in italics refer to illustrations and captions, those in boldface to pages in this volume.

Credits

Legend: a=above; c=center; b=below; l=left; r=right

Archivio Giunti (in alphabetical order): 230b, 275a (Atlantide/Stefano Amantini); 14-15b, 19al, 133 (Atlantide/Massimo Borchi); Giuliano Cappelli, Florence: 201cr; Claudio Carretta, Pontedera: 28b; Dario Coletti, Rome: 82cr, 229b; Patrizio del Duca, Florence: 81br; Giuseppe De Simone, Florence: 103bl; Antonio di Francesco, Genoa: 125br; Jona Falco, Milan: 48a; Stefano Giraldi, Florence: 35bl, 101bl, 161al, 165ar, 279ar, 279bl, 287a, 287br; Nicola Grifoni, Florence: 16b, 17b, 19br, 28-29, 33, 34bl, 34r, 44, 50, 54al, 60b, 63bl, 66al, 69a, 72-73, 73al, 76-77, 79, 80ar, 80bl, 80-81, 81ac, 86bl, 88ar, 89bl, 89br, 90b, 91ar, 92-93, 94, 94-95, 98bl, 100 bl, 103a, 106-107, 112a, 114br, 116, 124r, 135b, 139bl, 140al, 143c, 143br, 144al, 144ar, 145ar, 146r, 214bc, 214br, 215al, 216ar, 216-217, 217ar, 217bl, 217br, 220, 220-221, 222-223a, 222-223b, 224al, 224-225, 225a, 225cl, 225cr, 227b, 228cr, 228b, 229cl, 233br, 234al, 234-235, 235r, 236cl, 238a, 259ar, 290; Aldo Ippoliti, Rome (Concessione S.M.A. no. 945 of 18/11/1993): 43c; Nicolò Orsi Battaglini, Florence: 62ac; Marco Rabatti-Serge Domingie, Florence: 62l, 142, 278a, 286-287, 296; Humberto Nicoletti Serra, Rome: 99bl, 118l, 146, 147a, 147cl, 230a, 232r, 305br, 322ar, 326-327, 326-327; Gustavo Tomsich: 305ar.

Atlantide, Florence (in progressive order): 40-41 (Massimo Borchi); 41a (Stefano Amantini); 55br, 69b (Massimo Borchi); 160br (Guido Cozzi); 163a (Stefano Amantini); 186ar (Concessione S.M.A. n. 01-295 del 21/06/1995); 294bl (Guido Cozzi).

Contrasto, Milan: 98a, 215br, 262cr, 302-303, 307bc, 315bl (Erich Lessing); 317c (Gamma), 329cr (Erich Lessing), 330 (Gamma); 352a, 352b (Erich Lessing); 356a, 356bl, 357a (Gamma); 358-359 (Massimo Mastrorillo); 359a (Wes Thompson); 359c (Massimo Mastrorillo); 359bl (Alexis Duclos); 364bl (Craig/ Rea); 368b (Massimo Mastrorillo); 370al (Gamma); 371a, 371c (Gianni Berengo Gardin).

Corbis/Contrasto, Milan: 14c (Karen Huntt Mason); 16-17 (James Davis); 26-27 (Yann Arthus-Bertrand); 27 (Roger de la Harpe/Gallo Images); 32al (Earl & Nazima Kowall); 34al (Archivio Iconografico, S.A.); 35r (Paul Almasy); 36b (Ric Ergenbright); 37a (Ruggero Vanni); 43br (Adam Woolfitt); 48bl (GE Kidder Smith); 49a (Chris Lisle); 51c (Paul A. Souders); 52r (John Slater); 55a (John Dakers); 56 (Macduff Everton); 58-59 (Angelo Hornak); 60-61 (Christine Osborne); 61ar (Eric Dluhosch, Owen Franken); 66ar (© Bettmann/Corbis); 67br (Chris Bland); 68-69 (Joseph Sohms/Visions of America); 71a (Oriol Alamany); 71br (Philip Gendreau); 73br (Dave G. Houser); 74al (Sandro Vannini); 78r (Adam Woolfitt); 83l (Werner Forman); 96ar (Ruggero Vanni); 97b (© Bettmann/Corbis); 100br (Gillian Darley); 101a (Adam Woolfitt); 104 (Archivio Iconografico, S.A.); 104-105 (Adam Woolfitt); 107b (Harald A. Jahn; Viennaslide); 110b (© Bettmann/ Corbis); 111 (Gianni Dagli Orti); 112-113 (Roger Wood); 113 (Kevin Fleming); 117 (Paul Almasy); 119br (Diego Lezama Orezzoli); 121al (Sandro Vannini); 124l (Mimmo Jodice); 125bl (Vittoriano Rastelli); 129b (Paolo Ragazzini); 130-131 (Robert Holmes); 134-135 (Kevin R. Morris); 136-137 (Pierre Colombel); 137a (John T. Young); 141 (Mimmo Jodice); 146l (Araldo de Luca); 148-149 (Yann Arthus-Bertrand); 149ac (Philippa Lewis); 149br (Macduff Everton); 152a (© Historical Picture Archive/Corbis); 152br (Lindsay Hebberd); 153a (Sheldan Collins); 153b (Stephanie Colasanti); 154al (Paul Almasy); 154b (Charles Lenars); 154-155 (Kevin Schafer); 155c (Gian Berto Vanni); 157a (Robert Holmes); 157b (Joseph Sohm); 158bl (Cuchi White); 159a (Robert Holmes); 161br (Dallas and John Heaton); 163cl (Marc Garanger); 163cr (© Corbis); 164b (Andrea Jemolo); 165al (José F. Poblete); 166 (Paul Seheult); 167b (Sakamoto Photo Research Laboratory); 168-169 (Michael S. Yamashita); 170cl, 170br (Andrea Jemolo); 171b (Archivio Iconografico, S.A.); 178 (Ruggero Vanni); 181r (© Bettmann/Corbis); 182 (Archivio Iconografico, S.A.); 183c (Gillian Darley); 184b (© Lake County Museum); 188cl (Layne Kennedy); 188cr (Angelo Hornak); 189al (Raymond Gehman); 190c (Werner H. Müller); 193ar (Richard Schulman); 194r (Macduff Everton); 195a (Yann Arthus-Bertrand); 195c (Pawel Libera); 196ar (Grant Smith); 196bl (Craig Lovell); 197bl (G.E. Kidder Smith); 201b (Michael S. Yamashita), 202a (Michael Nicholson), 202-203 (Gian Berto Vanni); 203 (Michael S. Yamashita); 204 (Yann Arthus-Bertrand); 206-207 (Paul Almasy); 207b (Diego Lezama Orezzoli); 208al (Dean Conger); 209a (Nik Wheeler); 209b (David Forman/Eye Ubiquitous); 210l, 210r, 211c (Roger Wood); 211a (Paul Almasy); 211b (Nik Wheeler); 212-213 (Charles & Josette Lenars); 213bl (Chris Lisle); 213br (Roger Wood); 218 (© Bettmann/Corbis); 218-219 (Michael Maslan Historic Photographs); 221c (Roger Wood); 222b (Wolfgang Kaehler); 223br (James Davis); 226c (Chris Lisle); 227cl (Richard T. Nowitz); 227cr (Ruggero Vanni); 231c (Jonathan Blair); 233bl (Richard T. Nowitz); 234bl (Roger Wood); 236cr (Chris Ellier); 237c (David Lees); 238b (Paul H. Kuiper); 239a (Adam Woolfitt); 239b (Andrea Jemolo); 240l (Vanni Archive); 241l (Ruggero Vanni); 242 (Aaron Horowitz); 243l (Sandro Vannini); 243r (David Lees); 244l (Carmen Redondo); 244r (Lucidio Studio Inc.); 245cl (Pierre Colombel); 245cr (Archivio Iconografico, S.A.), 245b (Dave G. Houser), 247r (Adam Woolfitt); 248 (Roger Wood); 249cr (Carmen Redondo); 250 (Richard T. Nowitz); 251a (Luca I.Tettoni); 251b (Christophe Loviny), 252b (Charles & Josette Lenars); 252a (Jack Fields); 253c (Lindsay Hebberd); 253b (Earl & Nazima Kowall); 255 (Ruggero Vanni); 256a (Paul Almasy); 256c (Gian Berto Vanni); 257a (Patrick Ward); 257c, 259cl (Angelo Hornak); 258b (Vanni Archive); 260a (Franz-Marc Frei); 260b (Gail Mooney); 262cl (Carmen Redondo); 262b (Bob Krist); 263cl (Vanni Archive); 263cr (Mimmo Jodice); 264b (Michael Busselle); 265b (Andrea Jemolo); 266, 267ar (Archivio Iconografico, S.A.); 266-267,267br (Adam Woolfitt); 268cr (Ruggero Vanni); 268b (Paul Almasy); 270c (Richard List); 272a (Dennis Marsico); 273b (Ruggero Vanni); 274cr (Sandro Vannini); 274b (Dennis Marsico); 275c (Bob Krist); 275b (Chris Bland/Eye Ubiquitous); 276cl (Martin Jones); 276cr (Archivio Iconografico, S.A.); 277a (Carmen Redondo); 277cl, 277b, 280-281, 281cr (Wolfgang Kaehler); 282ar (Paul Almasy); 283al, 283b (Adam Woolfitt); 284a (© Alfred Ko); 285br (Pierre Colombel); 288, 288-289 (Macduff Everton); 296-297 (Araldo de Luca); 298-299 (John Heseltine); 299ar (Araldo de Luca), 300cl (Francesco